Charlotte Wacker $3.00

11/93

W9-BRM-768

ALSO BY ANN KAISER STEARNS

Living Through Personal Crisis

COMING BACK

COMING BACK

Rebuilding Lives
After Crisis
and Loss

Ann Kaiser Stearns

Random House
New York

Grateful acknowledgment is made to the following for permission to reprint
previously published material:

Alfred A. Knopf, Inc.: Excerpts from "On Children" reprinted from *The
Prophet* by Kahlil Gibran. Copyright 1923 by Kahlil Gibran, renewed 1951
by Administrators C.T.A. of Kahlil Gibran Estate and Mary G. Gibran.

Cherry Lane Music Publishing Company, Inc.: Excerpts from the lyrics to
"Perhaps Love" by John Denver. Copyright © 1980 Cherry Lane Music
Publishing Company, Inc. All rights reserved. Used by permission.

Little, Brown and Company: Excerpts from *Chancing It* by Ralph Keyes.

Macmillan Publishing Company: Excerpts from *Brainstorm* by Karen Osney
Brownstein. Copyright © 1980 by Karen Osney Brownstein. Reprinted
with permission of Macmillan Publishing Company.

Parade Publications, Inc.: Excerpts from "Our Right to Independence" by
Ted Kennedy, Jr. Copyright © 1986. Reprinted with permission of the
author and *Parade*.

Psychology Today: Excerpts from "Psychological Hardiness: The Role of Challenge in Health" by Maya Pines, in *Psychology Today*, December 1980, Vol.
14, No. 7. With permission of the author.

Robinson Risner: Excerpts from *The Passing of the Night* by Robinson Risner.
Copyright © 1973 by Robinson Risner. Ballantine Books (paperback) 1975.
Reprinted by permission of the author.

Al Siebert, Ph. D.: Excerpts from "The Survivor Personality" by Al Siebert
in the *Association for Humanistic Psychology Newsletter*, August-September 1983,
p. 19. With permission of the author.

Simon & Schuster, Inc.: Excerpts from *Keeping It Off* by Robert Colvin,
Ph.D., and Susan Olson, Ph.D. Copyright © 1985 by Robert Colvin,
Ph.D., and Susan Olson, Ph.D. Reprinted by permission of Simon &
Schuster, Inc.

Library of Congress Cataloging-in-Publication Data

Stearns, Ann Kaiser.
Coming back: rebuilding lives after crisis and
loss/Ann Kaiser Stearns.
p. cm.
ISBN 0-394-56936-9
1. Bereavement—Psychological aspects.
2. Deprivation (Psychology)
3. Life change events—Psychological aspects. I. Title.
BF575.G7S73   1988   87-26575
158'.1—dc19   CIP

Manufactured in the United States of America
98765432
First Edition

To
My Daughters,
Amanda Asha and Ashley Anjali
and
To the Memory of
Richard A. Goodling,
My Teacher, Spiritual Father, Mentor, and Friend
1924–1986

*"The world breaks everyone,
then some become strong
at the broken places."*

—Ernest Hemingway,
A Farewell to Arms

PREFACE

This book is about those who survive painful experiences, but it is also about triumph and going forward. The healing stories of dozens of men and women are recorded here. These are the stories of people who have coped with tragedies, disappointments, and losses of many kinds and who have gone on to live fulfilling lives. Each person has shared his or her story with the earnest hope that others who struggle with crisis can be helped to move beyond pain, hopelessness, and discouragement. In the book are revealed some of my own battles and their lessons. I also researched the strength factors of other victorious survivors in the literature pertaining to trauma.

Building a new life wasn't easy for these "triumphant survivors," as I call them. In most cases, years were required for recovery, growth, and the development of a fulfilling and happy life. Those who have triumphed over adversity offer the best instruction on how comebacks are possible. The dynamics of successful psychological adjustment are apparent as the story of one individual after another unfolds.

Having had more than one million people read my first book, *Living Through Personal Crisis*, I wanted to take the healing process several steps further. Words of appreciation from hundreds of individuals who wrote to me, or whom I met while lecturing around the country, revealed that people were grateful for and comforted by what I had written yet were open to receiving more help. Clearly many people are seeking to continue a mending process now well under way.

My goal is to offer concrete and practical help to those of you who are trying to transcend the pain in your lives. My guidelines for rebuilding a life are also intended to assist the friends, family members, and helping professionals in your life. These people care about your healing, too.

ACKNOWLEDGMENTS

I am especially grateful for the support, many talents, dedication, and hard work of Hilda Zink and Ilene McGrath for their superb word processing and editorial skills, respectively, and to the Ballantine Editor-in-Chief, Robert Wyatt, for assigning himself to be my editor. Also with me from the start to finish of a long project were Terry O'Malley and Rose Roberts, each woman a confidante who played an important supportive role. My friends Marian Wattenbarger, Dorris Hoyle, the Reverend Jack and Peggy Compton, and Beth and Ray DePaulo read large segments of the manuscript in progress and provided significant encouragement and feedback. Research assistants Barbara Holtan and Debbie Phillips Ford made a valuable contribution, as did Judith Vetter Douglas, who helped disguise some of the triumphant survivors' identities, and Linda J. Walter who helped me with copy editing and proofing the manuscript and galleys.

CONTENTS|

AUTHOR'S NOTE

This book features dozens of true stories told to me in hundreds of hours of interviews. In many instances certain identifying information has been changed to ensure confidentiality. While to the best of my knowledge each story is true, the names of all major characters in the book are fictitious except for the following persons, whose actual first or full names are used with permission: Robbie Risner, Gloria Back, Hope and George Curfman and their children, Jan and Ed Romond and their children, Ken and Sam, Georgia, Daniel Brewster, Elane Stein, Steven and Naomi Shelton, Dave and Mary Sanborn, John Liller, Jim Townsend, Ray Bevans, Charles, and Meritt Stark.

COMING BACK

PEOPLE WHO | 1
MAKE COMEBACKS |

In the middle of the journey of our life
I came to myself within a dark wood
where the straight way was lost.
—DANTE,
THE DIVINE COMEDY

We can encounter many traumatic and painful experiences as human beings, events that shatter our dreams and force us to struggle with suffering. At first when a crisis occurs we search for the strength and skills just to get through the pain, to survive. As the years go by, we yearn to know how to rebuild our lives, to make a comeback.

"It is important to learn to see life as a story yet to be completed," said my former professor, mentor, and friend Richard Goodling. His personal credentials for having such an insight were impressive: When Dr. Goodling's wife died, he was in his early forties and had five young children to bring up on his own. His children are grown now, most of them finished with their formal education, and all are doing well.

Dr. Goodling and I were recalling a time in my life when my marriage had just ended and I was devastated. My husband was my everlasting love, a person I had fully trusted. When he unexpectedly left me, on my twenty-seventh birthday, my emotions exploded in many directions like loud fireworks on the Fourth of July—but I wasn't celebrating.

I made a decision that day to go back to graduate school and obtain a doctorate. Yet for more than two years my reasons for living fought furiously with my yearnings to die.

Late one night, about six months into my single life, I felt especially depressed and hopeless. In desperation I called friends in Michigan and made arrangements to fly there early the next morning. There was no early flight from Baltimore, so I booked a plane leaving from Washington's National Airport, a ninety-minute drive away.

It was dark and the road was icy as I started my drive to Washington. Conditions seemed to worsen along the way. I wondered why the salt trucks hadn't begun to work the road. Aware that I was driving much too fast under these dangerous conditions, I remember thinking, "If I get there, fine; if not, that's all right, too."

Reaching the Washington Beltway, which encircles the nation's capital, I saw that the roads and bridges were frozen and treacherous. A dense fog covered the area, making for poor visibility. Still, I drove fast, tempting fate.

Then something forced my Volkswagen hatchback to a halt and shook me to my senses. The flashing lights of a state trooper's car caught my attention. A tractor trailer carrying milk had jackknifed in the middle of the highway. Broken bottles and crushed cartons spread a white trail of milk and glass over three lanes of highway.

Seven or eight automobiles were scattered about like bumper cars at a carnival. They faced in all directions, after having crashed into each other or the guard rails. Some of the people were still in their crashed cars, and no medical emergency vehicles were there yet.

I parked my car on the shoulder and walked onto the highway. Someone lay flat on his back in the middle lane, and a small group of people had gathered. The state trooper had fallen on the ice and seemed to be badly hurt.

I removed my chocolate brown, ankle-length, hooded cape from my shoulders and placed it over the trooper's coatless body to warm him. Standing in the cold, I surveyed the scene and had a chilling confrontation with myself. "For crying out loud," I muttered silently, "you could easily have been the one who caused an accident like this. You could have killed somebody."

Feeling guilty and ashamed yet glad that the accident was not my fault, I waited until help came for the trooper and the injured. Then I drove slowly to the airport, knowing that doing so would cause me to miss my plane.

"What a tragedy," said Dr. Goodling, "if you had taken yourself out of history." At Duke University twenty years before, I had been a student of Dr. Goodling's. Now I was visiting Duke as an author and guest lecturer. "It's so important for people who are hurting," he continued, "to know that the story hasn't been finished. Things are terrible now, but there's more to the story."

ROBBIE RISNER: A PRISONER OF WAR

On August 18, 1965, Air Force pilot Robbie Risner kissed his five children goodbye as they slept. One month later he was shot down over North Vietnam and taken prisoner. During his seven and a half years as a prisoner of war, he was to remember a thousand times the scene of his wife waving goodbye in Okinawa. He would not see her again until February 20, 1973. When he came home his little toddler would be eleven years old and his high school–age son would be a twenty-four-year-old graduate student.[1]

During Robbie's seven-year separation from loved ones, he endured human cruelties on a diet of bread and water. He had to learn to cope with years of solitary confinement and ten continuous months of almost constant darkness. In a cell seven feet square with a walking space two feet wide and a concrete bunk, he lived with rats, lizards, insects, untreated sores and open wounds on his body, excruciating loneliness, and boredom. Repeatedly and savagely tortured, suffering in anguish for weeks at a time, he managed to maintain his sanity and his will to live.

Psychologists have long relished the study of individuals like Robbie Risner, who cope remarkably well with extreme circumstances. If we examine his suffering as a POW and the traumatic events with which he was forced to do battle, we can learn a great deal about how it is possible to survive almost anything.

Robbie Risner's survival skills and resources for courage and strength were tested in the hottest fire. We can learn from him.

JAN AND ED: BEREAVED PARENTS

At the end of Michigan's winter in 1982, a young mother and her little boy got into their car, which was parked in front of their house. They were about to drive off to the nearby school when a group of children from young Mark's first-grade class appeared; they yelled from across the street, asking Mark to walk with them. Jan, Mark's mother, gave her permission, and the boy eagerly jumped out of the car to join his friends. Witnesses say that he looked quickly both ways, yet as Mark was running across the street, a speeding car struck him down. His mother and friends watched in horror.

At the hospital Mark was in a coma, but his vital signs were good for the first two days. The doctors said he would be fine and told Jan and her husband Ed to bring in photos of Mark so that when he awakened he would know who he was.

On the third day the bottom fell out of Jan and Ed's lives: Mark's cranial pressure went up and his doctors said that Mark was dying. Later that day Jan and Ed lost their beloved seven-year-old son, a little blond miniature of his dad (complete with a dimpled chin) who loved to swim and was taking lessons, and who was just starting to learn to play the fiddle. He was a bright, determined, curious, and inventive kid who was capable of great kindness and who liked pizza and cartoons, loved running and being active, and could argue his parents blue in the face.

The hardest thing for this couple was waking up every morning and realizing that they hadn't died, too. They wondered how they could live day after day with overwhelming suffering.

"I couldn't understand why trees were growing and why spring came," Ed explained. "It just didn't seem possible that, with Mark dead, people went on with their lives, that lightning bugs still flew."

Yet it *is* possible to undergo what is said to be the most dreaded, agonizingly painful loss to bear, the loss of a child, without becoming permanently embittered, broken, and joyless. A way *can* be found to rebuild a family, eventually reexperience pleasure and happiness, and go forward in the throes of a wound that never completely heals.

When the ache of a loss that has been experienced affects and alters, for months and years, one's moods, attitudes, values, relationships, daytime fantasies, and nighttime yearnings—somehow it still is possible for people to go on with their lives.

GLORIA BACK: THE MOTHER OF A GAY SON

Gloria Gus Back's son didn't die, but there was a period of several years when she often felt that she had lost him forever. Her younger son, Ken, was nineteen when he first tried to tell his mother that he was in love with another man, but Gloria was unable to hear it. One parent receiving such news wrote Ann Landers, saying he preferred that his son die of cancer than be a homosexual.[2] Gloria was worried. A psychologist friend reassured her that it was a phase Kenny was going through since he had recently lost his father from leukemia.

Two years later Gloria had remarried and was living in New York City when Kenny called from Maryland and said he was bringing a college friend, Clem, home for the weekend. "It was during that particular visit that I finally consciously grasped the truth," Gloria explains in her book *Are You Still My Mother?*[3] Hearing her son address his friend as "dear" finally made her ask Ken the question she probably had been avoiding for years.

She waited until Ken returned to Maryland and then phoned him. "What is Clem to you?" Gloria asked. "What's going on?" The derisive words "fag," "fairy," "pansy," and "queer" were tormenting her. She had to know about her son's sexual orientation.[4]

Ken explained that yes, he was gay and that he and Clem were lovers. "I've always been gay and I've known since I was about ten. It's the way I am. I can't help it. It's a built-in condition like the color of my eyes," Ken told her.[5]

Gloria felt that her son was showing contempt for the values she had always taught him. "You know I never let you sleep with anyone, any girlfriends or anyone, in my house," she told him, remembering when he used to bring girls home. Ken had betrayed her, she said, by sleeping in the same bedroom on the pretense that he and Clem were friends. If she had known they were lovers, they would not have been allowed to visit. How could Ken behave so disrespectfully? Gloria asked angrily.

"Kenny, you cannot treat me this way," Gloria declared. "You'll see a psychiatrist or you can forget you have a mother."[6]

Ken hung up. Mother and son did not speak a word to each other for the next six months. Each withdrew in hurt, anger, and bewilderment.

Gloria tossed and turned in her bed at night to the extent that her husband Gene once commented that he felt like he was sleeping on a trampoline. Usually she could confide in Gene, but she couldn't bring herself to tell him why she was feeling so miserable. What would her new husband think of her if he knew she had produced a homosexual son? What would he think of Kenny? Gene was a U.S. Department of Defense attorney who had represented the government against homosexual security clearance applicants and had been picketed by gay rights groups. Gloria wondered if Gene would lose his own government security clearance if word got out about Ken.

Gloria felt depressed, ashamed, indignant, angry, and wounded. She doubted whether it would ever again be possible to take delight in her son's accomplishments or feel again the closeness they had always shared. Had these events taken place in the 1980s and after instead of the 1970s, Gloria would also have struggled with the fear of losing her son to AIDS.

How does one deal with the pain of a lost dream? How is it possible to get beyond feelings of disappointment when a beloved family member follows a path in life outside the range of what one feels able to understand or accept?

In addition to offering insight and help to parents suffering an estrangement with an adult child, Gloria's journey can offer hope to those who yearn to get beyond grief and anger in a variety of other life circumstances.

ALEX: A FORMERLY OBESE MAN

He is a lean, handsome, athletic man, thirty-eight years old. People respond with amazement when they learn that he once weighed 325 pounds. Having lost 150 pounds and maintained it for fourteen years now, Alex is among only 2 percent of the population successful in maintaining a significant weight loss after seven years. Recent reports indicate that at least two thirds of those who lose weight gain it all back, and then some, within a few years.[7]

At the age of twenty-three, positioned in his first full-time job, Alex put himself on a drastic diet. Fourteen weeks later he had lost 150 pounds. He was undernourished, had low blood pressure and a low pulse rate, and was in a dangerously weak condition physically and psychologically. His shoe size went down two sizes and his ring size was reduced more than four sizes. "For most of my life," Alex says, "people thought I had inherited my mother's face, which was round. It turned out that I had an oblong face like my father. No one knew that, including me."

As he lost the first thirty pounds, people who knew Alex scarcely saw any change because he still weighed so much. When he continued to lose ten pounds a week, people started noticing and looking at him with puzzlement. He was changing before their eyes.

Alex ate one meal a day at seven in the morning, drank eight glasses of water a day, and ate no other food after breakfast. Every day he ran. He hated to run. For the entire first year he had to force himself to do it. After eleven weeks, he had lost a hundred pounds. He would pass out while running at the YMCA; his legs would start to feel like rubber and then he would wake up on the floor.

Fortunately Alex had an incredibly strong heart, in both senses of the word. What a determined person that young man was—yet he was lucky he didn't permanently damage himself following such a severe diet with no medical supervision. He lost weight in a dangerous way and would not have survived had he not eventually learned more healthful habits.

As the diet went on, Alex felt less and less like himself. For about six months he went through a period of what psychologists call "depersonalization." His sense of self, the person he had so long known himself to be, was gone. He wondered who he was now and what his life would be. When he looked into a mirror, he no longer recognized himself. He had been overweight all of his life, significantly so from the age of thirteen. Now he looked like another person.

The dramatic physical change also resulted in a loss of co-ordination. He had been somewhat fluid before; in high school he had wrestled and had played some football. Now he was as awkward as a year-old baby taking its first steps.

Talking about the life of a greatly overweight person, Alex described to me how it felt to experience society's contempt for obese people, both as a group and as individuals. It was excruciatingly painful to be obese. During all those years when many of the other boys were dating and excelling in athletics, he was terribly lonely. "I can't tell you," Alex explained, "what a shock it was, after I lost the weight, to find that women were attracted to me. I had the self-concept of someone who had been literally and physically a laugh to people."

Some years earlier, as a college student, Alex had dieted without lasting results. He had lost a hundred pounds over a period of five months, but in three subsequent months he gained back the hundred pounds and added another fifty, arriving at his top weight. He didn't do anything more about it for four years, and the next time he was successful in dra-matically losing weight and maintaining it.

Alex's recovery is typical of many who eventually triumph over an obstacle, an addiction, or a tragic loss in life. For many the story begins with a series of failures or disappointments, bouts of depression, unfulfilled dreams, promises unkept, feel-ings of hopelessness, and even periods of despair.

"THERE'S MORE TO THE STORY"

Robbie Risner, Jan and Ed, Gloria Back, and Alex are among the scores of men and women featured in this book. Some have endured a violent or virtually unbearable loss. Some have suffered abandonment, rejection, failure, or abuse at the hands of another human being. Most have battled such consuming emotions as disappointment or disillusionment, fear or terror, anger or rage, sorrow or anguish, regret or remorse, embarrassment or shame, helplessness or hopelessness, discouragement or despair.

You the reader are likely to find in this book someone whose life situation or loss experience resembles your own. Perhaps you are trying to rebuild your life after a loved one's death or a shattered love relationship, a disabling accident, or the diagnosis of a serious, possibly life-threatening illness. Perhaps you are addicted to drugs, alcohol, or food. You may be struggling with family estrangement or grievously regret past actions still difficult to live with. You may have been victimized by violence or suffered the loss of a dream. Perhaps you have lost a symbolic or literal part of yourself or your future—through infertility, surgery or other medical treatments, the loss of a job, public embarrassment, or a financial loss.

You can come through the pain and rebuild your life, whatever the nature of your personal situation. You may be able to learn as much from POW Robbie Risner or Jan and Ed and other bereaved parents as from a person whose crisis is similar to yours. You may be surprised at the lessons to be gained from a person who has struggled with and conquered a loss quite different from your own, such as Gloria Back's struggle to accept her gay son, Alex's laborious effort to maintain his 150-pound weight loss and to find a new identity, or the pain and triumph of those whose stories will be told here.

This is a book about triumphant survivors. They have weathered torrential storms, some of them capsizing in the deepest, coldest sea—still to survive with a sense of personal hope, a sound mind, and a heart able to throb with warmth and vitality. What all of us can learn from these resourceful, spirited men and women can hold us up and move us beyond almost any crisis.

DEALING WITH THE 2
PAIN COMES FIRST

The first and necessary step of grief is discovering what you have lost. The next step is discovering what is left, what is possible.

—PSYCHOLOGIST JOHN SCHNEIDER,
MICHIGAN STATE UNIVERSITY

Most of us deal with trauma and crisis by moving through some or all of the following phases of mourning: shock or disbelief; a necessary preoccupation with self and with sad feelings; vivid and sweet or sorrowful remembrances that utterly absorb us; feelings of regret, guilt, or self-blame; physical symptoms such as anxiety reactions, sleeplessness, bodily aches and pains, or changed appetite; feelings of intense fear or anger; a loss of interest in things once pleasurable; social withdrawal or other efforts to avoid having to confront our loss in the presence of others; and periods of depression that can last months or intermittently for years.

After we have adequately mourned and protested the way things are, we finally accept our changed circumstances. Things will never again be as they were or as we thought they were, we realize, and gradually we set out to make the best of it.

"Mourning is the necessary process of returning back to life after we have been jolted from its road," writes Jim Froehlich, a clergyman graduate student I taught at Loyola College. "It involves leaving behind what needs to be left behind, bringing along what needs to be brought along, and learning to distinguish between the two," Froehlich continues. "It must be undergone."[1]

ESTABLISHING POSITIVE MEMORIES

Seven-year-old Mark Romond died in his hospital room, never regaining consciousness after being struck by a speeding car three days earlier. His parents requested that the medical staff remove all of the life support equipment and the tubes attached to Mark's body, had them bring a rocking chair, and asked to be left alone with their son. Jan and Ed had brought Mark's blanket from home with Charlie Brown, Snoopy, and other *Peanuts* figures printed in bright red, blue, yellow, and green. They wrapped their little boy's body in the blanket and rocked him in his hospital room for about three hours after he died. Fortunately, nobody asked them to leave.

This couple listened to their inner need to replace their last memories of Mark lying in a maze of equipment with memories of closeness, gifts of love, and parental adoration. Without consciously intending to do so, Jan and Ed began to reshape the circumstances of their terrible loss. In so doing, they contributed to their own healing. Warm, sacred memories are part of what eventually enables people in anguish to go forward with life.

In the days immediately following Mark's death, Jan remembers, "our family and friends came from all over the United States. There was nobody we were close to who didn't come. The neighborhood opened up its homes to our friends, providing beds for whole families." One friend, a physician, left her busy professional life for an entire week to be a comfort and help. "She cried with us," says Jan, "fixed food, and took care of us as well as everybody else. I have felt many times that this is a little piece of what heaven is—all these dear people who weren't yet acquainted loving each other immediately."

It was one of the most memorable, powerful, and healing experiences of Jan's life to be enfolded in the gentle and caring presence of loved ones. "That's how I could put one foot in front of the other," she says. "That's how I could stand in a room and look at my son in a coffin—because our family and friends literally held me up. It wasn't just that Ed, our surviving son John, and I had lost Mark—we *all* had lost him."

Jan's sisters Patty and Mary came to stay for a time with the couple and pitched in with the tasks of day-to-day functioning. They also helped with the funeral arrangements. The sisters and their brother Chuck helped most of all by expressing their love at the time of Mark's death in ways that will always be a part of Jan and Ed's loving memories of that time. At the funeral home, for instance, Chuck said, "If Mark had lived any longer, he couldn't have been more loved." When the couple was agonizing about how it would ever be possible to continue living in the house where they had lived when Mark died, Chuck's words again were meaningful. "Don't forget," Jan's brother tenderly reminded them, "this is also the house where Mark lived. He had a lot of happiness here."

Sister Juanita, the principal at Mark's school, was especially helpful. She had come immediately to the scene of the accident after Mark was struck down and stayed long hours with the boy and his parents at the hospital. Sister Juanita saw to it that attractive booklets were made up for the people who would attend the funeral service. On the cover of the booklet, another nun from Mark's school drew a picture of a small child reaching for the hand of God. Enscribed in a circle around the drawing were the biblical words, "Let the little children come to Me" and "the Kingdom of God belongs to such as these."

Ed asked a priest friend from college to say the funeral mass for their son. The couple wanted to be sure to have the most understanding and sensitive clergyperson available to perform the service. They planned the service with much care and chose the music with great love. Ed especially put a lot of time into finding just the right readings.

"In memory, thanksgiving, and prayer for Mark Romond," read the opening page of the funeral service program. He "lived and walked with us as son, grandson, brother, nephew, student and friend."

Mark's fiddle teacher and another musical friend played the music and led the singing at the funeral mass. The boy's first-grade class sang the closing song. "Weave me the sunshine," sang Mark's sad little friends, "out of the falling rain."

Says Jan, "We felt that putting together a caring, beautiful service was in a way a last gift to our son, and it was helpful in the excruciating pain of those early hours of loss to have something concrete and positive to be pouring our energy into."

At Mark's funeral, during the service of Holy Communion (which commemorates God's love and enduring presence and involves the breaking of bread), a recording of John Denver's touching song "Perhaps Love" was played. The words, perfectly appropriate, seemed to echo what Jan, Ed, and many others were feeling:

"*Perhaps Love*" by John Denver

Perhaps love is like a resting place,
A shelter from the storm
It exists to give you comfort,
It is there to keep you warm,
And in those times of trouble
When you are most alone,
The memory of love will bring you home.

Perhaps love is like a window
Perhaps an open door,
It invites you to come closer,
It wants to show you more,
And even if you lose yourself
And don't know what to do
The memory of love will see you through.

Oh, love to some is like a cloud
To some as strong as steel
For some a way of living
For some a way to feel
And some say love is holding on
And some say letting go,
And some say love is everything,
And some say they don't know.

Perhaps love is like the ocean,
Full of conflict, full of change,
Like a fire when it's cold outside,
Or thunder when it rains,
If I should live forever,
And all my dreams come true
My memories of love will be of you.[2]

Without really being aware of it, Jan and Ed, as well as their lost son's other family members, teachers, and friends, were helping themselves to heal by participating fully in the tributes to Mark and his memory. The psychological benefits of the funeral, burial, Christian wake, or Jewish shiva period are well established and widely recognized. Psychologists have seen, for example, that those who are denied the opportunity meaningfully to ritualize their loss have more difficulty (as time goes on) releasing their preoccupation with thoughts of the dead person. The primary benefit of mourning is the eventual "ability to go on."[3]

DEALING WITH FEELINGS OF UNWORTHINESS

"In the early part of this century fifteen percent of all deaths were of children," explains psychologist and bereavement expert John Schneider of Michigan State University. "It was expected that many children would die, and everybody knew several people whose child had died. It was more fair because it happened to more people." These days the death of a child is unusual. According to Schneider, "People now stand so isolated, feel so singled out."[4]

"How can you be a good person if your child dies?" Jan wondered. Seeing it as having been her job to take care of Mark, Jan felt like a bad person and was unable to love herself. Her witnessing of the accident and feeling so powerless haunted her. "My God," she thought, "what if I have years left of feeling this way, that I don't deserve to live?"

Two weeks after Mark died, several people in the neighborhood called with requests they often had made before Mark's death. The women asked Jan to watch their children while they were out for a while. Jan couldn't understand why her neighbors would still want to leave their children with her. "Aren't they afraid of me?" Jan remembers thinking. "I'm not a safe mother." The first few times it happened, she watched the children like a hawk.

Distraught with grief, Jan felt unable to concentrate on anything but her loss, unable to cook or clean, absorbed in feelings of self-blame and unworthiness. Her once positive image of herself was shattered. "I'm lucky I can still dress myself," she remembers feeling. "What a gift those women gave me when they handed their children over to me. It didn't occur to them that I wasn't a safe person."

BEING PREPARED FOR CRISIS

How well we live with a significant loss can be greatly influenced by caring people who share with us our time of crisis and its aftermath. We remember vividly the circumstances surrounding a major loss. If our memories are of unkind and insensitive interactions with friends, family members, and the people representing various institutions, our torn emotions can be difficult to mend. Essential to the strength of the fabric of our lives is the knowledge that other human beings can be trusted in our times of greatest vulnerability.

At the hospital where I teach young physicians training to be family doctors, I have emphasized the importance of helping people to prepare for crisis. We know from numerous scientific studies that those who thoughtfully select and nurture a strong support system are less likely to become mentally or physically ill. They get well faster when they do become injured or ill, and they fare much better when a loved one dies or other personal crisis occurs than those without such systems.

The characteristic attribute of such a healthy support system, writes psychiatrist Gerald Caplan, is that the individual enjoys relationships in which he or she is respected and is dealt with as a unique individual. When others are sensitive to the individual's personal needs and speak his or her language, they buffer the impact of crisis and stress.[5]

Although one can never be adequately prepared to lose a daughter or son, Jan and Ed had built and maintained a strong network of love and support long before it was necessary to call for help in a time of desperate need. They had made an effort to remain in contact with old friends over the years, despite the hindrances of geographical distance and busy lives. Their friends lovingly embraced them and helped in a variety of practical ways during their most difficult periods of mourning.

SHARING LOVING MOMENTS WITH OTHERS

Jan and Ed were themselves caring individuals who had chosen a close association with people able to share human vulnerability. "It helped that our friends understood that it could have been their child, that we weren't the only ones who had no skin," Jan says.

She feels it was also helpful at times to be able "to laugh and socialize" with their family and friends even as they mourned together. There were sweet, funny stories to remember about young Mark, such as the time he had invented a sandwich "with everything in it but the kitchen sink," Jan recalls. "He put mustard, mayonnaise, ketchup, olives, raisins, pickles, lunch meat, peanut butter, jam, and I don't know what else into the sandwich. We just about turned green watching him eat it and politely declined when he offered to make us one." The intimate sharing of these tales brought the healing balm of laughter which washed into tears.

As month after anguishing month passed, Jan and Ed were comforted in their longing for their lost son by the poems, cards, phone calls, letters, and other tributes they received. Friends and family continued to "keep" and honor Mark by donating money in his name to children in need, by freely talking or writing about him, and by remembering him on special occasions such as on his birthday or holidays.

The first Christmas after Mark died, a neighbor Jan knew only slightly telephoned. She must have realized how difficult Christmas would be for Jan and Ed after losing their elder son. "I don't know if I should call," she said, "but I was just thinking you won't be buying Mark any presents this year. . . ." The neighbor suddenly stopped talking and started crying.

Jan responded, saying, "It must have taken a lot of courage to call and say that." Now weeping also, Jan explained, "I'm not crying because your words hurt me but because it's a gift that you are remembering Mark."

Not only did Jan receive comfort from people like her neighbor whom she didn't know well, she responded in a way that helped to establish new friendships. In a time of need and painful vulnerability, Jan helped to shape the circumstances surrounding the event of her loss. She contributed positively to the permanent storage of memories. That repository will always be present now, yielding mind pictures associated with losing Mark other than the memory of watching her little child being hit by that horrible car.

For all the years of life that remain for Jan and Ed, each will carry the precious memories of loving moments shared with others and every caring word and action spoken and received.

SEARCHING FOR ANSWERS

After Gloria Back found out that her son Ken was gay, she felt he was no longer the "golden boy" whom she could brag about. If others knew that her son was homosexual, she reasoned, it would damage her image as a competent mother and her reputation in the community, and it might even damage her new husband's legal career in the U.S. Department of Defense. Gloria had always taken pride in both sons' accomplishments and had derived from these accomplishments a sense of personal worth. She felt now that she was no longer a good person.

Feeling alone and dismayed, Gloria searched every corner of her brain for an explanation. Had she been too hard on Ken when he was growing up? Too easy? Maybe she shouldn't have sent him to summer camp as a boy. Had a male camp counselor molested him? Had she secretly wanted a daughter after Kenny's elder brother was born? Had she cut his hair soon enough?

Was it Fred, Ken's dad, whose influence had brought about Ken's homosexuality? Fred had been a strong yet supportive and kind father, a good role model. She wondered how such a splendid combination of fatherly traits could do a boy any harm.

Was Fred rolling over in his grave? What would her friends think if they knew one of her sons was homosexual? Her parents' approval always had mattered so much. How would *they* react?

When Gloria finally did bring herself to tell Gene and her elder son about Ken's homosexuality, her husband was relieved. Gloria's moods, sleeplessness, and strange behavior had made him start to worry that something was wrong in their marriage. Reassured that Gloria hadn't been secretly thinking about a divorce in the months of her obvious withdrawal from him, Gene's reaction to the news was surprising. "So what? He's still Ken," Gene responded. Ken's brother's way of answering was also helpful and reassuring. "What else is new?" asked Jeff.

Finally one autumn day the phone rang; it was Ken calling from Maryland. "Hi, Mom, are you still my mother?" he asked. Little did Gloria know that she would someday write a book based on those words: *Are You Still My Mother?*

As Gloria recounts in her book, she felt a tugging sensation in her chest and stomach. "Had I actually turned away my son," she thought to herself, "because he was honest and trusting enough to tell me who he was?"

" 'Mom, are you there?' Kenny's voice was insistent.

" 'Sure, sure, Kenny, of course. I'm still your mother. What could ever change that?'

" 'Mom, you'll work it out. You'll see, you just need time,' "[6] Ken said. He sounded much older than twenty-one.

MARKING THE MILESTONES

Gloria examined her options and came to some conclusions. They "had always been close," and she "would not lose [her] child just because he was gay."[7]

Gloria traveled down one road and then another in an effort to come to grips with her son's homosexuality. A series of "dawnings" or realizations were the milestones that marked the way.

She asked herself many questions. "How would Kenny have any children? Would he walk alone through life? What about the police? Did they entrap homosexuals? How would he socialize? And with whom? What would the world do to him?"[8]

Gloria realized that she had a lot of work to do. She wanted to understand what it meant that her son was gay, how he had gotten that way, whether he could change, and what kind of a life he was going to have. She wondered how it would ever be possible to give up her hopes and dreams for Kenny. Clearly this was not going to be the life she wanted for him.

She sought out the counsel of a medical doctor, Robert Laidlaw, known to be knowledgeable on the subject of homosexuality. A gentle and empathic psychiatrist, Dr. Laidlaw first gave a name to Gloria's struggle. What she was going through, he explained, were the stages of *bereavement*.

Looking at Dr. Laidlaw sitting in his wheelchair, Gloria thought he looked like her hero, Franklin Delano Roosevelt. So *that's* what her feelings of bewilderment, hurt, guilt, anger, fear, and disgust were all about: She was mourning her homosexual son!

Dr. Laidlaw fielded Gloria's questions and guided her into a reading program that would go on for several years. A great deal was still being learned about homosexuality, so scientific materials on the subject could be seen as most informative. He explained that what causes a person to become gay or straight still is not known. It is believed that a person's sexual orientation, if not determined before birth, is established by an early age.

He told her that homosexuality is no longer described as an illness in standard psychiatric texts and other medical literature.[9] We do not yet understand it but know that homosexuality is not a simple "choice" and that it is linked, like all sexuality, to a strong biological drive.

Gloria tried to absorb the new information. If, as she was being told, homosexuality was really something essential about a person's identity, she would have to learn to accept it.

There was at least one good thing in all that Dr. Laidlaw had told her. With more than twenty million gay men and women living in America, about 10 percent of the population, Kenny would have lots of friends![10]

Having the name "bereavement" attached to her troublesome feelings didn't make Gloria's pain and discomfort go away. The label did, however, help her to think that perhaps her turbulent feelings wouldn't last forever.

Aided by Dr. Laidlaw and the books she fervently read, gradually Gloria began to map out the journey toward understanding and accepting Ken's orientation. It was a long trip that would take her about six years to complete.

STRATEGIES FOR SURVIVAL

Certain circumstances are so overwhelmingly difficult that the best we can do to promote our eventual healing is simply to mark time, stay alive, and bear up under the worst of our suffering. Recovery begins with doing whatever is necessary for survival.

A woman I know lost her husband by suicide and was left a widow at the age of forty-one, with three young children to raise. When I met her within a year of her husband's death, the woman told me that she swims a mile each day and runs about five miles daily. The young widow had read in my *Living Through Personal Crisis* that losing a loved one by suicide is one of the most traumatic losses a person can bear, and she was worried about her "drivenness" to be physically active. What a relief it was to this troubled, grieving woman to hear that my new research has shown that she is behaving like a "triumphant survivor." Particularly in the early months of a crisis event or when a traumatic loss has occurred, we sometimes survive dramatic circumstances by taking drastic action.

When POW Robbie Risner was first placed in a dark, desolate cell in North Vietnam for what would become ten months of constant darkness, he quickly became so agitated that he couldn't sit still. "I jumped up and ran and ran and ran," Robbie remembers in *The Passing of the Night*. "Sometimes I switched to push-ups and then sit-ups. It was a couple of hours past the nine-thirty gong when I finally stopped that first night after hundreds of push-ups and as many as a thousand sit-ups."[11]

To combat his panic, Robbie would run as many as *twenty-five* miles a day. As he did throughout his imprisonment, he kept track of how many miles he was running by knowing how much time or how many steps it took him to run a mile.

Sometimes it gave him relief to scream. "When I thought I was going to die if there was not a change," he writes, "I would hold something in my mouth and another rag over my face and just let myself holler. Other times it seemed to help to cry. To keep the guards from seeing me or hearing me, I buried my head in the blankets."[12]

Earlier another POW had taught Robbie how to conjure up and solve simple math problems. Using equations to figure out problems involving such things as square roots and fractions, Robbie also solved for three unknowns in his mind. "Math became something like a personal friend," he explains. "It was one of the few things to provide a break in my twenty-four hour routine of panic,"[13] which lasted for ten months in a blacked-out cell.

PAIN IN SMALL SEGMENTS

Many people who have come through a personal crisis will tell you that they did so "one day at a time." Almost any bereaved parent, victim of violence, or other person suffering a traumatic loss initially survives in this way—counting days, hours, and sometimes minutes at a time.

Virtually every person recovering from an alcohol, drug, food, or tobacco addiction reports that the initial recovery process is all about coping with small increments of time that finally accumulate. Dealing with the cravings and symptoms of withdrawal and accomplishing wrenching behavioral change usually is possible when one moves a step, an hour, a day, a week at a time.

A friend got through the early months of the painful end of her marriage by plunging herself into workaholism in the daytime and dancing herself into a near frenzy at night. Choreographing interpretive dances to loud, intense music and rehearsing them over and over until she literally fell in exhaustion onto the floor was her way of surviving. Through expansive leg and arm stretches and high flying kicks, she pushed herself to her limits of exertion and got by her suicidal fantasies—a day at a time. She sought the aid of a friend who was a pastoral counselor and relied heavily on the support and caring of other friends, yet it was still a matter of managing day to day, week to week, off and on, gradually feeling better over a period of about two years.

When Robbie Risner was put in leg stocks, he figured out how to deal with the hours, days, and weeks of extreme physical pain. First he tried planning his oldest son's college education. After a few hours he abandoned such thoughts; it hurt too much to try to envision something so close to his heart that he might not live to see. Robbie then began to remember different flights and refueling stops from California to Hawaii, Guam, the Philippines, Bangkok. That also proved too difficult; such thoughts made a man who loved the freedom of flight yearn for a glimpse of the open sky now denied him. Neither the future nor the past was helpful to him. Finally, he found that what did work was to focus on one day, on the here and now. Talking was not allowed and would lead to more punishment. He would try to communicate with someone in another cell by using the tap code, a Boy Scout survival code that the other men knew. Robbie worked hard not to think ahead. It helped him not to look too far down the road, not to imagine how long his suffering might last. Like the

Hiroshima survivors who were unaware of the effects of radiation and kept expecting their grotesque wounds to heal, Robbie was better off not knowing what torment was yet to come.[14]

He survived numerous episodes of torture as well as years of physical discomfort and psychological trauma by separating the pain into manageable segments. "I would wake up and think of my plans for the day," Risner told me. "It wasn't necessary to find light at the end of the tunnel because my life was only a day long."

During ten months in desolate darkness, Robbie even found that cold terror could be broken down into tiny pieces. A sense of panic would grip him whenever he sat still. In all those months he never ate his food without pacing in his cell like an animal. He had to keep moving hour after hour after hour. "Robbie," he told himself, "you can make it one more minute." Regardless of what happened, he knew he could take sixty more seconds.

Robbie used a nail to scratch a mark on the wall every evening to keep a one-month calendar. Especially in periods when he was being savagely tortured for days or weeks at a time, the calendar brought comfort. "Another day down. How many to go I didn't know, but at least another one had passed. It was as if I had won one day's victory."[15]

PRAYER

Strength comes to people in different ways. Prayer during the most difficult period of a crisis or on a routine basis is helpful to many. Prayer can provide an outlet for haunting feelings of fear, yearning, anger, guilt, or loneliness. Meditation and prayer can provide a sense of hope, courage, calm, or simply the feeling that one is doing *something* and is not completely powerless.

Every morning during his imprisonment Robbie Risner began the day with prayer, asking God to bless his wife, Kathleen, and their children and to protect them, thanking God for the blessings that had been his. He prayed for his wife and children, each one of the other prisoners, every friend and relative back home, and the leaders of the American government. Mentioning names in prayer, says Risner, bonded him to others in a meaningful way.

There are many times when the only significant or meaningful thing Robbie could do was to pray. During one period he was placed in leg stocks for thirty-two consecutive days. He lost control of his bowels and was forced to lie in his own waste for days at a time. He was hungry, cold, and miserable. Open sores formed on his ankles where the metal from the leg shackles cut into his skin. "When the pain started really ripping me," he says in his book, "I began desperately to pray . . . I cried, 'Lord, you promised grace to bear anything. But this pain . . . I can't stand it . . . God! Help me, please help me!' "[16]

Robbie experienced God's presence, which helped him to bear the pain of torture and the mental pain which resulted when he was forced to yield to his captors. It was necessary for all of the POWs who were tortured to yield eventually to some extent. The North Vietnamese were especially harsh with Risner because he was the highest-ranking officer in captivity, a full colonel who had appeared on the cover of *Time* magazine and whom the North Vietnamese saw as a celebrated hero in America.

On many occasions when Robbie was savagely tortured, he prayed by the hour. "It was automatic, almost subconscious," he writes. "I prayed God would give me strength to endure it. When it would get so bad that I couldn't take it, I would ask God to ease it and somehow I would make it. He kept me."

Once, in leg stocks and wristcuffs for ten days, Robbie's pain and fatigue were such that he could not even remember the names of his wife and children. When the pain became unbearable, he prayed, "Lord, I have had all I can take. I am asking you to take me out."[17] Finally he was released from the cuffs and stocks, and a medic was allowed to treat his worst infections and give him an injection for blood poisoning.

Robbie hated himself when he was forced to give in to his captors, write confessions, lie into the camera, and make propaganda statements. He repeatedly needed God's help to just get through the toughest times.

RECOGNIZING HUMAN STRENGTH AND ENDURANCE

Julius Segal, a psychologist, was a member of the special health team assigned to the fifty-two American men and women held hostage in Iran from late 1979 to January 1981. In a 1985 *Washington Post* article, "Underestimating Hostages—What Psychologists Ignore Is Just How Tough They Are," Segal wrote that he has been inspired by his more than three decades of studying victims of overwhelming trauma. "Concentration camp survivors, POWs liberated from years of captivity, terrorized hostages, [and] bewildered refugees," he wrote, "have shown a pattern of coping and conquest" as opposed to "one of deficit and defeat." There is a remarkable "human capacity for endurance" under "crushing stress," says Segal.[18]

The psychologist quoted former Iranian hostage Bruce Laingen: "We're like tea bags. We don't know our strength until we get into hot water." Segal also quoted the authors of a newly released study of Holocaust survivors now living in Montreal and affirms "the magnificent ability of human beings to rebuild shattered lives, careers, and families, even as they wrestle with the bitterest of memories. Buried in the human breast are undreamed-of powers of healing and even growth in the face of stress," he continued. "We are rarely as fragile as we imagine ourselves to be."[19]

GETTING THROUGH GRIEF | 3
TAKES LONGER THAN
MOST PEOPLE THINK

*Patience is power;
with time and patience
the mulberry leaf becomes silk.*
—CHINESE PROVERB

S aid Merlin the Magician to King Arthur in T. H. White's novel *The Once and Future King*, "The best thing for being sad is to learn something." The main problem for people who are dealing with the loss of someone or something precious is that the kind of personal growth and learning necessary for healing takes a long time.

A few years ago I became aware of a study conducted in New England which reported that the average widow, widower, and divorced person needed about four years to get beyond grief and thrive again. I had already seen this hypothesis tested in many years of counseling with individuals and families.

In the aftermath of a host of bereavement situations—involving not only divorce or death but also a wide range of other loss circumstances—it had seemed to me that many people required several years to resume full functioning and a fulfilling, energetic, vital life.

In cases where there had occurred a debilitating illness or

accident, cancer, a rape or other assault, the loss of an important part of one's body or identity through surgery, the loss of a dream or sense of purpose in life or when there was a situation of ongoing family estrangement, when a handicapped child was born or a loved one suffered permanent brain damage or became senile, and in many other loss situations— it was my observation that making peace with the life crisis event took longer than most people would have expected.

In conducting my own research, I sought those who were down the road in the process of rebuilding a life. I wanted to know how people doing well now had handled their crises in the earlier months and years.

Almost everyone I interviewed for this book, the triumphant survivors I studied, were at least four years distant from their crisis, loss, or transition event. An exception was someone who had lost a beloved animal and was two years from her loss event when I interviewed her. I have included this woman's story early in this chapter as a way of illustrating that even the death of a beloved animal takes longer to cope with than most people think.

GEORGIA: DEALING WITH THE LOSS OF AN ANIMAL

She is in her late forties now, a person whose one regret in life is that she and her husband were unable to have children and never adopted them. A nephew lived with the couple in his adolescent years, and he, his wife, and their child still remain emotionally close to them. Georgia also enjoys a fond relationship with several friends and their children. Her family, however, consists primarily of the horses, dogs, and cats she has loved and cared for through the thirty years of her marriage. A woman who has always lived in the country and enjoys working outdoors, Georgia is a knowledgeable and skilled animal trainer whose animals clearly reciprocate her devotion and affection.

Georgia's most-loved animal was Fancy, a purebred, smooth-gaited Tennessee Walking Horse. Georgia groomed and trained Fancy as a foal and delighted in riding her on trails, in parades, and in competitive horse shows. For more than a decade, a special bond existed between the horsewoman and Fancy; it had begun when Georgia was the first person to ride Fancy and the horse didn't even buck her.

"The reason I have horses is that they usually live past thirty, longer than most other domestic animals," Georgia explained. Two years ago Fancy and her companion horse were killed by a bolt of lightning. Although Kookie, the beautiful pinto that also died, had been Georgia's pet for fifteen years, Fancy's death hit her harder. She was grief-stricken.

"Fancy had a heart good as gold," Georgia remembers. "If I was riding her wrong she'd go along with me and try to learn to change. She never attempted to hurt or kick anyone. If I put a child on her back, she seemed to have a natural instinct to keep her head up so the child wouldn't fall off." Fancy loved people, had a good disposition, was playful and tender. "She was as close to perfect as a horse could be. She was quite a girl."

Georgia had to struggle with guilt feelings: She had not brought the horses in from the field that day as she usually did before a storm. It was a hot day—100 degrees Fahrenheit—and she remembers saying to her husband, "I'll bet the rain feels good to them." She heard thunder and saw lightning, but it hadn't seemed like a bad storm. Georgia was shocked on finding the horses dead the next morning. Soon afterward she fainted in the yard. She was so emotionally upset that a doctor had to prescribe tranquilizers.

Georgia felt angry that lightning had struck her horses yet had not touched the horses grazing in open fields on neighboring farms. The other animals, she said, were owned by people "who just buy and sell horses and don't really love or take care of them the way I do." Deeply depressed, she wished at times that she had died too.

An uncomfortably heavy air settled over the farm like a fog, covering Georgia with a feeling of emptiness. For the first time in fifteen years there were no horses to water, feed, groom, train, show, or ride.

On her birthday a few days later, Georgia's husband gave her a blank check and wrote on the bottom of it: "For a Tennessee Walker." Jim said he knew she loved "the girls," which is how they always spoke of Fancy and Kookie, and he wanted her to get another horse. Georgia stood in the kitchen and cried because Jim's understanding meant so much to her.

Her friends, also horsewomen, said, "We know you'll never be able to replace Fancy, but why don't you get another horse? You love them so and work with them well."

MAKING A DECISION TO REINVEST IN LIFE

Wrestling with feelings of depression, guilt, and anger, Georgia grieved for many months. Each positive step would be a small battle. Georgia, finally deciding that she couldn't keep living on Valium, stopped taking the pills and started to travel around with her friends to look at horses. "I'm just not the type of person who sits around staring at the TV," she told herself, as she became more and more active. She made a conscious decision to buy a mare in foal so that a colt or filly would soon be born to raise as she had raised Fancy. Georgia hoped for a filly—"another girl."

Three weeks after the fatal thunderstorm—probably too soon to try to get attached to another animal—Georgia bought Souvenir, a golden palomino Tennessee Walker. When a little filly was born shortly thereafter, Georgia's sorrow somehow felt more manageable. Making an early statement about the healing she hoped the foal would bring, Georgia named her Sunshine.

For some months after the mare and her foal came home, Georgia couldn't let herself get attached to them. "What am I doing here with you?" she asked, addressing the new stable boarders. In her grief Georgia often didn't feel like going out to care for the horses. Every day she nevertheless spent many hours looking after the mare and working with Sunshine. She brushed, groomed, and played with the foal and led her on a halter across the paddock, a small training area. Gradually Georgia helped the filly get accustomed to a towel touching her, human arms over her back, walking with a lead, being led from both sides. It took Sunshine about two weeks to learn something new from the training activities which were repeated, over and over, seven days a week. As the foal grew, it became apparent to Georgia that her hard work was producing results. "It takes time," she says, "when you hand-raise them, if you want a horse you can really trust."

Being constantly busy with the horses, Georgia found there was little time to think. "In the back of my mind I said, 'Getting really busy is what I need.' " Friends helped by regularly coming by to see the foal.

A year passed before Georgia felt like riding horseback again. She had tried riding the mare, but Souvenir was "such a pistol, a sassy horse" that Georgia neither trusted nor enjoyed riding her. Souvenir, who had come with that name, which means "reminder," was a big horse like Fancy, nearly sixteen hands high, but there the resemblance ended. Watching her every day was a painful reminder to Georgia that the mare could never take the place of the gentle and lovable Fancy.

Georgia had taken Fancy to an annual competitive horse show during May, a month before she died. The following May, Georgia agreed to ride a friend's horse. She knew in order to go forward she needed to resume her involvement in shows, trail rides, and parades. When her friend's Tennessee Walker won two blue ribbons with Georgia showing the horse, Georgia felt happy and proud. There was also sadness, for she had never won a blue ribbon in a show ring with Fancy.

Her many mixed feelings were typical of a normal healing process.

THE REWARDS OF CARRYING ON

With Gabriel and Pumpkin, a huge mixed-breed shepherd and a beautifully colored rust, gray, and white kitten, at our heels, I follow Georgia to the stable. Sunshine whinnies with excitement as we approach; she nuzzles her nose against our hands, arms, blouses, and jeans while we pet her. She is a beautiful horse—a reddish brown, almost two-year-old with a white blaze running the length of her face. Fancy had had a white blaze marking, too, Georgia explains, and was similarly affectionate and well-mannered. "Sunshine is a real sweetheart," her owner says.

This is the kind of horse, I realize, you can't help loving. She's so gentle, it seems unbelievable that the filly hasn't yet been "broken," has never had a rider on her back. Georgia expects that because of her tranquil, moderate treatment of Sunshine, there will be no resistance when a rider does mount Sunshine for the first time.

"You're a wonderful horse!" I tell Sunshine, stroking her ears. I renew my own lifelong love of horses. Sunshine whinnies repeatedly from the stable as we walk back to the farmhouse.

On the country kitchen table, Georgia spreads family photo albums featuring thoroughbred show horses, German shepherds, miscellaneous cats, and humans. She points out handsome pictures of Fancy and the pinto much as many other persons coming back from grief have shown me photographs of lost family members.

In a photo that especially catches my eye, Georgia is wearing an ankle-length pink-and-white calico dress and matching bonnet. She is proudly astride Fancy in a parade. Their relationship was very special, and Georgia continues to miss her. "The

Tennessee Walker is the best breed there is," says Georgia. "They're so smooth-gaited, I could ride Fancy all day long and not get tired."

She places several loose photographs on the table before me. They have captions like "Sunshine: A Few Hours Old" and "Sunshine: First Day on Earth." Georgia lights up a Marlboro, vows to quit smoking by autumn, and speaks of an approaching, much awaited trip to Hawaii that she and her husband began to plan with friends shortly after losing the horses. Clearly her healing process continues. By degrees, Georgia has been able to allow herself a strong attachment to Sunshine. She is making plans individually and with her husband for continued health and recovery.

On recent trail rides with a friend, Georgia explains, she has felt reunited with nature's beauty. "I can feel the life back in me," she says.

It took Georgia a long time, about eighteen months, to feel "exuberant" again, even with her admirable decision actively to get reinvolved in life. She has weathered the storm.

BETTY: LEARNING TO LIVE WITH THE PAST

Betty was a student in a college course I was teaching called "Helping People in Crisis." In her mid-fifties, she was a brunette with a young-looking, pretty face and soft features. One day after class she approached me and asked if she could see me privately.

Sitting across from me in my office, looking down at her knees, Betty confessed her secret to me: Many years ago she had given up a baby for adoption. Approximately five million birth mothers in America have made the same decision.

With my hand on my forehead, I propped my elbow on the desk and gazed at her intently. I had long held a picture in my mind of the desperate women who relinquish their children. It puzzled me that Betty didn't fit my mental photograph.

She seemed a well-integrated person, self-confident, resourceful, articulate, and happy. I had heard her speak fondly of a husband and children and had observed her full involvement in my psychology classes. In fact, I saw Betty as the type of student I most admire: a woman who has the courage to come to college and begin a new life for herself after being a homemaker for thirty years. Surely somebody who gives up a child for adoption wouldn't be such a capable and resourceful person as the woman who sat across from me, her eyes now focused directly on mine.

Betty nodded her head and smiled. We concluded our brief, private conversation, and I continued to enjoy her many contributions to my subsequent college courses. Betty's secret was not spoken of again until several years later when I was interviewing "triumphant survivors" for this book. I decided to satisfy my curiosity; I looked up Betty's phone number and asked if she would share the rest of her story.

UNDERSTANDING PAST ACTIONS

Sitting at her kitchen table, I saw a striking alteration in Betty's appearance. The competent and poised middle-aged college student underwent a metamorphosis before my eyes. She became a young girl, innocent, inexperienced, and afraid. There was no resemblance between the young girl with tearful, halting speech and the mature woman who had greeted me at the door.

When she was twenty-one years old, she had been living in her mother-in-law's home and was the mother of a one-year-old son, Adam. Her husband had returned from military service in Germany and suddenly announced that he no longer wanted the responsibilities of a marriage and family. He even asked Betty if she would co-sponsor the German woman he was now in love with so that the other woman could immigrate to America!

Feeling devastated and angry but holding these feelings within herself, Betty swallowed her pride and wrote a letter to her elder sister and brother-in-law, asking if she and the baby could move to Pennsylvania to live with them. She felt she couldn't move back to her father and stepmother's house, which she had left at marriage. While it was clear that her sister, a minister's wife with two small children of her own, had mixed feelings about the added responsibility of two more people living in a crowded parsonage, Betty and the baby were given one of the bedrooms.

Living in Pennsylvania, Betty grieved about the end of her marriage. She also felt sick. Finally she went to a doctor and learned that she was pregnant. Desperate and still in love with her husband, she had slept with him one more time after he told her he wanted someone else. Now overwhelmed with depression and consumed with worry, Betty wondered how she was going to take care of fifteen-month-old Adam. "I majored in cooking in high school," she explained to me. "I had no other talents that I was aware of then."

She made a trip back to Baltimore to tell her father she was pregnant. While she was there, her stepmother gave her a piece of paper and said, "Elizabeth, if you want to take care of this, go to this doctor and you won't have to worry about having this baby."

Betty was frightened. It was the mid-1950s, and abortion was both illegal and dangerous. "I was too afraid to go through with an abortion," she said. "I didn't know this doctor and I didn't have good feelings about my stepmother. I couldn't be sure that I'd be safe."

It was difficult to approach him, but Betty felt that she had to ask her father for advice. He was a stoic man of German descent who rarely spoke about feelings or even addressed events of major consequence to the family. Engulfing the family in mystery, he had never, for example, told his daughters the cause of their mother's death when Betty was ten years old.

"Betty," her father said, "why don't you just go through with having the baby, pretend you're having an operation, and give it up for adoption. Just pretend to yourself that the whole thing never happened."

"I took my father's advice," explained Betty, thirty years later, "because I was a very obedient child and I really didn't question him. I trusted my father and I thought, 'That's what I'll do.'"

Betty's brother-in-law took her to a Lutheran Social Service agency in Pennsylvania, where she initiated the process of giving up the baby she was carrying.

Some months later an old boyfriend, Dennis, began to correspond with her and often drove up from Baltimore. Dennis played with baby Adam, took Betty out for good times as she grew increasingly large from the pregnancy, and began to speak of marriage. "I'm making seventy-five dollars a week," Dennis said, as the end of her pregnancy drew near. "If you want to keep this baby, it's okay, and I think we can make it." He was giving mixed messages, however. Earlier Dennis had wondered aloud if he could successfully parent *two* children fathered by a man he had known for many years and never liked.

Betty's decision had already been made. Once the baby was born and given up for adoption, she would finally be free from the husband who had hurt her so deeply. "When I give birth to this baby," she thought to herself, "it's going to clean me of Harvey Wilson."

Betty also clung in those days to a biblical verse from Corinthians beginning with the words "Love bears all things," a concept that took on special significance. "I was going to bear this child and give the baby to responsible parents who could provide care, a good life, and the love that I couldn't give," she explains.

Betty gave birth to a baby girl. Her sister told the nurses

not to let Betty see the infant, since she was to be given up for adoption, but hospital policy dictated then that a woman had to carry her baby out of the building when it came time to leave.

"A nurse brought the baby to me," Betty explained, "and laid her on the bed. The first thing I saw was her forehead and I thought, 'That's Harvey Wilson's forehead.' This was Harvey's baby, our baby, and I guess I was explaining to myself why I had to give it up. I thought she was really cute, but I don't remember having any motherly feelings. I just kept worrying about how Adam was handling my being away from him for three days."

Walking out of the hospital and approaching the car, Betty was anxious to see Adam. Her sister took the infant and settled into the front passenger seat. Betty got into the back seat where Adam was waiting and held him on her lap. Her brother-in-law drove directly to Lutheran Social Services and Betty's sister carried the new baby in. "I stayed in the car with Adam on my lap," Betty remembers. "When my sister came back we went home and I absolutely forgot the whole thing as my father had told me to do. Anything unpleasant, like my mother's death, you just wipe right out of your mind. To this day, I have never again spoken of this event to my sister."

Betty and Dennis were married, and her new husband took over where her father, first husband, sister, and brother-in-law had left off, taking care of Betty and telling her what to do. Within a few years two more sons were added to the family and Betty was busy with Adam and the two babies.

GETTING HELP TO FACE LIFE SQUARELY

Twenty-one years after relinquishing the baby girl, whom Betty had named Elizabeth after herself, Betty sat in a psychiatrist's office. Adam was now twenty-three years old and had been diagnosed as having schizophrenia, a severe mental illness characterized by bizarre thoughts and behavior. The young man had begun what would become a series of hospitalizations. Betty was distraught with grief over the poor prognosis. She needed the psychiatrist's help to understand why Adam's illness made him so disruptive to the family. It was hard to accept the fact that the young man would probably have to live the rest of his life in halfway houses—residential centers for the mentally ill.

Betty saw the psychiatrist for nearly ten years. After the first three years Dennis urged her to quit therapy, but she continued without telling him. The doctor helped her to realize that Adam would grow by being on his own, that she had to cut the apron strings even with a boy who was ill. He also encouraged Betty to listen to her own inner yearnings and enroll in some college courses, an important step in her growing independence. He encouraged her to stand up for what she wanted.

The psychiatrist also opened Betty's eyes to the kind of childhood she had had. She began to realize how detrimental the mystery surrounding her mother's death was. The atmosphere her father had created by insisting that unhappy events and feelings were best hidden or ignored had made it impossible for her to mourn her mother's death. Having learned so early that troublesome feelings are dangerous, years of therapy were now required to bring to awareness many hurtful events and her feelings about them.

EXAMINING EVENTS FULLY AND ACKNOWLEDGING ONE'S FEELINGS

Deciding that the truth was preferable to living with mystery, Betty asked the doctor to obtain the medical records from the hospital where her mother had died in 1941. She was shocked to learn that her mother, who already had three children under the age of fourteen, had died trying to give herself an abortion.

Betty mourned the loss of her mother, releasing the sorrow stored within from the age of ten.

"What irony," she told the doctor, that both she and her mother had had pregnancies by their husbands, felt desperate, and made costly decisions. If abortion had been legal in 1941, she reasoned, her mother wouldn't have died. If Betty had had the mother love that was missing, perhaps her own life would have been different, she said. If her father hadn't lived such a life of self-deception (he continued thirty-five years later to deny that his wife was even pregnant when she died), perhaps she could have learned earlier the importance of living in the truth.

In mourning, a current loss often triggers a reliving of loss events in the past, painful experiences never adequately examined or mourned. Grieving Adam's illness came first, then the mourning of her mother. Finally Betty came upon the long buried feelings of sorrow over her first husband's rejection and abandonment, but especially her sorrow over having relinquished her only daughter. Also, she had recently had a hysterectomy. It was no wonder, her therapist explained, that she had been walking around tearfully holding her stomach. The operation had removed her last and only connection to her daughter: the womb that had carried a baby girl.

"When it finally dawned on me that I had given up my own flesh and blood," Betty explained, "I was angry at everybody. Angry at Dennis for not trying to convince me to keep this baby. Angry at my father. Angry at other relatives. Angry at the church. I had come from a huge family. Why didn't one of my aunts come forward and say, 'I'll help you raise this baby'? All my life I heard about how church people help others. Everybody in the local church knew I was pregnant and was going to give the baby up. Why didn't they help me?"

Guilt, absent from Betty's conscious reactions at the age of twenty-one, loomed over her at the age of forty-six. She decided she had to know what had become of her daughter. She contacted the Lutheran Social Service agency in Pennsylvania.

A social worker from the agency explained to Betty that, according to court precedent in that state, identifying information about the birth parent and the adult adoptee could be shared only with the permission of both parties. The agency could, however, release certain general information: The adoptive parents had chosen to keep the name Elizabeth. The baby had been adopted at the age of one month and apparently had had a happy childhood. She was an honor student, had a bubbly and cheerful personality, played the piano, sang in the church choir, and in high school had been chosen to study abroad.

LIVING IN THE TRUTH

Betty felt a sense of peace when she learned that Elizabeth was alive and well. She was delighted that her daughter had been reared in a religious home and had enjoyed many pleasures in life. She authorized the agency to release to Elizabeth information about her identity as the birth mother, in the event that Elizabeth contacted the agency to learn about her birth family.

Elizabeth did contact the agency. For several months the social worker carefully established that both Betty and Elizabeth wanted to meet each other and that each was reasonably prepared psychologically for such an emotionally wrenching experience.

"I looked at all of my life as one big lie," Betty told me. Now, as a result of her therapy, she was going to find the strength not only to admit to herself the events of the past but to meet the daughter she had given up and to tell her three sons about her as well.

The social worker made the arrangements, and the birth mother and daughter met in a tearful encounter. Betty explained the circumstances of Elizabeth's relinquishment, telling the young woman about the passivity and dependence that for so many years had characterized her mother's personality. Betty also explained that she had only recently gained the courage to face the truth. She answered Elizabeth's questions about her father, brother, and other members of the birth family. They talked for several hours.

The impact of Betty's personal growth was summarized in a letter she received from Elizabeth several months after their meeting. "It takes such courage," wrote young Elizabeth, "to face up to your past actions and try to set things right by telling Adam about his sister and by going to a therapist." The young woman wrote that she herself "felt more complete now," even though it was "mind boggling to know so little one day and so much the next day."

In the aftermath of the meeting with Elizabeth and the disclosures made to all of her children, Betty has continued to feel that "I'm no longer evading things. I'm being honest with myself and with those closest to me in my family. I'm a much happier person."

GROWING IN SELF-ACCEPTANCE

Betty is now more assertive with her family. She is not afraid to express her opinions, and she is continuing her college courses. Over the years her husband has slowly adjusted to the new Betty.

It has taken Betty a long time—thirty years—to let go of the nonproductive "if only" way of thinking and to live fully in the present. "I came to an understanding," she says, "that giving up my daughter was the only thing I could do at that time. I also had to learn that I don't have to suffer forever and ever because I gave up a child." She has come to believe "in a God who knows that we all solve our problems in imperfect ways."

Betty's life offers hope to those who are disheartened by the fact that crisis events in the distant past can be difficult to acknowledge and can require many years to resolve. Her healing story is not so much related to the fact that she and Elizabeth decided to meet each other. Rather, it was Betty's decision to admit *to herself* the events of the past, to mourn her losses, and to go forward in the truth that has set Betty's new life in motion. She has accepted responsibility for her past actions, has forgiven herself, and continues to grow in self-understanding and independence.

BATTLING HEREDITY AND OTHER FORCES

Alex had had a weight problem throughout his life. After his dramatic weight loss, he was still not able to see himself as the accepted and attractive person others saw. That took the passage of some years, along with personal counseling. As far back as he could remember, he had coveted the popularity and admiration that athletes seemed to receive. Now he turned out to be a good athlete himself, doing long-distance running and playing racquetball. Other men noticed his athletic capabilities and potential. Women were attracted to him. The whole thing felt good, but it also felt awkward and frightening. While it was satisfying to be able to run ten miles very quickly, Alex still had memories of not being able to run a mile in the ninth grade and being the object of ridicule. "I always felt uncomfortable when people complimented me," Alex explained. "While it greatly encouraged me to be praised, I was afraid that in a year I'd be my old self again, that I'd gain it all back. I knew that losing that weight was just the beginning."

Certain people criticized Alex for spending so much time looking in the mirror, as if excessively self-absorbed. "I remember thinking," said Alex, "why do you think I look in the mirror so much? I'm a whole new person!" He finds it hard to put into words "how it feels to not know that you're you." People would say, "You're good looking," and he'd say "Me?" It didn't jibe with his own view of himself.

During his intense dieting, Alex learned that any time his routine changed, such as weekends and holidays, if he let himself slide he could easily gain weight—five pounds in just a weekend or twenty pounds on a vacation. On numerous occasions, discouraged by the difficulty of his diet, he would go on eating binges and then need to lose ten pounds. It has now been ten years since Alex has gone on an eating binge.

"I know that I don't want to be three hundred pounds anymore," he explains. "I don't think I knew that in the first three or four years. Now I know I don't want that other person back." For the first year he was never sure who he wanted to be, whether he wanted this new, unfamiliar person or the old person he had been. "I think that during the binges I went back to a sense of safety when I ate ten brownies. It felt good at the time. The feelings of 'Who am I?' have been gone for a decade. I know I'm me now."

As obesity studies demonstrate, Alex found himself fighting a battle against heredity and certain powerful physical forces that cause animals and humans to maintain a certain weight. Many people who have lost pounds can remain at their new weight, if they consume about 25 percent fewer calories than someone normally at that weight.[1] The new research is showing what people with weight problems have known for years: Most can't eat what lean prople eat to stay lean themselves. It is necessary for people with a history of obesity or yo-yo dieting to eat significantly less. Thus, to maintain his new weight of 175 pounds, Alex has found it necessary to restrict himself to 1,500 to 1,800 calories per day—a remarkably low intake for a six-foot-two-inch man who plays racquetball or runs five miles daily, seven days a week!

EXPERIENCING A CRISIS OF FAITH

In the long, anguishing months following the loss of their seven-year-old son, Jan and Ed remembered the words of a friend who had hugged and held them at the hospital after Mark died. The friend had said, "If I were God, this never would have happened."

Both Jan and Ed found that their trust in the fairness of life was now shattered. "I used to think that if you do all the right things, life will be fair," said Ed. He was a physician dedicated to working with cancer patients. "I learned we can't count on life to be fair to us," he continued. Ed saw that he could save lives and make miracles happen for people as an oncologist, but he couldn't save his own son. "There is no dispensation," he said. "I never before had to face, in such a radical sense, the issue of whether there is something to ground us, why life is important, if there is something to live for. I never had to decide whether I was willing to make some commitment to the fact that there is a religious dimension."

Their irreparable loss also caused Jan to doubt whether she could any longer trust in the God she had embraced since childhood. If God exists, she decided, "I'll have to be careful how I respond to Him because maybe He'll do something [horrible] to us again."

She had been brought up a Catholic, and for her "there was an answer to every question. Now none of the answers held anymore." Whatever people said about losing a child didn't do anything for her.

Jan experienced a longing for God, a yearning for some ultimate hope in life. Most of the time during the months immediately following Mark's death, however, Jan felt she couldn't go to church. When she did attend mass she left "feeling so empty."

On one occasion when Jan and Ed participated in a religious service, the biblical story was read in which Jesus healed a sick person and said, "Your faith has made you whole." Jan felt angry when the priest said to the congregation, "You also must have faith." She felt he made it sound as if Mark had died because her faith was inadequate. She felt the church was judging her rather than upholding and supporting her as she mourned.

Jan approached the first Mother's Day after losing Mark with pain and dread. Reluctantly she went to church, feeling a desperate need for something to be said to bring her comfort. Jan was outraged to discover that the subject of the entire sermon that Sunday was abortion. "Can you imagine—on Mother's Day!?" Jan exclaimed. "I was horrified and wanted never to go to church again." Making pronouncements about abortion on Mother's Day, Jan felt, was like giving a caustic sermon to the people who come to church on the subject of people not attending church.

"How can that priest be so far away from all of us and our suffering?" Jan asked her husband after the service. "I know there were other people in the congregation who are suffering. Many of them are out of jobs."

Fortunately, a few months later Jan and Ed met a priest who was able to meet them in the darkness of their mourning. Father Jake understood their anger at God; he felt with Jan and Ed their powerlessness, rage, and anguish. Jake told the couple about times when he had given his all, with prayers and acts of caring, and still he had been powerless to save a life. With kindness and acceptance, without judging them and without defending God or the church, Father Jake walked with them through their crisis.

Rabbi Kushner's words in *When Bad Things Happen to Good People* came to have a special meaning to this couple. " 'God's language is people,' " Jan said, quoting Kushner. "That's part of my simple new faith. The people who helped me have a God are the people who let me be angry at God without feeling like a bad person, who let me have my doubts, who just loved us and hurt with us."

The powerful, healing presence of Father Jake, many other

friends, and several close family members also helped Ed re-establish a belief in the religious dimension of life. "God understands us and relates to us through caring human beings," he decided. Ed came to feel that he could participate in a religious community because he could now experience "God as one who shares our joys and sorrows, who truly suffers Mark's loss as much as we do, and who will go through this with us."

Jan and Ed stayed away from the church where the priest talked about abortion on Mother's Day. They found comfort and sanctuary at the place where Father Jake offered the prayers and gave the sermons. "Some of the most healing experiences of my life" took place at these services, Jan says. The couple's relationship with Jake repaired many injured and unhappy feelings about the church. "He was truly an instrument of God's peace," Jan remembers. "He introduced us to God as a griever, who felt sad with us, by being that *himself*."

A crisis of faith is common in a bereavement experience, particularly for persons for whom religious faith and the church or synagogue have long been a source of strength. When we are suffering terribly, it is often hard to hold fast to the belief that God is with us and to experience God's comfort. Through caring people who merge with us in our pain and who love us unconditionally, usually it happens that over time we find our faith renewed and ourselves once again grounded in the knowledge of God's love.

ENCOUNTERING EPISODES OF TERROR

Black ink surrounds a number of calendar dates in Jan's brain. Indelibly encircled in her memory are Mark's birthday, his death date, their first holidays without him, and other dates that held a special meaning. One such occasion was the day before Jan's thirty-fifth birthday, her first birthday without Mark.

On that day, Jan waved a casual goodbye to her seriously ill mother, who had come to live with Jan and Ed for the last months of her life. Jan hopped into the car and drove to the nursery school to pick up her four-year-old son, John.

Other parents' cars were lined up in the driveway ahead of her in front of the school. Like the others, Jan waited in the car for the teachers to bring the children out to their parents. She began to have vague feelings of nausea and faintness. Her limbs felt numb except for a tingling sensation, and her mouth felt dry. "I must be coming down with the flu or something," she thought to herself.

John got into the car, and mother and son greeted each other. As Jan began to drive away, her physical symptoms intensified and her breathing became labored. Concentrating on the road ahead became an enormous task; she began to drive block by block. "I'm dying," Jan remembers feeling. "I'll never make it home." Finally, when they did arrive, Jan somehow got herself and John into the house. "Mom, I can't breathe," she pleaded. "You have to get help!"

An ambulance arrived with a group of paramedics, who took Jan's blood pressure. Lying on the couch in the living room, she heard a medic say how high her blood pressure was. She grew even more frightened and thought, "For sure, I'm stroking out; I'm going to die."

One of the paramedics said, with no apparent compassion, as if he were reading from a textbook, "Has anything been bothering you lately?"

Struggling to breathe and terrified, Jan replied, "My son was killed a few months ago."

"Well, sometimes people get upset and need to talk," the medic continued. "I think you're just hyperventilating." His words were still not empathic, and he was not helping her terrifying symptoms to go away.

Another paramedic asked questions that sounded more medically appropriate, such as "Have you taken any medications lately?" He seemed to take Jan seriously and helped her to feel that they weren't going to let her die.

In the hospital emergency room, Jan's breathing finally became easier. By remarkable coincidence, the doctor who treated Jan had treated her mother several times in the emergency room when she was struggling to breathe. He knew well the deteriorating heart condition from which her mother suffered. By another fortunate coincidence, he was the doctor who had given Mark emergency care immediately after the accident that took his life.

The doctor was a caring man and a thorough physician. After examining Jan carefully and ordering lab studies, he assured her that he thought she would be all right. Because of his comprehensive examination, Jan could listen to his reassurance. "How terrifying that experience of being unable to breathe must have been for you," he said, acknowledging her feelings.

Breathing normally now, Jan reflected on the scene where her feelings of sickness emerged and her terror had erupted. It was John's first day of school. Waiting in the car with the motor running, she was again in the position she had been in when Mark had gotten out of the car to cross the street that day.

"What I am feeling," Jan realized, "is totally out of control. I've lost Mark and I'm losing Mom. And I can't make sure that my son John can get into my car and be guaranteed to be one hundred percent safe!" Jan wondered, "How am I going to let another child go to school?" She understood now what her desperate panic was about. How could she live and breathe under this burden of never being able to safeguard, with absolute certainty, the life of her surviving son?

Jan's horrifying fear of again suffering one of life's most unspeakable, unbearable losses reminded me of a woman I met on a lecture tour in Oklahoma. Although the woman was only in her forties, she had already experienced the death of her daughter and of two beloved stepchildren. The teenage and young adult children had died from completely unrelated causes and situations over a period of several years. At the funeral of the last child to be buried, she remembered her husband's saying, "Well, there's one good thing. This can never happen to us again."

A horrible loss feels like being swept on a torrential ocean tide that will crush our bodies and skulls against the sea wall. Excruciatingly difficult to live with is the fear, usually requiring years to diminish, that a similar loss might happen again. I understood the husband's brokenness and his odd-sounding, bitter sense of relief.

I also understood how Jan wondered whether she could bear to watch her son John going to and from school every day.

Following her day of acute crisis, Jan's women friends took turns riding along with her when she picked John up or dropped him off at nursery school. Jan knew that the accompanying friend could drive for her, if needed, although it was never necessary. Each day, as the car approached the school, she trembled and wept. It took about two weeks before Jan felt she could drive there alone. Once she started driving by herself again, Jan "felt afraid of feeling afraid" but no longer cried or felt shaky or tingly.

Jan experienced other panic attacks in connection with driving. Fortunately the attacks were never as severe as her first terrible episode. Jan found that once she "had a label for it," the anxiety would go away if someone sat with her and she was able to cry. She says she was amazed to realize how much she wanted to live despite the anguish over losing Mark. "Before I knew I was having a panic attack, when I actually believed I was facing my death, I saw that I didn't want to die!"

The panic episodes occurred less frequently as the months went on. More than a year passed before Jan's anxiety attacks stopped entirely.

Panic attacks and other physical symptoms such as disturbed sleep, appetite changes, bodily aches and pains, rest-lessness, and fatigue are not uncommon experiences in a bereavement process, especially in the first three to six months of grief. Usually physical symptoms diminish, as one identifies and expresses troublesome feelings, or they subside with the passing of time. If the symptoms cause alarm or persist, it is always a good idea to consult with your family physician.

HELPING A CHILD TO EXPRESS GRIEF

Jan and Ed's redheaded, blue-eyed son John was three and a half years old when his seven-year-old brother died. At the funeral parlor, where bushes and blooming plants decorated the front of the building, John went outside and picked a flower. He brought it in and put it in Mark's casket, placing it in his dead brother's hand. Observing the behavior of adults, John figured out what was appropriate and acted on his own. Another child might have needed help or suggestions to offer some expression of love and grief.

After the funeral Mark's body was cremated. Because the parents knew they would be moving within a few years, his ashes were placed temporarily in a mausoleum. Three years later, when they left Michigan, the family took Mark's ashes with them, and Father Jake came to Kentucky to be with them for Mark's burial.

Although three years had passed since Mark's death, John's continuing feelings about his brother's death were vividly apparent. John wanted to do something for Mark, to put something in Mark's grave. He decided he wanted to place acorns there so that Mark could have an acorn collection. The day before the burial John went with his mother to a park to collect the acorns. He was nearly seven years old now. As they collected acorns, John said, "Mom, I'm afraid I'm going to die when I'm seven, too."

John's mother put her arms around John and held his little

red head close to her face. Wisely she never told him that she sometimes had similar fears. Jan's knowledge of the irrationality and normalcy of such feelings hadn't made her own fears go away, yet her knowledge did help her to comfort John.

Reassurance was needed and an acknowledgement of the boy's fearful feelings. John needed to hear his mother say, "Oh, honey, it's scary for you but I think you'll live for a long, long time. I'm sure you'll do what you can to be well and safe, and I will, too."

When a child dies, the children who were close to that child often have lingering fears that death will strike them prematurely as well. The opportunity to voice troubled feelings and to receive reassurance is critical to healing and may be necessary from time to time, over a period of many years. Earlier, when his parents had been debilitated by their own grief, John had benefited from being held, loved, and played with by other relatives and family friends. His parents were more able now to provide John with needed reassurance.

CONTINUING TO STRUGGLE WITH PAIN

In the early months after seven-year-old Mark was struck by a car and killed, his little brother's questions were like sharp needles plunged into their mother's ears: "Where is heaven?" asked John, three years old. "Why did that lady kill him? Why isn't she in jail? What is forever?"

One night Jan's grief was especially fierce as she listened to John say his prayers. "Thank you, God, for Mark," prayed John, "but why are you keeping him so long?"

"As time goes on," says Jan, remembering her first year of mourning, "you get subtle messages from people that things should be much better. To the contrary, on the first anniversary of Mark's death I couldn't believe how overwhelming it still was.

"How can I hurt this badly for the rest of my life?" Jan

remembers asking herself. "How can I possibly endure it?"

Jan realized that healing was taking place, although her pain was often intense. "I didn't cry all day anymore, and I wasn't awake all night. There were concrete ways I could measure feeling better. My heart would still ache unbearably at times, however, and my arms would still feel so empty."

With the passing of time, Jan's suffering has diminished, yet it returns as various life events arise. "Things don't hit you all at once," she explains. "The second-graders started school without Mark. They made their First Communion without him." Again and again she has been struck with the realization that a whole series of events keep happening without Mark and will continue to happen. "He won't get to learn how to play any more songs on his fiddle. He will never get to see any of the sequels of the *Star Wars* movie which he loved so much. He won't get to play soccer, graduate from the eighth grade, make love to anyone, have children of his own, and he won't bury me."

Jan has gradually realized in the deeply hurtful moments that occur over days, months, and years that she will no longer have the joy of watching Mark Aaron Romond grow up and build a life for himself. Initially such realizations produce excruciating pain. As time goes on, the feeling provoked is "more like a dull ache," she says.

Mark was seven years, two months, and eleven days old when he died. Nearly four years later Jan and Ed found themselves nervously counting the days as John approached the exact age that his brother was at death. The couple's fears were not assuaged by knowing that the anxiety they felt was based on the irrational and superstitious notion that fate would prevent any of their children from growing past that particular age. "If I could have physically kept the days on the calendar from turning," says Jan, "I would have done it, even if it was irrational."

Finally John was seven years, two months, and twelve days old. Jan thought, "We've made it!" and the couple's anxiety passed. For a while, says Jan, "I felt rage at the impossibility of the whole situation: My little boy is now my big boy!" Jan felt the sorrow of "leaving Mark behind on a new level" and her anger passed after a few days. "A new era has emerged," she continues. "I've never parented a child older than Mark was when he died. Now John is my oldest child, the one we'll practice on."

Jan knew that each May 22, the anniversary of Mark's death, would be difficult. In the earlier years that date was practically unbearable, and probably it will be a hard day for Jan and Ed to get through for some years to come. Seldom in a lifetime, however, will a twenty-four-hour period be approached with the dread and endured with the anxiety of that day in the life of young John's parents, the day before he became their oldest son.

HANDLING AWKWARD QUESTIONS FROM OTHERS

One of the hardest things to deal with can be the questions raised by people who are not aware that a loss has happened. To a bereaved parent, for example, the simple question "How many children do you have?" can stir mixed emotions. On the one hand, the parents may not feel comfortable telling a stranger that their child has died, thinking it an event too emotionally laden or personal to reveal. On the other hand, a parent may feel that it somehow dishonors the lost child to refrain from bringing him or her into the conversation.

I usually recommend that grieving people do what feels most comfortable to them. They can decide to maintain their complete privacy or to explain the fact of a loss in some limited way. In either case, it can help to rehearse in advance the exact words one wishes to say. "We have one living child whose name is John" or "We have a son who is in the first grade" are both responses suitable for strangers. With new people with whom there is the potential for an enduring relationship, such as neighbors, teachers, selected work associates, or new friends, it could make sense to answer more fully: "We were blessed with two sons. Mark died in 1982 after being struck by a car and John is seven."

Whatever the nature of your loss, it's fine to be vague in response to others' comments and questions and not to render yourself needlessly vulnerable. A major change or life readjustment takes a long time to complete. A painful loss, a bitter disappointment, a difficult addiction to break, a physically or emotionally brutalizing experience—each of these requires a gradual recovery process for the restoration of a sense of wholeness, comfortableness in the presence of others, and the resuming of an energetic life. Replanting the forest with strong, healthy, firmly rooted young trees usually takes at least a few years.

GETTING UNSTUCK BY RECOGNIZING WHAT'S HAPPENING | 4

*The woman who cherished her suffering
is dead. I am her descendant. . . . I
want to go on from here . . . fighting
the temptation to make a career of pain.*

—ADRIENNE RICH

It can be very difficult in the midst or aftermath of a personal crisis to see clearly what is happening to us. There is the sense that we aren't doing well, things aren't right somehow. We may experience widespread confusion, depression, discouragement, sorrow, or anger yet not know how to make ourselves feel otherwise.

We may succeed at carrying on our usual responsibilities at home or work while feeling emotionally batted about by every wind that blows our way. It is easy to get stuck in one stage or another of the grieving process, struggling repeatedly with painful memories, anger, hurt, guilt, or self-pity.

If we examine what others have done to clarify their problems and then start to feel better, we can see that the process of getting unstuck consists of a series of emotional and mental changes, including certain decisions and actions. People who have felt they were walking a treadmill, every day moving in place, finally begin to gain ground when they can observe their situations with objectivity. Once insight comes, it is possible to outline a way to improve the crisis situation, actually to change things and go vigorously ahead.

COMBATING FEELINGS OF HELPLESSNESS

A famous experiment conducted by Curt Richter, involving two groups of wild rats known for their astonishing vigor, has enabled us to learn an important survival lesson. One group who had their whiskers sheared and a second group with whiskers were thrown into warm water. The length of survival time for the whiskered rats was significantly longer (by 60 hours!) than for those rats without whiskers. Was it the presence of the whiskers themselves that enabled this group to fight and struggle? No, something had happened to the rats that were restrained and sheared. They had fought the investigators who were shearing them, but to no avail. Because struggling the first time didn't do them any good, when thrown into water the whiskerless rats quickly gave up and drowned. Unlike the whiskered rats, who fought a good fight, they had learned helplessness from their previous experience.[1]

For human beings, having a sense of hope and personal power can also be a matter of life and death. Every step of the way as feelings of helplessness are combated, the individual gains the strength to fight and endure. It is terribly important to avoid being victimized by our own feelings of powerlessness.

You can take actions to make things better for yourself. You can initiate change. Once it has become your clearly identified goal to make the best of a situation, you will be surprised at the improvement in your life.

All of us have known people who seem to lack the will or heart to overcome obstacles, whereas others readily find the resolve to surmount them. The difference may be that the triumphant ones refuse to give in to feelings of powerlessness; they take decisive action to counter those human feelings.

LEAVING ENCUMBRANCES BEHIND

Through most of the years that I was a young college and graduate student, I worked several jobs in order to finance my education. I worked long hours, was frequently sick, and often felt quite sorry for myself. I resented this situation and looked with envy on friends whose parents were paying their way.

On one occasion Waldo Stevens, an undergraduate professor, approached me with a question that sounded unsympathetic, and yet I still remember it nearly twenty-four years later. "Would you pack two suitcases full of bricks," Dr. Stevens asked, "and carry them around with you every day, all day long?" Unfortunately I wasn't able, at age twenty, to take his words to heart.

I finished school and married. After my marriage ended, I added the bitterness from that loss to my then ten-year-old resentments about paying for my own education. A few more years passed, and I fell in love again. When that relationship ended, I felt resentful and had a hard time releasing myself from the attachment. A year or two later I found myself in love still again, but that relationship also did not work. These experiences added a medium-sized carrying case of additional bricks to my matching Samsonite ensemble.

Finally the luggage got so heavy and burdensome that I couldn't carry it anymore. I reached out for professional help. Dr. Rose helped me unpack.

"Well, you got through college and graduate school, didn't you?" she asked. She had been listening to me and to my ancient resentments for many months. "You've built a good life?"

"Yes," I answered.

"And you did it *yourself*," the gray-haired doctor continued. "You're not beholden to anybody."

"That's right," I said.

"So what are you bitter about?" Dr. Rose exclaimed, gesturing with open palms and waving arms. "You've earned something on your own that no one can ever take from you, something you can always be proud of because you accomplished it yourself. What's to be angry about?"

I straightened myself in the comfortable wing chair in my therapist's office and stared blankly into space. "She really seems to have a point there," I acknowledged to myself. The corner of my lip curled up into the trace of a smile. "What I have achieved belongs to me and I can respect myself for it," I told myself. "I don't have to hold on to all those resentments toward the people and circumstances that made it hard for me to be where I now am. I am *here.* I can let go of the bitterness and go on with my life." It was a life-changing realization. I was thirty-five years old and ready for a new perspective.

Past events, which I long remembered and resented, came to be seen as critical happenings in molding my character, shaping my sensitivities and capacity for empathy, even bestowing a gift of self-confidence and independence which would always belong to me. With the passing of time and Dr. Rose's help, I also eventually released my resentment toward my former husband and toward the other two men who had been important in my life. I realized that each of these experiences had taught me something. I had grown wiser about the world and more self-sufficient. Most important, I had learned not to define my value as a person and woman according to the presence or absence of a man in my life. In subsequent relationships, I also learned to choose my male companions more carefully.

Feeling angry and expressing anger to a trusted confidant can be an important part of any healing process. It is also necessary for most of us to feel sorry for ourselves for a time in order to come to terms with a loss. It is when what may once have been an appropriate emotional reaction becomes a lingering, festering, nonproductive bitterness or self-pity that therapeutic action of some kind is called for. In my case I used professional counseling.

Even when one is the victim of a tragedy such as incest,

rape, the senseless premature death of a loved one, or a grievously debilitating illness or accident—there comes a time to
lay down the mantle of being a victim and leave grievances
behind.

Dr. Joy Joffe, formerly of Johns Hopkins Hospital, described her work with incest victims and others suffering a
traumatic loss. After assisting in a period of mourning and
reflection, she said, "Sometimes I have to say to people, 'What
happened to you was truly horrible. But you have a choice.
You can live the rest of your life as a memorial service or you
can put it away and get on with it.' "

Sometimes, continues Dr. Joffe, she asks her patients to
leave their guilt, anger, unresolved conflicts with their parents,
and other troublesome feelings in a little chest in her office.
"I always say," she says, smiling, "if you find you can't live
without it, give me a call and I'll make arrangements for you
to come by and get it!"

What is wonderful about Dr. Joffe's approach (in addition
to the obvious realism and good humor she utilizes) is that she
helps people to objectify their troublesome emotions or circumstances. She makes it clear to her patients that their anger,
for instance, is not an inseparable part of their being—it is
something from which one can separate and with which one
can do something. People get stuck when they think they *are*
their feelings or will *always have* a particular troublesome emotion or haunting memory. Things can be left behind.

Finding a way to unload or walk away from our encumbrances, which heretofore we have insisted upon carrying, is
like dieting, losing thirty or forty pounds, and finding that we
had forgotten how it felt to walk with a bounce in our gait
and be infused with energy.

NEEDING OR DESIRING TO FORGIVE

A year and a half after Jan and Ed lost Mark, Jan felt a need to meet the woman whose car had struck Mark and killed him. The still tormented mother felt she needed to forgive the person responsible for her little boy's death.

First she talked it over with Father Jake, expressing her intense desire to tell the speeding driver what it was like for her that Mark was dead. She also discussed her need to forgive. "It feels like my bitterness toward her will kill me," Jan explained to the priest. "I don't want to walk around with this hatred and anger for the rest of my life. It just feels crushing— like it will consume me and kill me."

Father Jake was present in a human way; clearly he was a friend who shared Jan's suffering. He understood why she yearned to confront this woman, so he made arrangements for the three of them to meet in his office several days later.

The light in Jake's office was soft. There were lounge chairs a few feet apart. Books and personal mementos gave the room a comfortable feeling. Jan saw that the woman, in her mid-forties, was wearing a dark suit with a white blouse and bow. "She looks like a nice lady," Jan thought.

Father Jake first prayed with the two women. He said a prayer about courage and prayed that they would be open with each other. He prayed for their healing and then he left.

Jan started: "The report that we got a year after Mark died said that you were speeding. But because of Mark's age, it was assumed that it was the child's fault. You didn't even get a ticket!"

She paused, then continued, "*Your* children are perfectly alive. Our family is devastated. We'll never get over this. And you are perfectly free."

The other woman said she knew what it was like for Jan and her husband to lose their son because she had lost a parent. Jan felt that her loss was being minimized and was discouraged about how the talk was going. Losing your parent and losing your little child were not the same kind of loss.

"I teach second graders," the woman continued. She must have realized the feebleness of her first response to Jan's anguish. "Every day I have to go to work and look at a room full of little boys your son's age. For a while it was horrible, and I was going to just quit teaching forever. But then I decided I had taken the life of a child and I owed something in return. I couldn't give back the boy's life but maybe, I decided, I could go back and work with those children and do the very best possible job." Suddenly Jan experienced the person who had robbed her of Mark as a human being who had made a terrible mistake. Jan was actually able to feel some compassion toward the teacher, even though the woman had been the instrument of her son's death.

"I want to forgive you," Jan explained, starting to cry, "even though I don't feel like forgiving. I want to be alive for my son John, for my husband, and even for myself."

"You don't have to forgive me," the schoolteacher replied, now weeping with Jan. "I would understand if you couldn't forgive me."

"But I need to forgive you," Jan said. The two women embraced. For a moment they wept in each other's arms and experienced the tragedy that had brought them to this place. Neither would ever be able to forget that terrible day. Mark had been struck as he crossed the street in front of his own house while his horrified mother watched helplessly from a short distance and the schoolteacher, stunned, sat behind the steering wheel in a state of shock. The memory of those moments would never adequately fade.

They said goodbye, after wishing each other whatever goodness life could offer. A friend of Jan's had come along to drive her home, not knowing what kind of emotional state would follow such an ordeal.

"That meeting," remembers Jan, "was one of the hardest things I've ever done."

Years later I sat talking with Jan and her husband in a cluttered office at the Kentucky hospital where Ed works with cancer patients and she trains bereavement workers. It is obvious that their loss of Mark continues to be deeply felt. Retelling the story is meaningful because Jan and Ed want to help others by talking about their lost son.

"I'll read about a child hit by a car," says Jan. "When a person is sued or jailed over an injustice, I'll wonder if I should have taken the woman to court. I feel angry again. Then I think nothing that could happen to her would bring Mark back. It doesn't fix what happened.

"I think what Mark would want from me is that I be fully alive. That's what I can give him now, two gifts: one is to grieve because that's the healing, and then to live life in a full, living, loving, giving way."

Jan was courageous in initiating an action which she hoped would ease her tormenting rage. There was always the risk that meeting the other woman would intensify her pain and anger. Jan chose the setting of a trusted friend's office. Her friend, the priest, could influence the meeting which was to follow by his simple yet caring and sensitive prayer. She took care of herself further by bringing along a friend, who could provide emotional support and help after the meeting.

Not everyone who suffers because of another's direct negligence or violence feels a need or desire to forgive. Some are not plagued by feelings of rage in the way that Jan was. Others understandably want the one responsible for their loss to be punished. They believe a successful lawsuit or criminal conviction could bring relief.

Jan's wisdom was in deciding upon an action that could promote healing. Many successful lawsuits, criminal convictions, and especially executions provide a sense of retribution but don't effectively aid healing. Each person must search his or her own heart to establish a plan of action. What is needed are the actions most likely to result in a renewed freedom to live one's life productively.

FINDING PEACE THROUGH EXTRAORDINARY FORGIVENESS

One day a newsletter came from a New York retreat center Jan and her husband had once visited. Jan put it on her bedside table, where she could look it over later. That evening she discovered in the newsletter an extraordinary story. A religious sister was recounting a meeting that had taken place in Switzerland in the 1950s. The story was astonishingly relevant to Jan's continuing struggle.

The American sister had been washing dishes, along with an Englishman and a German, at the spiritual retreat house. They spoke about the international conference they were attending and shared memories of past events from their respective countries. All three of them, they realized, had been in the military service in World War II.

The Englishman, who had been a Royal Air Force bomber pilot, said his most horrible memory was of directly hitting a hospital in Dresden. He could remember flying low and seeing the white cross painted on the roof of the building before dropping the bombs. The event was not an accident; his orders specifically read that he was to bomb the hospital. He said he continued to feel tormented with guilt, remembering the destruction and death that day which he had personally wrought upon innocent civilians.

The German stood motionless and looked stunned. He knew well the day and the event. "My wife was giving birth to our first child that night," he said, "and they were both killed."

With a look of terror on his face, the Englishman reached out to embrace the German. "Oh, please forgive me! Oh . . . ! Forgive me!"

"I already have," the German replied, "long ago."[2]

Jan placed the newsletter back on the nightstand. She saw the ongoing horror experienced by the Englishman. It was chiseled into the ceiling as she lay on the bed staring at the shadows overhead. How incredible and miraculous a gift it was, she thought, that the Englishman could be forgiven. In a most concrete, human way he had been forgiven by the only person who could forgive him. Otherwise, she realized, the Englishman would have spent his entire life never able to be at rest.

"For the first time," Jan recounts, "I felt really free from the pangs of 'Did I do the right thing? Was I loyal to Mark?' All those feelings just left when I could see a similar story in a situation that will never be fair."

Jan had the sense that she also had been in a position to give forgiveness when it cost a lot to give it. She was glad that she had been able to come forth.

"From that moment," Jan explains, "I stopped feeling confused about forgiving the schoolteacher for my son's death. It was a really wonderful, wonderful feeling.

"I feel free now from my doubts," she continues. "I feel no regrets at all. I feel a peace from the knowledge that forgiveness doesn't have anything to do with justice or fairness or my loyalty to Mark. I feel solidly at peace about it."

MOLLY AND BEN: MAKING A DECISION NOT TO REMAIN PASSIVE AND POWERLESS

When parents lose a young adult child to a religious cult, their grief can parallel that of losing a child by death. The loss of a daughter or son is life's most difficult loss to bear.

Molly and Ben's daughter Dorrie was an able student who left a prestigious New England college to join a religious cult. In the early years of their daughter's membership in the group, the couple knew very little about cults, mind control, or brainwashing. They watched with bewilderment as their beloved Dorrie became remote both from them and from her previous emotional, spiritual, and intellectual self. The cult members saw the group's guru as their lord, their ticket to heaven. Cult members were led to distance themselves severely from previously held ties, loyalties, and values. Molly and Ben were troubled, deeply distressed. Often it was hard to pay attention to other family matters, to their work, and to anything else in their lives.

Watching their daughter lose her individuality and self-determination was difficult. "We were certainly angry with Dorrie," Molly remembers, "but we never got to the place of utter alienation with her. We never gave her an ultimatum, and we never would have."

Dorrie's parents had urged her to come home as often as she could. Whenever possible they sent letters and phoned Dorrie, always telling her good news and speaking of happy things at home. They sent CARE packages with clothing and food. Molly and Ben made a decision to do everything within their power not to lose their daughter.

The tragic story of the masses who committed suicide in Jonestown, Guyana, in 1978, intensified the couple's fear for their daughter's well-being. On the other hand, so powerful was the spell under which Dorrie lived that her parents at times thought of her as being already dead. "Sometimes I wondered," explained Molly, "would it really be so awful if Dorrie were killed in a car crash? It would be no worse than it is now."

ACTIVELY LEARNING ABOUT THE PROBLEM

One of the chaplains at the university where Ben was employed, arranged for several authorities on cults to come speak on campus. Molly went to the lectures. She heard about mind control and for the first time met other parents in their situation. Molly reported what she had learned to Ben, who could not attend. "It was as though we were being shot with electricity," she says.

The couple was particularly impressed by the message given by Margaret Singer, a psychologist at the University of California at Berkeley. She spoke about the psychological state of cult members, how hollow these persons are, and how their confidence and decision-making power is almost nothing.

Molly and Ben experienced a turning point as a result of Dr. Singer's presentation. She had explained to them what had happened to their child. "We were set afire with the sense that we had to do something to free our child from her psychological bondage," says Molly. "Dorrie had been controlled for such a long period of time, we realized, that she couldn't free herself from this powerful mind control."

They saw that in the beginning Dorrie had been drawn to the cult by her desire to learn the type of meditation that it taught. Once she was lured away from college and family, there had been a surrendering of free will as the result of subtle coercion. Dorrie was vulnerable to psychological coercion because she was young, confused, and unhappy at this particular time in her life. She was a gentle soul who saw the group members as living a simple life of kindness to each other. The cult's alleged intention to help indigent people also appealed to Dorrie. She was unable to recognize the manipulation that occurred at the hands of a cult leader obsessed with power and money.

Molly and Ben decided to do something for Dorrie that was uncustomary for them. They would have to try to free her. "You always hope," says Molly, "that your child will have enough self-will from growing up in your family. It was pathetic to see how Dorrie lacked this will."

Regularly participating in Sunday morning services at the church, Molly and Ben started sitting closer to the minister. They were looking for help in every possible place. Says Molly, "I was listening with different ears, and there was always something that would help me."

Molly read about cults and attended more lectures and workshops. She tried to contact every individual she could who might know something about the subject. Her search led to many blind alleys but also put her in contact with a number of people who were very helpful. Some parents told her of their failures in attempting to have their children deprogrammed. One described precautions that she and her husband could take to increase the chance of successful deprogramming.

Present at one of the many workshops Molly attended was a father whose daughter had once been in the same cult as Dorrie. The young woman, already deprogrammed, sat next to her father. She seemed so pert and normal that Molly kept thinking, "Dorrie once again could be like this instead of the sad sack she is now."

TAKING DECISIVE ACTION

Hiring a professional deprogrammer was expensive—and the stakes were high. They knew they couldn't afford to fail. Their plan had to be meticulously, secretly developed over a period of months and carefully executed. Some of the planning sessions were held in secret places; Molly and Ben felt like spies, sneaking and plotting.

Dorrie was twenty-five years old and had been a cult member for six years when her parents and three siblings stole her away for deprogramming. She was home for a brief family visit and the family had just finished dinner at her sister's house. When it was time to leave, Ben drove to pick up a hired security person, who hurriedly jumped in the car and took over the driving. Held in the back seat of a two-door car where she could not jump out, Dorrie said, "I thought you were too smart for this."

She told them horror stories of other cult members allegedly injured in various ways by efforts to deprogram them. She had been warned that deprogrammers would violate her and try to take away her faith. Dorrie felt betrayed.

They drove to a secret rented house in the country where cult people could not interrupt the deprogramming. Security was needed also to prevent Dorrie from hurting herself and necessitating a trip to a hospital, where she might "spill the beans."

Her parents and siblings worked with Dorrie, helped by two deprogrammers, one a former cult member and the other a professional flown in from California. For five days every effort was made to cause her to reflect upon her cult experiences and to think for herself.

Dorrie was never left alone. She was fed in the deprogramming room, someone always stayed with her at night, and her mother accompanied her to the bathroom.

Dorrie was required to listen to audiotapes in which former cult members told of their experiences. A tape was played of the Phil Donahue television show featuring former cult members who had escaped Jonestown. The tape seemed to have a great impact on Dorrie. As she later told her parents, she saw that she was just as capable of killing herself or someone else on her guru's order, as were the people in Jonestown. Dorrie also was greatly influenced by the fact that her parents' assertive behavior had been so untypical of them.

Escorted by the professional deprogrammer, Dorrie flew to a rehabilitation center on the West Coast, where she remained for several months. Having just spent six years of her life with no ability to make decisions for herself, Dorrie was intoxicated with her new freedom. The idea of simply choosing what things to eat and what recreational activities to pursue was overwhelming at first and then exciting. Her childlike delight was reminiscent of prisoners of war emerging from the darkness of enforced captivity following years of imprisonment.

REMAINING STEADFAST

It's true that in most situations parents find that it is wiser to accept rather than try to change their adult children's values, lifestyles, choice of love partners, political activities, religious beliefs, and the like. The circumstances faced by Molly and

Ben were extraordinary in that an "uncustomary intervention" was deemed necessary.

The lessons learned by this couple are valuable for every parent. They remained steadfast in their expressions of caring and love for their child and set about to learn everything possible about the world in which she lived. They struggled to maintain communication with their daughter even while she turned her back on their values and rejected their concern.

Molly and Ben did not become "stuck" in anger or despair but looked to new sources of help—their minister, other parents of cult members, professionals. They attended lectures, read books and articles, and painstakingly researched the matter of deprogramming. They refused to remain passive and powerless in a situation which was causing them great pain. They methodically set about to learn what they could do to change their situation. Obtaining the advice of experts and trusted others, this couple had the courage to take decisive action.

During the years Dorrie was lost to them, Molly and Ben followed a normal grief process: they suffered depression, confusion, guilt, sleeplessness, physical ailments, anger, and other symptoms of bereavement. Their situation changed, however, because Molly took the lead and brought her husband along, in a passionate effort to learn and grow.

Dorrie needed a healing period of several years. Eventually she went back to an Ivy League university and finished college. She graduated Phi Beta Kappa, with highest honors. At the age of thirty-two, Dorrie graduated from the Stanford Law School.

REACHING OUT TO OTHERS— SOMETIMES EVEN STRANGERS

In *Brainstorm*, Karen Brownstein tells the harrowing story of her ordeal with a malignant brain tumor. She reached out and carefully selected those who would give her professional, emotional, and practical support.

Knowing that she needed people at her side, Karen called friends and relatives from near and far and asked them to come. She asked her parents to help with the children. She openly and frequently confided in her husband. She called a doctor friend for advice in selecting a neurosurgeon. She sought out a psychiatrist who was caring yet knowledgeable about her medical condition. After hair loss from radiation therapy, she found a good wig manufacturer and took a friend along in a serious effort to find attractive wigs. She had long talks with an understanding rabbi, who was an old friend.

At a preliminary diagnosis of a brain tumor, one doctor was straightforward to the point of brutality. Several physicians and other health care providers were simply clumsy in their handling of her human feelings. To cope with them, Karen reached for all the empathetic support she could find from friends, family, and those health professionals who were sensitive to the emotional dimension of her medical situation.

Once Karen even lunged after a complete stranger, strongly suspecting that he could help her when she first entered the waiting room where patients sat awaiting radiation treatment. She had thought the other patients looked like the "congregation of the damned," that they all looked "so terminal." Out of a treatment room "trotted a tall, shamelessly fit man in his middle forties." Her eyes followed him as the athlete jogged down the hall, then she chased after him, finally grabbing the man's sleeve at the elevator.[3]

"Please," she said, as she describes the scene in her book. "Please don't go yet. I have to ask you something . . . I'm a new patient," she continued.

"Oh," the man said, "I'm an old patient. Tomorrow is my last treatment." She noticed he was grinning.

"Ah," she said, now with a smile on her own face, "so you are both. Both an escapee and a survivor."[4]

They exchanged a few more words before she closed with,

"I'm glad to have known you." The stranger smiled and softly touched her hand. Those who intend to fight for life often reach out to others who can reassure or inspire, wherever such bearers of encouragement are to be found. It is smart behavior.

"OLD EGGS": WORKING THROUGH FEELINGS OF DISCONTENT

When I was thirty-nine I developed vague feelings of depression. I felt unmotivated, tired, and unfulfilled.

Finally I went in search of a professional opinion from someone who, like myself, held a doctor's degree in psychology. She was in her late sixties and not very sympathetic about my feeling old. "Too old for what?" she asked.

All I knew was that I felt terrible. After several weeks of carefully examining my feelings, it finally hit me. "I have wonderful friends, new wallpaper on the walls, and a pretty house. I've also reached my goal of becoming a full professor by age forty but—oops—I'm getting too old to have children!"

My ex-husband and I had not had children. A significant part of how I survived the painful end of that marriage was by plunging myself into work, building a career, and completing my graduate studies. Now I saw in a *Time* magazine article that a woman's eggs are whatever age she is and become "old and tired" at about thirty-five. "Too old to have young eggs, that's what!" I reported to my therapist. My biological clock was running out.

I thought about one of my closest friends, who had given birth to a stillborn baby. Naomi was about my age and her baby had died with a chromosomal abnormality. Even if I did marry now, I couldn't face the possibility of bringing a child into the world with a genetic problem. My belated need to be a mother had to be resolved another way, I decided.

I enrolled in a course for prospective adoptive parents. "I respect you that you're not going to marry some jerk just to have children," said a woman in the class. The man I was dating wasn't a jerk but I still didn't want to marry him.

Then a woman entered the classroom with her two little daughters from India. Suddenly I was certain about the direction my life would take. It was necessary for me to grieve the biological child I would never have, but it wasn't necessary to mourn very long. I was going to adopt a baby from India!

My depression lifted. Most women gain weight during their pregnancies, but I literally lost forty pounds as I awaited my adopted baby. Deciding to take action and go after the family I yearned for caused the depression to evaporate.

There were certainly struggles. I worried whether I would be a good mother. Would I even like motherhood and the way it would change my life? How would members of my family and others accept my child? How much social prejudice would there be toward a little brown child with a white mother?

I grieved for the baby—one of literally thousands abandoned by a mother unable to care for a child. India is a country whose population of poor and hungry people outnumbers the entire United States population. I grieved for my baby's mother and prayed for her to have enough food.

Like most children relinquished in the Third World, my child would never learn the identity of her biological parents, know her medical history, or understand the exact circumstances that had rendered her birth mother unable to take care of her. For this and whatever inevitable feelings of rejection my daughter might suffer in later life, I felt sad. I also had a melancholy feeling that I would never have beautiful brown skin and brown eyes like my daughter in order to have us look as much like each other as possible. Although she was not even conceived yet, I worried about my baby's premature birth, low birthweight, and the struggle she would face just to survive.

Later, after my daughter arrived, it would become exceedingly clear that no child in the world was preferable to this one. I still went to the mirror with my babe in arms and wished to be a brown person, wished I had one of those more-or-less regular families with a husband for me and a father for her, and wished especially that my child wouldn't someday have her own grief to bear in relation to her biological mother or birth circumstances. I was somber when I realized that I had become a mother because of another woman's pain. At the same time, a pervasive and abiding joy filled my being. I wouldn't have traded this beautiful little baby for any biological child or traditional family situation.

Grieving what isn't possible in life, we eventually become free to celebrate fully—with thanksgiving, delight, and a sense of wonder—what *is*.

THE CRITICAL COMPONENTS OF RECOVERY

According to Dr. Robert Weiss, formerly of the Massachusetts Mental Health Center at Harvard, "the process of recovery has three components, interrelated but to some extent independent: cognitive resolution, emotional resolution, and appropriate identity change."[5]

Cognitive resolution involves "making sense of an event," says Dr. Weiss. We need to understand the why of a loss and how it happened, what lesson was learned or what value obtained from our adversity. Efforts to "figure out" a personal crisis contribute to the ability to move away from a fixed state of distress.[6]

The "emotional resolution of a traumatic event," continues Weiss, "is usually harder to achieve than cognitive resolution and takes longer." Others and we ourselves may think we are going over and over the same troublesome feelings and reviewing all the same memories and issues even while movement is taking place, says Weiss.[7] We know that healing is taking place, however, because gradually our ability to function in a world with other people improves. Our capacities for concentration and productivity slowly return along with an ability to love and work without constantly focusing on ourselves or our hurtful memories. Grief pangs can return from time to time, but these painful remembrances no longer "own" us and shape our being and our thinking in the ways they once were capable of doing.

The third critical component of recovery articulated so well by Dr. Weiss has to do with the necessity of reshaping our self-concept. Following a major loss or crisis event, we can neither remain the person we once were nor view ourselves in the same way. In order to go forward it is necessary to integrate the changes that have transpired into our daily activities, our philosophy of life, our relationships with others, and our approach to the future. Recovery means accepting our changed circumstances to the degree that is necessary in order once again to find pleasure in life and something to live for.

STRATEGIES FOR BECOMING "UNSTUCK"

The following guidelines can help you to take some positive action in order to regain a degree of control in your situation. Pursuing at least some of these suggestions can provide you with a greater feeling of personal power, optimism, and hope:

- Make a conscious effort to identify what is not making sense to you about your loss or crisis. Ask yourself: What is it that is most puzzling or troubling me?
- Name the emotions you are feeling as precisely as possible—hurt? anger? shame? guilt? regret? yearning? wondering "why me"? The process of labeling them will cause them to lose much of their power.
- Specific actions promote healing. Ask yourself what actions in the past were helpful to get you moving.
- Confide in someone. Be sure to choose someone who is

a good listener and a nonjudgmental, caring, positive individual.

☐ Search out the opinion of an expert or professional who is knowledgeable about problems like yours—a teacher, counselor, doctor, nurse, clergyperson, social worker, financial advisor, or lawyer. You want someone who is qualified to address your particular concerns yet who also has the human characteristics listed above. If you must get advice from an expert lacking in such human qualities, take a caring friend along with you to humanize the encounter.

☐ Look for books that pertain to your situation, or ask your physician, counselor, or clergyperson to recommend reading material that could be helpful. Try to learn something new which will give you insight for understanding your situation and skills for coping with it.

☐ Bring more order into your life. It will help you to feel better simply to straighten up the house, clean out a workroom, balance your checkbook, pay the bills, or accomplish other practical tasks. While there are certain stressful events over which you have little control, it is especially important to take charge in other ways.

☐ Take a positive action that will lead to a better understanding of your situation or help to resolve some lingering troublesome feelings. For example, write a letter, speak to a particular person, make a necessary decision.

☐ Take a good look at the positive qualities that have gotten you this far in life and will carry you the rest of the way. What long-standing strengths and new perspectives will enable you to go forward?

☐ Make plans for your future. Start to reinvolve yourself in life. You can aid your own survival by doing something of benefit or helpfulness to others. Also, you can do something for yourself, something that you've always wanted to do.

TURNING | 5
POINTS |

*If you always do
what you've always done,
You'll always get
what you've always gotten.*
—ALAN COHEN,
THE DRAGON DOESN'T LIVE
HERE ANYMORE

In order for a turning point to occur in a troubled life, someone or something has to change. Turning points in most cases represent a departure from the usual. One's path is cleared of mental or physical obstacles blocking the way, or the tollgate to a brand new highway emerges, seemingly from nowhere.

HAVING HEART-TO-HEART TALKS

Gloria, whose story about accepting her gay son was told earlier, made a decision to get to know her son all over again in order not to lose him. That decision was a turning point in her healing story.

"A gay child is the same person the day after telling his parents that he is gay that he was the day before," explains Ken, "but there is a whole new perception on the part of the parent. Now the adult child is seen as looking at other gay men instead of at women."

For mother and son to resume their close relationship, it would be necessary for Gloria to allow Ken to be himself instead of the person she wished him to be. She would have to learn, she realized, how Kenny felt about things and what *his* view was of the kind of a life he was going to have.

After several months of seeing Dr. Robert Laidlaw, a psychiatrist knowledgeable about homosexuality, Gloria got up enough nerve to take some of her questions directly to Ken. With a gentle curiosity, and at her own timid pace, Gloria came forth with one or two inquiries at a time. "How do you know you love Clem?" she would ask. "Did anything ever happen with the girls you dated in high school to turn you off to women?" After Ken's reply, Gloria often changed the subject to something less personal. "Where are we going to dinner?" she would wonder aloud. Perhaps later in the conversation or during another visit or phone call, Gloria would ask, "What about Clem attracts you? Are you sure this isn't just a phase you're going through?"

Much of his attraction to Clem, Ken told his mother, was *affectional*. He was in love with Clem, he enjoyed Clem's companionship and engaging personality, and he hoped they would have a lasting relationship. What he was looking for, he said, was exactly what most straight people want in their love relationships: mutual commitment, lifelong sharing, and a sense of family.

Ken explained that his attraction to certain gay men was not merely a sexual attraction and that gay people don't constantly have sex on their minds any more than straight people do. Homophobia, society's intense and irrational fear of homosexuality, he said, causes stereotyping and perpetuates many myths about gay people and their lifestyle.

"But you'll get hurt," Gloria told Ken. "Society doesn't like homosexuals. People will try to hurt you physically, they'll prevent you from getting work, and they won't let you get ahead."

Ken tried to answer his mother in a way that would reassure her regarding his personal safety, yet he had to agree that there was considerable validity to many of her concerns. Gay people are sneered at, and many gay people are victimized by acts of ridicule, bigotry, and violence.

Eventually it was Dr. Laidlaw who helped Gloria to feel that "thank goodness Ken was going to do something with his life [become a psychologist] where he wouldn't be hurt by society's prejudice against gays." The psychiatrist explained that although gay people contribute to every occupational group and are represented in every socioeconomic class, as a psychologist Ken would be working with educated people who are not as subject to prejudice.[1]

Ken, gratified that his mother was getting professional help for herself and no longer insisting that *he* see a psychiatrist, opened up to his mother. He told her that from the age of ten he had undergone a "terrible internal emotional struggle" in an effort to accept his homosexual fantasies. Outstanding in school, both academically and socially, Ken dated girls while secretly sharing his true feelings with a buddy who was also discovering himself to be gay. "He knew enough to say nothing to anyone, thinking that he would magically outgrow his fantasies about men," Gloria recalled in her book. "He knew his feelings would have created a crisis in [his] traditional family."[2]

Gloria felt compassion for Ken as she realized how long her son had carried his secret. Remembering what Dr. Laidlaw had said about a person not having a simple choice of whether to be straight or gay, she felt sad that society would judge her son for something that was "an immutable fact of his life."[3]

LEARNING FROM RESPECTED PERSONS

Several times Gloria and her new husband, Gene, traveled from New York to Maryland to visit Ken. On one occasion, they had dinner with Ken and Clem at the elegant country home of Clem's parents. Gloria and Gene discovered that Ken's lover was witty and bright, had been a medic in the military service, was sophisticated, had a master's degree in psychology, played the piano and violin, and spoke three languages. Clem's parents, likewise, were ambitious, refined, respectable people.

The environment from which Clem had come clearly was not the "lowlife" or "dregs of humanity" Gloria's mind had previously associated with homosexual people. Gloria and Gene liked Clem and his family and saw that almost anyone would. However, Gloria was chagrined by the fact that Clem's parents seemed quite unaware of their son and Ken as a gay couple, at least on a conscious level. To them, they were just good friends.

During another visit to Maryland, Gloria and Gene brought along Gloria's longtime best friend, Ida, who "became enamored of Clem." Ida, of course, was not attached to Ken in the way that his mother was; she could be matter-of-fact about Ken's gay qualities and enjoy Ken and Clem as a couple.

Ida's smooth and easy acceptance brought about a turning point for Gloria. If a nice person, someone whom she respected, could so readily accept her son and his lover, then she could begin to accept them too.

AN INTERLUDE: LETTING GO OF
FALSE HOPES

About the time that Gloria was taking significant strides in a long journey toward viewing gay people and especially her son in a new way, Ken and Clem's relationship ended. Terribly hurt after the breakup, Ken started dating a girl and continued to see her for about nine months. Gloria felt hopeful that her son might develop a relationship with a woman after all; she stopped asking questions and stopped the process of trying to get to know her son all over again. It is typical of parents of gay people to so hope their child will turn out to be heterosexual that they hastily deny all strong evidence to the contrary.

Ken eventually realized, "This is phony; I'm gay," and broke off the relationship with his girlfriend. Knowing that he had dated her to avoid the pain of losing Clem, whom he missed mightily, Ken traveled for nine months around America and North Africa to pull himself together.

For more than a year Gloria clung to the hope that Ken had suddenly dismissed all attachments to men. Such denial and false hopes are often part of a healing process leading to acceptance. When one reason for hope after another proves unwarranted, an individual is helped gradually to face reality. Gloria was to find out that Ken's recent interest in having a girlfriend was merely a short interlude. He was ultimately drawn to her as a friend, not a life partner.

False hopes finally seen for what they are can be a turning point. Herman Wouk wrote in his novel *Inside Outside*, ". . . once things are hopeless a [person] can laugh again; it is clinging to an eroding hope that sickens the soul."[4]

CHALLENGING STEREOTYPICAL ATTITUDES

In the year that followed his world travels, Ken's sexual and affectional orientation became clear again. He moved to California to pursue his doctoral studies, and he and his mother resumed their monthly telephone conversations in which Gloria sometimes asked general questions about the life Ken was living. Eventually Ken began to mention the name of someone named Sam, a medical student, the first man he had allowed himself to trust since the painful breakup with Clem. A couple of years passed.

Six years after Gloria learned that Ken was gay, Gloria and her husband Gene traveled to California to spend Christmas vacation with Ken and Sam. As visitors from the East, they were the guests of honor at a Christmas party in San Diego, given by Gloria's son and his lover. The festive dinner party was to be a major turning point for Gloria and would permanently change her view of gay people and their lifestyles.

The crowd at Ken and Sam's house included numerous close family members, friends of Sam from medical school, professors from the university where Ken was a doctoral student, a gay barrister from England, who was accompanied by his Mexican-American lover, a straitlaced but fun-loving navy commander, and a few elderly people who lived in the same apartment house. The guests were old and young. They were gay and straight. Almost everyone brought a dish of food to share, and Gloria thought the conversation sparkled. An outgoing woman, Gloria found the party stimulating and enjoyed the people she met.

"My mother saw how thoroughly integrated our gay lifestyle was into a normal life," says Ken. "Mom realized that we could have a good life and be a gay couple and that we weren't doomed to the lonely and unhappy life she thought being gay was all about. I think my mother realized that there are far more similarities between gay people and straight people than there are differences. The same is true of many types of people. If you're a white person and you don't know any black people, you don't know that they have bookends on their shelves, that they send flowers on Valentine's Day, and that they use washing machines like everybody else."

Meeting Sam, Gloria found she warmed to him easily. She liked his sense of humor and obvious intelligence. She was impressed with the thoughtfulness and hospitality Sam showed his guests, including his divorced parents, their dates, and Ken's brother Jeff, along with Jeff's wife and child.

There was something else in Sam's favor. "If Kenny had to have a male lover instead of a pretty young wife," wrote Gloria in her book, smiling at herself for being the stereotypic Jewish mother, "at least Sam would be a doctor!"[5]

What had happened in Maryland, when Gloria met Clem and his parents and saw what fine people they were, was happening again in California. Gloria was quite "taken with" Sam and with his parents. She was also impressed by the fact that so many people whose lives she admired, such as the navy commander and his psychologist wife, obviously accepted Ken and Sam. Here were respectable people who were comfortable in the home of a gay couple and who clearly cherished Ken and Sam as their friends. Just as Gloria's friend Ida had readily accepted Ken and Clem several years earlier, now literally a houseful of interesting, accomplished, lovely people were demonstrating *their* full affection for her son and his lover.

Waves of a changing perspective came over Gloria like a gentle tide drenching the sand. Observing others, Gloria had her first glimpse of what it could be like truly to feel comfortable with Ken and Sam. For the first time she caught a picture of her son and his lover as having a life she could respect.

SERENDIPITY

Sometimes a turning point comes in the form of a gracious event of the kind M. Scott Peck has described in *The Road Less Traveled*[6] as "the miracle of serendipity." At the time most needed, "highly unlikely beneficial events happen to us," softly knocking on the door of our awareness, awaiting our openness, recognition, and response. "Serendipitous events occur to all of us," Peck writes, "but we fail to take full advantage of them."

In *Some Survived: An Epic Account of Japanese Captivity During World War II*, Manny Lawton tells the story of himself and thousands of other American and Filipino soldiers who were taken prisoner by the Japanese and subjected to the infamous Bataan Death March of 1942. More than eleven thousand of the men perished in the grueling six-day, sixty-mile journey under a burning tropical sun. Those who survived the death march were loaded onto trains for a time and then continued on foot to a slave labor camp, where they were interned.

During the next several months they were moved twice to other POW camps. On the second move, in October 1942, they were again loaded onto a crowded freight train, which stopped at every station along the way. The men, anguishing in hunger, thirst, and sickness, were losing all hope. They were wondering what it was all for. Did the people of the Philippines appreciate the sacrifices the soldiers were making? Did they even care?

It was at the fourth stop that the significant event occurred. A group of local Filipino children—eight small boys—were standing at the end of the station platform, humming a tune. Manny Lawton and many of the others could see the boys, since the freight train doors had been left open for fresh air. "In perfect pitch they rendered their melody over and over until the train pulled out." Explains Lawton, "They hummed, for the lyrics would have infuriated [their] Japanese captors." The boys "might have been imprisoned, or shot." They were humming "God Bless America."[7]

That expression of support made a great difference to the Americans. The remaining two hours of the train ride were "not nearly so miserable" as they might otherwise have been. "The musical incident," recounted one survivor, "had refortified our will to endure." The Filipino children had shown where their allegiance lay and had demonstrated their affection and appreciation toward the soldiers.

"In any circumstance in life," says Lawton, "man is always seeking approval and encouragement. To receive it spurs him on to greater effort; to be denied it, or to be derided, can destroy him."[8]

A serendipitous event can present itself in any crisis if we are open to receiving it. Sometimes it is necessary to wait long and patiently for help or a message of hope. If we listen and look carefully for the inspiration that can come from supportive people, and if we know how to interpret events, we can find the strength to triumph over most of life's difficult, seemingly hopeless situations.

Ellen Goodman, in *Turning Points*, wrote, "A turning point is not a doorway which we pass through in a neat completed motion. It's rather a chain of reactions."[9] It's true that we never know what one event will lead to.

A friend of mine, married six years, was concerned about an infertility problem. She found help in an interesting way. A member of the international organization MENSA, the group for people who have high IQs, she wanted to get on the mailing list for a local chapter in order to attend their social and intellectual gatherings. She saw in a newspaper article the name of the chairman of MENSA, a doctor, and decided to write him for information on the organization. She looked up the doctor's address in the phone book and wrote him a letter of inquiry. The doctor replied to her on his office stationery, and the letterhead indicated that the man was an obstetrician/gynecologist "specializing in infertility." My friend said: "It was the first that I knew there was any such thing as a medical specialist to whom one could go to try to get pregnant. So I called his office and made an appointment. We have two children now," she added, laughing at the fortunate events that transpired. A series of serendipitous events worked together on my friend's behalf because she took the initiative to follow up on a valuable new piece of information. Usually it is necessary for a person to respond to the opportunities that present themselves in order to experience the full benefit of a serendipitous happening.

A chance comment somebody makes, something read in a book or article, a timely conversation with an acquaintance, friend, elderly neighbor, grocery clerk, or even a stranger, an encounter at a party or one's place of employment, or a chance meeting with someone associated with the school one's children attend—in any of these situations a serendipitous event can occur to a person ready to hear, receive, or ask for insight or assistance. You may find a new job, make a decision to pursue a certain college, find out about a career training program, or be helped to solve any number of important personal problems simply because you allowed yourself to be open and responsive.

GRETCHEN: THE POWER OF A SYMBOLIC ACCOMPLISHMENT

Gretchen was a high school physical education teacher, a lacrosse coach for a girls' team, the mother of two teenage boys, and an unhappy wife. "For many years," she explains, "I knew Greg was having extramarital affairs, but I didn't confront him and insist he stop for fear he would leave." She worked full time and had all the responsibilities of the home and children. Greg would not help. Yet at the same time she was paralyzed; she just couldn't do anything for herself to try to make things better.

After five or six years of feeling depressed, unfulfilled in her marriage, and angry about her husband's infidelity, Gretchen made a decision to pursue a master's degree in music with the goal of teaching in a music school and having private students as well. She knew her marriage wouldn't survive and expected that it was only a matter of time until her husband left her. She wanted a more secure way to support herself. It took Gretchen four years to complete the master's degree. Once she had that, she began openly to confront Greg concerning his behavior and entered into her own extramarital love relationship. By then she had been unhappy for about ten years.

Situated finally in a secure full-time position as a music teacher, Gretchen left her husband. For five years she enjoyed a passionate love affair with the man with whom she had fallen in love. She had also joined a string quartet and was performing with them at various places in the community. Since she had studied violin from the age of ten but had had no outlet for her love of music for many years, Gretchen's musical pursuits were very important to her during this transitional time. She was growing in self-confidence. No longer paralyzed because she felt she could not change her life, she gradually seized her own power and became self-reliant. The accomplished and joyful artist giving recitals seemed far removed from the unhappy, frustrated, and powerless wife and mother who was terrified of being abandoned by her husband.

Gretchen found, however, that all the things she once had feared did eventually occur—but not in the way she envisioned. Five years after leaving her husband and the financial security of his highly paid position in a brokerage firm, she discovered that this second important man in her life was having a torrid affair with a very young woman. "For years and years I feared that my family life would break apart and that I would be left alone," she explained. "That is exactly what happened."

Struggling with feelings of disillusionment and anger, Gretchen also battled severe bouts of depression for two years. She was determined to learn to live on her own, without the prestige and economic advantages of her husband's important position and without her former lover's companionship.

During this long period of estrangement, her husband Greg had a change of heart. He accepted full responsibility for the breakup and tried very hard to regain Gretchen's respect and love. Gretchen, however, was finished with the marriage, despite the fact that they were not yet officially divorced. She was learning, albeit painfully, that she could survive independently.

As is typical in a recovery process, Gretchen wondered if she would ever learn to cope well with her changed situation.

She often felt that she was on a treadmill going nowhere, when in fact progressive steps were being made in the direction of healing.

One day Gretchen made a crucial decision. She decided on an impulse to sign up for a mountain climbing school she had read about in a travel magazine. Located in the Grand Tetons, south of Yellowstone Park in Wyoming, the school afforded Gretchen and a group of other novices an opportunity to undertake the unusual confidence-building experience of climbing to the top of a major mountain. There was a week of training sessions during which Gretchen and the others learned to follow behind their guide on the end of a rope, crawling over rocks and down through cracks and trusting their leader to get them over very steep inclines. After the seven-day period of gaining stamina and courage, middle-aged Gretchen, along with several young men and their leader, climbed up to the 13,000-foot summit of the Grand Teton. Combating throbbing headaches and nausea resulting from the thin air, Gretchen and her companions accomplished the climb in just under nine hours. "What a sense of exhilaration it was," Gretchen remembered, when finally she reached the summit to behold the magnificent sight of a 360-degree view of miles and miles of nothing but nature. Gretchen felt that in accomplishing this feat, she was making a statement to herself that "I have strength sufficient to manage my own life."

"I had no support from anyone in my family to undertake this venture," Gretchen remembers. Her former husband and her children were amazed, when they learned of the feat, to see how much strength and endurance Gretchen had. She rather surprised herself as well.

"The Grand Teton climb," says Gretchen, "was a way of dividing my life into before and after. Just a year earlier," she recalls, when she was mourning the breakup of her love affair, "I was reduced to being upset if nobody would go grocery shopping with me. Despair is a terrible thing. But now I'm full of hope and excitement about tomorrow."

Before the climb, Gretchen had come a long way in recovering from the depression and anxiety brought about by a
succession of major losses. "All of a sudden I felt myself to
be in a new place, but really my growing in strength and self-
confidence was a long time coming," she explains. The Grand
Teton climb was a symbol of personal resourcefulness. Here
was a woman who used to be afraid to go shopping alone. As
she puts it, "Nobody can ever take away from you what you
have done for yourself."

"I always felt I had to be a coach, athlete, and physical
education teacher," continued Gretchen, "*or* a classical mu-
sician. My recognition that I was both of those things and that
I didn't have to be one or the other helped me with the process
of finding myself after losing the things in life [marriage and
love] which I felt were so important."

Climbing the Grand Teton was a turning point in Gretch-
en's adult life, as was the composite effect of the public musical
performances she had given several years earlier. A pretty
woman with a bouncing energy in both her voice and graceful
bodily movements, she looks much younger than fifty and
clearly is happy and contented now. "I feel reconciled within
myself," she says. "The fragmentation is gone."

Last year she bought her own home, "a handyman's special," and she has done most of the work on it herself. She
took down old wallpaper, repapered, painted the inside and
outside, paneled the basement, and supervised the remodeling
of the kitchen and bathroom. She is now going to apply her
newfound hobby of collecting antiques in order to furnish the
new house. "Self-sufficiency is a very important part of my
being able to feel at one with myself," she explains. "I know
now that I can provide the things I want for myself. Except
for friendships, I'm independent. Before the Grand Teton
climb, I had never felt this way."

It is not necessary for everyone to climb a 13,000-foot
mountain in order to experience a powerful symbolic accomplishment! Other more modest triumphant achievements can

similarly empower: speaking or performing in public, learning to drive, joining a social group, eating in a restaurant alone, going to a strange place, flying in an airplane—any activity once feared but conquered can serve as a symbolic achievement that propels us forward.

SENATOR DANIEL BREWSTER: TURNING A LIFE AROUND

He was a golden boy in state politics, an attorney who had won twelve straight elections, a man remembered as a decorated war hero, wounded seven times while an officer in the Marines in World War II. In 1962 the people of Maryland elected Daniel B. Brewster to the United States Senate.

He was well tailored, handsome, distinguished-looking, friendly, and gracious. A *New York Times* reporter wrote that "Nobody ever looked more like a senator than Danny Brewster."[10] Neither Brewster nor his constituents knew the implications of the fact that the senator had a family history of alcoholism. Brewster's grandfather had been an alcoholic, and his father had died of acute alcoholism when Dan was ten years old. His personal chemistry, along with the stresses and lifestyle of high-level politics, contributed to Daniel Brewster's life exploding into ruins.

Brewster fit a pattern commonly observed by family members of the ten million Americans who suffer from alcoholism.

Slowly, over a period of years, "normal, social, moderate drinking increased to the point that gradually I (and my friends) recognized that I had a problem with alcohol," Brewster told editor Blaine Taylor of the *Maryland State Medical Journal*. "It grew—again, gradually—and, from time to time, there would be periods when I would be 'on the wagon,' and periods when I would only drink moderately."[11]

Early in his life as a senator, Brewster recalled, there were times when his judgment and performance had been impaired by a misuse of alcohol. There were meetings he failed to attend, and others that he did attend where it was obvious that he had been drinking. At times his judgment and intellect were not sharp.

In 1964 President Lyndon Johnson asked Brewster to stand in for him in the presidential primary election in Maryland, running against Governor George Wallace. It was a "bitter, name-calling campaign" and Brewster was disheartened that his "old supports [among white people] in the blue collar districts had evaporated" over issues concerning racial tensions. Although he won the election, he defeated the Alabama governor by a mere four hundred votes—in his home county. He had won the Senate race by a 40,000-vote margin in the same county only two years earlier. "I was bitterly disappointed," Brewster told me in an interview twenty-two years later. "Amazed, staggered, and depressed," he seriously considered leaving politics.

From 1964 to 1968 Brewster's drinking increasingly affected his performance as a United States senator. "During this time," he said, "I periodically abstained from drinking. I tried every halfway measure there was—for example: *only* beer; *only* wine; *only* champagne; not *after* 5 P.M.; not *before* 5 P.M.; *not* in the state of Maryland; *not* in Washington, D.C.; *only* at meals, etc.; all *types* of controlled drinking, but I had now become an alcoholic. No halfway measures worked."[12]

His marriage broke up in 1967, and his two sons, aged ten and twelve, went with their mother. Years later one of these sons would write a book-length biography of Brewster for his senior thesis at Princeton. There "will always be a gulf" between the sons and their father, the son would explain, and he expressed disappointment that Brewster hadn't been a better father. The family breakup was the beginning of Brewster's "losing everything," as the senior Brewster puts it, "because of alcoholism and ambition."

By the time of his 1968 reelection campaign, Brewster's reputation for drinking had increased. His Republican opponent, Charles Mathias, Brewster remembers, "could capitalize on [the drinking problem] without ever openly attacking me or mentioning the subject. Mr. Mathias' campaign slogan was 'Reason for a Change,' which could be interpreted many ways, but the whispered campaign against [me] was that the 'reason' was that [I] drank too much."[13]

The senator tried to be very careful not to appear in public if he felt he had had too much to drink. There were times when he was not a good judge of his own fitness to appear, however, when his staff members had to protect him. There were numerous broken speaking engagements. On one occasion, scheduled as a principal speaker at a large political gathering, he arrived intoxicated and was unable to speak. The event, reported in the press, contributed to his subsequent defeat. "Alcoholism," he explained, "had dampened my resolve, impaired my judgment, and taken away the ability to act positively. I found myself only reacting to situations."

Brewster was devastated to have lost his seat in Washington to Charles ("Mac") Mathias. He must have noticed the stark contrast between himself and Mathias, an old friend from law school, the godfather of his eldest son. His friend's public service career was soaring while his own career had fallen into ruin. Brewster at the time was only forty-five years old.

On the heels of the election defeat came another devastating blow: Daniel Brewster was indicted for bribery and accused of accepting money in return for a political favor. Over the next few years his legal fees would be in six figures, he would stand trial, be declared innocent of bribery but guilty of accepting an illegal campaign contribution, and be sentenced to prison. The lower court verdict was overturned by the U.S. Court of Appeals with an option for retrial. Attorney General John Mitchell (who himself later would go to prison for the Watergate conspiracy under President Nixon) vowed to "try him again." Daniel Brewster saw himself as being on the political "hit list" that Nixon's attorney, John Dean, would describe during the Senate investigation of Watergate

The former senator's "almost continual" drinking from 1969 to 1974 led to several medical emergencies and brought him near death on at least two occasions. During these years he also married and divorced for a second time. Sometimes Brewster sat alone in a drunken state for days, unable or uninterested in returning even highly important phone calls from his lawyers.

BEING HONEST WITH ONESELF

A turning point came "sometime during 1975," says Brewster. He and I sat and discussed this in his farmhouse study. I had been wondering how a man could take such a long fall and still put his life back together again. I felt the presence of the distinguished government figures whose framed photographs loomed over us, seeming larger than life. In virtually every photo a tall and handsome Maryland senator stood or was seated proudly in the company of a vast array of political notables.

"I was sitting alone in this house," Brewster continued, "thinking of the great success I had enjoyed in my life from school days on—and now I was alone, my life in shambles, no friends, having lost everything. And the government wanted me [for a retrial on bribery charges]."

He had put himself in Hiddenbrook, a detoxification center in Maryland, and had undergone several thirty-day withdrawal stays there. During one of these month-long rehabilitation residencies, Daniel Brewster learned to his dismay that a bus trip was planned to a local Alcoholics Anonymous meeting. Fearing humiliation, since his name and face were widely recognized in his home territory, the former senator told the Hiddenbrook director, Joe Quinn, that there was "no way" he was going to appear in public at an AA meeting. Quinn replied, "Then you don't belong here. You're not ready to be honest with yourself because if you are, you're going to that meeting."

A critical moment of realization occurred in the life of Daniel Brewster because of Quinn's words of confrontation. "I've shown up at so many political meetings somewhat under the influence," Brewster said to himself. "What in the world is wrong with going out to a meeting where people are trying to get well?" Brewster acknowledged that his life had become unmanageable and faced himself honestly. He climbed into the Hiddenbrook bus and went with the others to the AA meeting.

Later Brewster recalled, "I never realized—and didn't admit to myself in all my years of public life—that I was an alcoholic. I thought I could control it, not knowing that control is impossible for the alcoholic.[14]

"The ability to be truthful with oneself is essential to recovery," the former senator declared, his wisdom hard won. It was important to sit alone in the farmhouse feeling desperate, lonely, and sick, and important to transport himself to an alcoholism treatment center. Even the thirty-day "dry-out periods," which were followed by more episodes of drinking and drunkenness, were part of the typical healing process that many alcoholics go through. The turning point for Daniel Brewster, however, was when this tough old Marine Corps lieutenant who had nearly died courageously leading his soldiers on Okinawa finally faced himself squarely and admitted that he was out of control and powerless. A man who had long been independent, a loner, and too proud even to pray for himself in times of crisis, Brewster finally was honest with himself and could receive the help from others that he desperately needed. It was to be the beginning of a new life.

STARTING ANEW

A horrible black cloud still threatened Daniel Brewster like the sky that fills the horizon before a tornado touches down—Brewster's indictment on bribery charges. To rebuild a life, sufficient light, a sense of safety, and the promise of a clear sky soon to come—all are necessary. "So I made a deal," he explains, "a plea of no contest to one count of accepting an illegal contribution." He paid a $10,000 fine and the government dropped the plans for a second trial.

"I gave up," he told Frederic Kelly of the *Baltimore Sun*.[15] "I simply quit. I had gone through years of pure hell and I was sick and tired of fighting. My health was broken, my career was gone and I had spent a small fortune in legal fees. I had to call an end to it. I wish now that I had stayed and fought another round and cleared my name. . . . I may have been careless about some things, but there was nothing illegal or corrupt in what I did."

Finally free and almost ready to devote himself to reclaiming his life, the former senator met Judy Lynn, a woman seventeen years his junior, who would become Daniel Brewster's third wife and a highly influential person in his rehabilitation. Judy went along with "Danny," as she calls him, to Alcoholics Anonymous meetings. They attended the meetings *twice a day*, *every day*, for an entire *year*. They married and thereafter attended AA meetings daily for several years. "Total abstinence, Judy's love and support, and the group therapy of AA finally made my compulsive urge to drink disappear," Brewster explained. They made a permanent decision together to serve no alcohol in their home and to allow no drinking on their property even when giving an occasional political fundraiser for a friend.

"All through my life I had been driven by ambition—another election, another legal fee, another girl. After 1975," continued Brewster, "I was unshackled by both ambition and alcohol. I'm retired, very quiet. I'll never run for office again."

A year after their marriage, Daniel and Judy Brewster's first new family member arrived. Their baby daughter was followed by boy-girl twins two years later. With Judy's two teenage children from an earlier marriage, they were a family of seven living together on the farm.

Judy's children are now on their own, but the rest of the family continue to live on the sprawling green-pastured horse farm where Brewster once lived the lonely life of a man owned and controlled by alcohol. The drug nearly destroyed three generations of men in Brewster's family.

"We run a reasonably active cattle and horse farm," says Brewster, a silver-haired, trim, and handsome man, not at all looking like a man in his early sixties. "Judy puts up all of our own vegetables and I'm a relatively competent 'jack of all trades.' We've built a very good life together."

"He's a gentle man and a wonderful father," his wife says. "The children adore him; he's not quick-tempered; he gives one hundred percent as a father and husband." The former senator drives car pools and never seems to mind a noisy house with three little children under ten. Brewster has especially enjoyed teaching the Girl Scouts about ponies, Judy says, spending time with a troop of little girls.

"I was no father at all to my first two children," he acknowledged. He was away from home five to seven nights a week during his first marriage. "If you were a congressman from Oklahoma," he remembered, "you moved your whole family to Washington. If you lived in Maryland, you were a local phone call from the U.S. Capitol and were expected in at every hour, night and day."

"All Danny wants out of life," Judy continues, "is peace, quiet, and his children. He wants to be at the dinner table and he wants the children there, wants the noise and the car pools." He's a man who likes to go to bed early, perhaps so that he can start all over again and fully enjoy the next day.

Although Daniel and Judy prefer a private, family-centered life, Brewster has maintained important friendships over the years with friends in the political arena. "Mac" Mathias, the man who took away his Senate seat, is one of his closest friends. "I admire the guy," he says. "Hell, I voted for him in 1974 and he's the only Republican I ever voted for in my entire life, so you know I have an awful lot of respect for him."[16]

INVOLVEMENT IN COMMUNITY SERVICE

In his new life, Daniel Brewster has been active in community service. He has testified candidly before legislative committees on alcohol-related issues and has also shared his personal story as a speaker for other groups. He often begins his presentation with the courageous words, "I speak to you today as an alcoholic."

As chairman of the board of Franklin Square Hospital in Baltimore, Brewster was instrumental in helping establish an alcoholism rehabilitation center. At a local Veterans Administration hospital he worked three days a week for several years in alcoholism peer counseling. He has served as chairman of the Governor's Advisory Council on Alcoholism and on the boards of directors of "quarterway" houses where alcoholics can go for thirty-day detoxification and treatment residences. "Part of my personal program in continuing *my* recovery from a renewed onslaught of alcoholism," Daniel Brewster firmly maintains, "is to help others individually and through service on these boards."

The blue and white cover of the July 1977 *Maryland State Medical Journal* fittingly announced its feature story on "one man's fight against alcoholism." Next to a close-up head shot photograph of Brewster at the height of his political career reads the caption: "Phoenix—The Rise, Fall and Resurrection of Senator Daniel Brewster." His emergence from the ashes to build a new life has progressed and advanced considerably in the more than ten years since the article appeared. Brewster's three little children have given him a chance to live out the life he missed the first time around.

KATHLEEN: OVERCOMING COMPULSIVE EATING

"Hi, I'm Kathleen. I've lost ninety-two pounds, and I've maintained my weight loss for eleven years." She is blonde, middle-aged, and wearing an attractive, diagonally striped black-and-white dress with a shiny black belt. Her personality is warm and engaging. I'm sitting in a classroom full of people at a place called Diet Workshop, watching her and listening attentively. Kathleen is the teacher and I'm there to take off some pounds gained during a recent lecture tour.

It's the day after Christmas. We are gathered like a congregation in search of atonement for our eating sins that undoubtedly included a 4,000-calorie Thanksgiving dinner and continued steadily through half a dozen Christmas parties, a gallon of eggnog, and an unbelievable amount of holiday sweets.

I have often looked at overweight people in shopping malls, in grocery stores, at airports, and at the beach, and a sadness comes over me when I watch them. Knowing that nearly every overweight person has dieted even more times than most smokers have quit cigarettes, I wonder why losing weight permanently seems to be such a monumental task. The people who comprise that mere 2 percent of the population that successfully maintains a weight loss, I decided, must be worthy of careful study.

Kathleen hadn't been fat as a child, she explained to me privately, yet some of the seeds of her eventual weight problem probably were sown then. An insecure feeling had existed in her home. She was the eldest daughter of an alcoholic father and an unhappy mother who couldn't bring herself to take her children and leave. During Kathleen's childhood most women caught in abusive, miserable marriages lacked the financial means to support themselves or a family. There was a constant turmoil and conflict in her family which the children were forbidden to protest outwardly. "We children were not allowed to show our parents or anybody else that we were upset about anything," Kathleen explains. "People didn't know what went on inside our house: My mother tried to keep my father's drinking quiet."

After she married and gave birth to the first of her five children, Kathleen began to suffer episodes of severe depression lasting several months. Just as compulsive drinking was the way her father had coped with depression, a combination of compulsive eating and getting high on diet pills was Kathleen's way of coping. Various physicians prescribed amphetamines freely, and Kathleen became dependent on the diet pills. She looked to the pills for the energy to care for her large family of small children and to aid her in weight control. "Hyped up on amphetamines," explains Kathleen, "I kept a super-clean house with no unironed laundry in the laundry basket. My house was so clean," she remembers, laughing, "that when we had a fire in the house one of the firemen made the others take their boots off when they came in the door!"

In her thirties, Kathleen would lose twenty to thirty pounds with the aid of the diet pills, gradually gain them back, seek another doctor some months or a year later, and take pills again. "After a while," she says "the pills only kept me functioning; my tolerance for the drug increased, and I gained weight up to 240 pounds *while taking* the diet pills!" At the age of forty-one Kathleen weighed a hundred pounds more than she had weighed on her thirtieth birthday.

During that time amphetamines were considered by some in the medical community to be so safe that one doctor prescribed amphetamines for Kathleen while she was *pregnant*. Since then, medical knowledge and public awareness regarding the medication have changed dramatically. Kathleen finally realized that the high doses of amphetamines were endangering her health. She quit the pills cold, became profoundly depressed, and spent her days eating and sleeping.

Kathleen ate when everyone else was in bed or while her husband and children were at work and school. She bought large bags of candy nearly every day, ate some of it and squirreled the rest away in the bathroom for secret snacks in the evening. She routinely ate entire cakes and pies and whole boxes of cookies.

"When I went to the store I bought one gallon of ice cream for my husband and children and one gallon for me! My husband would say, 'Who ate this ice cream?' and I'd say, 'Ask one of your children.' I wouldn't say I didn't do it. He'd ask three of the children—and with five kids I knew he wouldn't get through all five of them with the question—and then he'd assume it was the other two. I never let him see me eat—I always fed him and the kids and then I ate when nobody was watching, eating the food and candy hidden around the house."

Kathleen stopped frequently at fast food restaurants, where most of the offerings are high in fat content and calories. She always ordered two of everything, even sodas that she didn't want, to make it appear that she was ordering for two people. Never mind that the teenager taking her order was a complete stranger, as were the other customers who stood in line. Kathleen ordered two cheeseburgers, two orders of greasy french fries, and two desserts. She never ate in public, not even in her car in the restaurant parking lot. She ate the food at home or drove to a distant and empty library parking lot, where no one would see her. Fearing ridicule, Kathleen would not provide others with the opportunity "to watch a fat lady eat."

REACHING ROCK BOTTOM

In their excellent book *Keeping It Off*, weight loss experts Robert H. Colvin and Susan C. Olson piece together the puzzle of permanent weight loss. They carefully examine the stories of people who have lost twenty to 275 pounds and kept them off for more than five years. Many of these triumphant persons "remember a particular time or an event—a critical comment— that marked their start on the road to success."[17] An incident or series of events "that may span weeks or even months, often experienced as a particular moment in time," suddenly enables an individual to break free from previous immobilization.[18]

Kathleen overheard a conversation between her husband and a sister who was visiting from out of town. "Every time I come she's fatter," Kathleen's sister said.

"I know," replied Kathleen's husband. "Why don't you get her to see a doctor? She *never* eats!"

Kathleen remembers smiling. "I've got you fooled," she said, speaking silently to her husband. "That's good," she continued, "you're not blaming me." Deep within, however, Kathleen was troubled by hearing herself described as a help-less person growing fatter and fatter. She secretly knew that she was responsible for finding a solution to her eating prob-lem, yet she "didn't want to own up to it," she explains. "Whenever I thought about my problem, I thought of myself as weak, lazy, and lacking in willpower and discipline."

A great deal of shame surrounded Kathleen's approach to the world. Whenever she bought clothes and had to get a larger size, she would tell herself, "This is the last larger size I'll buy." She always went shopping with a plain brown bag so that others in the mall wouldn't see her carrying a sack im-printed with the name of the store for large women where she was forced to shop. On returning home she quickly ripped off all the size tags, fearing that her husband might see what size she was wearing.

Finally Kathleen came to the point of despair. "I felt really ashamed and powerless," she says. "I dropped out, quit going to church, couldn't face people."

"Why am I this way?" Kathleen wondered. "Why do I worry all the time about what I'm going to eat and when and whether there will be enough for me? My mother and sister aren't this way about eating," she reasoned. "Why do I have this terrible problem?" Finally she decided that "food was [her] drug of choice," that she was cut from the cloth of her alcoholic father. Her secret food purchases, squirreling away of food, and sneak-eating habits closely paralleled her father's approach to alcohol.

A certain readiness gives rise to the ability to make a major and permanent change. This readiness on the part of overweight people, write Colvin and Olson, almost always means "a letting down of the psychological defenses that kept them from admitting how they really felt about their bodies and, sometimes, about their lives in general."[19] Previous rationalizations, excuses, and self-deceptions no longer work. "Uncomfortable enough" to want to change, a person is "able to say sincerely, 'I know how I look and how I feel and *I hate it*!' "[20] In that moment of honest self-confrontation the seeds of a new beginning take root.

TRYING SOMETHING NEW

People who have overcome a self-destructive behavior of some kind such as compulsive eating, gambling, drinking, smoking, or drug taking usually will tell you that failures were necessary on the way to success. From failed attempts to give up a self-destructive behavior many have confronted the enormity of a problem and have begun to shape the highly individualized solutions necessary for overcoming their addiction or compulsion. The lessons of failure lead many to the tools of success.

Kathleen went with a friend to various diet doctors, tried hypnotism for a time, and attempted numerous diets over the years. As a favor to her friend, whose minor weight problem was rendered serious by arthritis, Kathleen agreed to attend a group known as the Diet Workshop. The meeting was being held far away from their neighborhood, and the friend assured Kathleen that no one there would know them.

"So we went together," Kathleen explains, "and the first thing I saw at the meeting was a room full of people who, compared with me, all looked thin. Then I saw a woman taking registration who was the mother of a classmate of my daughter. I felt really uncomfortable. To save face I decided to go through the motions and just never go back again: I didn't want that woman to go home and tell her family that the fattest person present didn't register for the program!"

Kathleen went into the private room where the workshop teacher weighed the participants. Although the most successful programs ask participants to set their own weight loss goals, Diet Workshop at that time still set the goals for members. "They set as my goal to lose eighty-four pounds," Kathleen explains, "and I just decided that was ridiculous and I wondered how I ever let my friend get me into this!"

Kathleen, who had never lost weight without the aid of amphetamines, looked at the low-fat, low-sugar, sensible, well-balanced basic diet advocated by Diet Workshop in their brochure. Seeing there was no miracle in the diet, Kathleen thought to herself, "This will never work. It's hopeless. I'll always be fat."

Kathleen's friend said, "Look at this—we can have ice milk and all the string beans, broccoli, and other low-calorie vegetables we want."

"I've never even heard of ice milk," Kathleen replied. "And none of that other stuff appeals to me. Look," she continued, finding fault, "there are no potatoes on the diet. I can't stand a diet without potatoes."

The course instructor gave the group an assignment that caught Kathleen's eye in a positive way because it was something new to try. Everyone was asked to eat all meals in the coming week, including all snacks, at the kitchen or dining room table. "Overweight people," the teacher explained, "rarely take time to eat three meals a day sitting at a proper eating place."

"I had never eaten any food with my family, not even dinner

in the evening. I was always busy waiting on my husband and all the kids. The course instructor said I should ask if the six of them had everything they needed, sit down for dinner, and explain that I'm not going to get up again. The idea appealed to me!"

TASTING SUCCESS

Kathleen was curious to see whether something new could indeed be learned that would enable her to lose weight. She didn't stick to the diet, but by observing one principle of behavioral change, sitting at the table to eat, she lost more than a pound in the first week. Kathleen thought it was remarkable that one small change in behavior could produce a weight loss in any amount. She decided to attend the Diet Workshop weekly meetings to discover whether any other behavioral changes could help.

By the third week Kathleen had lost seven pounds. She told the course instructor, "I don't want to think about losing eighty-four pounds. All I want to do is lose twenty-five pounds by Christmas."

"That's not very realistic," the teacher replied. "It's already November."

"Well, if I can't lose twenty-five pounds by Christmas," Kathleen retorted, giving herself an out, "then I'm quitting!" Expecting failure, Kathleen decided not to tell even her family that she was dieting.

Most successful dieters lose weight slowly, at a rate of about two pounds per week. The body hastens to regain pounds shed quickly, but it doesn't physiologically resist a slow weight loss in the same way.

The pursuit of small wins is an important concept in successful dieting. Research has shown that it is a good idea to lose weight slowly for psychological as well as for physiological reasons. Following the marvelous analogy of authors A. Kuhn and R. D. Bean, weight loss experts Colvin and Olson "liken small wins to the task of counting paper: the person who tries to count 1,000 sheets in a single stack risks having to start over completely if he loses track. Piling the counted sheets in groups of ten may take a little longer but the penalty of losing count somewhere between 990 and 1,000 is very slight!"[21]

By losing weight a pound or two at a time, one is not devastated by failures, since the individual fails only to lose a pound or two instead of failing to meet a major goal. An opportunity is presented, according to Colvin and Olson, "that leads to winning big with little danger of losing big."[22] Little by little, the individual learns what works and what doesn't work, and he or she is enabled to succeed in the long run. "Small wins—a small change in food preferences, a little increase in exercise, a slight boost in confidence—all move in the same direction, slowly and solidly building an unshakable foundation."[23]

Kathleen's goal of losing twenty-five pounds in seven weeks (an average of three and a half pounds a week) was a way of breaking down an inconceivable goal—eighty-four pounds—into something that felt more manageable. Many overweight persons find they need an early and significant weight loss as an aid to motivation and self-confidence. Still, Kathleen's initial goal was rather ambitious; a lesser goal would have been a more appropriate or helpful start.

"By December 23, at 8:00 P.M.," Kathleen proudly remembers, "I had lost twenty-five and a quarter pounds and received the certificate given for losing twenty-five pounds. That was a turning point in my life, because I knew from that point forward that I was going to lose the rest of that weight. I just *knew* it!"

Kathleen desperately needed a significant experience of success, and she made it happen for herself. Never mind that she was still so heavy that no one in her family yet noticed she was on a diet! Kathleen was determined to go forward. Accomplishing what she had believed was impossible, a considerable weight loss without the aid of diet pills, Kathleen gained a substantial sense of achievement and power. She felt, "I did this! And if I did this I can do the rest. There really is hope for me now."

GIVING A REWARD, SETTING MORE GOALS, LEARNING NEW SKILLS

Kathleen rewarded herself. On Christmas Eve she bought a pair of brown slacks a size smaller than her old black or navy blue slacks. She immediately set another goal, choosing Washington's Birthday as the date by which to lose another twenty-five pounds.

By February 22 Kathleen had not yet lost the next twenty-five pounds, but she was well on her way. Learning a new concept for behavioral change each week at the Diet Workshop meetings provided new knowledge and skills for coping with the often discouraging and laborious struggle to lose weight.

The following guidelines and dieting techniques became a way of life for Kathleen and have been useful to countless others involved in weight loss programs:

- □ Set small and achievable weekly goals, such as experimenting with a daily walking program or being satisfied with not gaining on a holiday.
- □ Weigh only once a week to avoid the intense discouragement of normal weight fluctuations or the absence of a weight loss.
- □ Sit away from serving dishes at parties or picnics, eat slowly, eat at specific mealtimes, and avoid becoming so hungry as to increase the likelihood of overeating.
- □ Use spare time doing an activity, even cleaning a closet or sweeping a garage, anything to become involved in something other than food.

- ☐ Have low-calorie snacks such as raw vegetables, hot air–cooked popcorn, diet gelatin, apples, grapefruit, and sugar-free products on hand at all times and avoid having high-calorie foods readily available.
- ☐ Avoid boredom by routinely eating a good variety of nutritious foods and by trying out tasty low-calorie recipes.
- ☐ Eat small amounts of the sweet or fatty foods which previously led to a binge, changing from thinking of these foods as forbidden.
- ☐ Shop for good-quality lean meats, fruits, vegetables, whole-grain foods, and low-fat milk products.
- ☐ Plan ahead when it is necessary to eat away from home, carrying along lower-calorie foods or diet products such as small packets of salad dressing.
- ☐ Order selectively from a restaurant menu or ask if the chef can cook the vegetables and entree with seasonings alone, omitting the butter and creamy sauces.
- ☐ Learn how to graciously say no to a hostess or host, remaining on a diet in social settings without calling attention to yourself.
- ☐ Routinely prepare low-fat meals for the entire family, including children over the age of two, permanently utilizing low-calorie cooking methods (broiling and baking without butter or cream sauces) instead of high-calorie preparations.
- ☐ Keep your personal goal in mind regarding appearance or health. Frequently remind yourself that taking charge of your food selection and intake is not an act of self-denial but of self-care.
- ☐ Accept the fact that times of discouragement and periodic setbacks are inevitable. When you "miseat" for one or more days, do not feel overly guilty about these episodes. Record in a journal your strategy for resuming control, or talk with a supportive friend about how to get on track again. Be patient with yourself.

When she had lost forty-seven pounds, Kathleen went to a beauty shop to have a bleach sensitivity test; she had always wanted to be a blonde. She made an appointment for ten days later, knowing that by then she would have reached her fifty-pound weight loss goal. Without telling her children or husband in advance, Kathleen had her long, dark brown hair becomingly cut and bleached on the appointed date. Kathleen's husband sleepily woke up that first morning after she had her new hairdo. Although he had seen her the night before, he rolled over in bed and saw a blonde woman, who after five months of dieting was not the same person she had been. "My God," he said, wondering for a moment if he had had an affair, "what have I done?" Old friends and some of the neighbors who saw Kathleen and her husband driving together also wondered at times whether he was having an affair. Kathleen was delighted. She received compliment after compliment about her appearance.

There were times when Kathleen grew sick of dieting and wondered whether she would ever reach her goal. She found it difficult to cope with normal family conflicts and problems that arise while dealing with the stress of dieting. Angry feelings particularly triggered an eating binge. Some weeks she gained rather than lost weight. Sometimes she felt alone, feeling that members of her family were insensitive to her battle. She felt resentful when one of the children brought high-calorie food into the house and left it in a conspicuous place or when family members expected her to continue to make chocolate Easter eggs and other tempting traditional treats. Finally she found it helpful to express her anger by writing in a journal or talking about it to family members. She also learned to discuss some of her feelings of discouragement and at times to ask her children and husband for support.

Losing the pounds between minus seventy-four and minus eighty-four were the hardest and most frustrating. Kathleen's weight loss was negligible then. Certain friends meant well but didn't help by saying, "Aren't you going to stop losing now? Your skin will start to look old if you continue to diet." Kathleen yearned to be finished with the effort to lose weight, and the friends' comments only made it harder for her to stay motivated.

Averaging a loss of approximately two pounds per week, Kathleen reached her eighty-four-pound goal after ten and a half months of dieting. She waited a few weeks before deciding on the perfect reward for her accomplishment. "I was looking for a pizzazzi new outfit," she says, "something very pretty." Two-piece pants suits were popular for women at the time, and eventually she chose a strikingly attractive black suit which cost more than anything she had ever worn before. "I deserved it," Kathleen remembers. The pants were a size twelve—down from size twenty-eight and a half. Kathleen had lost a total of ninety-two pounds.

"The reason I gained a hundred pounds after age thirty was that I never believed it could happen to me. With all the diets and the pills, I fully intended to lose weight and not gain it back. I'd look at certain people and say, 'At least I'm not that fat' or 'I was never fat at that age.' I was never going to be such and such a size, never going to buy clothes at the store for heavy women, never going to buy half sizes. Yet I did all those things. I know now that if I get out of control I might not make my way back again. The fear helps me maintain my weight now." Kathleen knows that being a formerly over-weight person is like being a recovering alcoholic, drug addict, gambler, or smoker—it would be all too easy to slide back into the old self-destructive habits that once controlled her life.

TEACHING OTHERS

Kathleen received a lot of pressure to join the staff at Diet Workshop, but she first resisted for fear of "having too much to live up to." Staff members were required to be successful dieters. Kathleen's accomplishment was a personal one: She wanted to maintain her new weight just for herself and not to meet a requirement of employment. While outwardly a new person, inwardly she carried the insecurities, vulnerabilities, and self-doubts of a fat person.

"Listening all those months to the problems of overweight people," Kathleen explains, "I had learned that I wasn't unique in my self-destructive eating habits. I learned to stop blaming others; I could make my own choices, and change was possible. I wanted other people to know that they could change, too."

One year after enrolling in Diet Workshop because the woman taking the registration happened to know her, Kathleen began her career as a diet course instructor in the room in which she had enrolled. "If you only knew how I was when I came into this room a year ago," she told her students, "you'd never believe it!"

A homemaker all of her adult years, never having done any public speaking, Kathleen at first felt nervous. Soon she became one of the city's most respected and popular weight loss instructors and now teaches a dozen classes, including on-site courses in large corporations.

Losing weight and maintaining a healthy body size, write Colvin and Olson, "is in some ways like raising a child: It's a relentless job, it requires constant attention, and it seems never to be done."[24] Those who, like Kathleen, are triumphant, "don't necessarily like to do all the things they must do to stay the way they are, but they can't bear the thought of becoming what they once were."[25]

Kathleen has developed a personalized weight control plan uniquely her own. Sometimes she "miseats," as she puts it, gains a few pounds, and "learns from such mistakes" what behaviors or eating habits undermine her. During one period, while on a leave of absence from her work as a diet course instructor, Kathleen regained fifteen pounds. With the support of her colleagues she dieted again. She resumed keeping a journal in order to study the events that trigger a loss of control. Resuming meaningful work outside the home also helped her reestablish her goal.

Kathleen has steadily maintained a ninety-two-pound weight loss for many years and continues to enjoy teaching the diet courses. She has weathered the painful loss of her husband (who died three years ago) and the departure of her children (who one by one are reaching maturity), as she continues to help others.

"People never get to know who you are as a fat person," she explains. "You hold back because you don't feel worthwhile. Assuming that others will reject you, you reject them first. Life feels too good to me now to ever want to go back to that," she says boldly.

Kathleen was able to orchestrate a series of turning points in order to achieve lasting success. When we are in pain or dealing with crisis, doing something or a series of things that we weren't doing before can alter our perspective and change our lives.

SAYING COMPLETE|6
GOODBYES|

And you learn . . . And you learn . . .
With every goodbye, you learn.
—ANONYMOUS, FROM THE POEM
"COMES THE DAWN"

This chapter is about looking back and saying goodbye. It's about looking ahead and going forward. There are specific and detailed guidelines which can enable you to bring healing and completion to a wide variety of losses from which many people never recover. The guidelines are practical, make sense, and have been proven effective by persons who have triumphed over some of life's most debilitating and painful crisis experiences.

STEVEN AND NAOMI: PARENTS OF A STILLBORN CHILD

When I appeared on *Donahue* after the publication of my first book, I brought with me several persons to illustrate the kinds of losses I had discussed in *Living Through Personal Crisis*. Along with a dentist friend whose house had burned down and a former nun who regretted never having had a husband and children, I took with me Steven and Naomi Shelton. The couple's baby son, a second child, had died after eight months in the womb and was stillborn one week later. A longtime close friend of the Sheltons, I felt certain their healing story would be an inspiration to others.

"The hardest thing about having your baby die before he's born," explained Naomi, "is that you never get to do any of those things for him that you planned to do." I was reminded that long before my daughter Amanda was born in India and came to me by adoption, I had taken her dozens of places in my mind—to Disney World, the National Aquarium, the zoo, in a stroller for long walks. In my fantasies I had already read many stories and colored in many coloring books with her, sat by her bed while she was ill, met her boyfriends, and sent her for the best education we could afford. I realized Naomi and Steven's parental hopes and dreams for their son were shattered.

Probably thinking how emotionally difficult it must have been for Naomi to carry her baby after she knew he was dead, Phil Donahue said, "That was a blessing, wasn't it?" referring to the fact that they didn't need to wait more than a week after they learned the baby had died.

"It was a blessing, Phil," Naomi replied, "but I have always felt that there was also a real value to that week that we spent waiting for the birth. We were able to make many of the arrangements that helped facilitate our grieving." It was their choice, she explained, to wait for labor and not ask their physician to induce labor in a hospital.

"This one main event in our lives," continued Steven, "the baby's death, was so much out of our control that we needed to take control of the pieces of it we could. We made arrangements for a funeral ceremony to reflect our beliefs, and we wanted to be in charge of the time we spent as a family, the circumstances we could control." They took care, he explained, to be sure that it wouldn't be necessary to deal with institutions that weren't "user friendly."

Steven and Naomi made arrangements to have their baby born at home. Two well-trained midwives would be present, and a physician who was aware of their situation was available, if needed. The Sheltons were simply afraid that their local hospital would not provide the emotional support and the private, sacred time together that they needed as a family. They feared that they and their lost baby would be handled according to hospital protocol and not according to their own values and needs. While many hospitals now have bereavement programs and trained staff members who can deal sensitively with situations such as a stillbirth, there was no such institution in their locality.

Steven held Naomi's hand while she was in labor and did the breathing exercises with her that they had learned in natural childbirth class.

Collin was born with several obvious abnormalities, including a cleft lip and the malformed ears associated with certain chromosomal abnormalities. He was also discolored because of having been dead for a week. There is an initial tendency of parents to be repulsed by or rejecting of such a child. Studies show, however, that most parents who spend time with the baby and have a naming or baptismal ceremony can get through that early reaction and begin to love and claim their imperfect child as their own.

After Naomi delivered their stillborn son, Steven wrapped the baby in a blanket and gently carried him to a rocking chair. With the tenderness of a man who loves fatherhood and deeply yearned to have a second child, Steven rocked Collin and sang nursery rhymes to him. He helped Naomi hold and rock the baby and helped their daughter Lea, age five, look at and hold her little brother.

Lea drew a crayon picture of Collin on the encouragement of one of the midwives. Drawing the picture helped the youngster discuss her feelings about Collin's death and his unusual appearance. A close friend of the family was by the child's side at all times, providing attention and caring, answering her questions, and occasionally offering distractions. The Sheltons chose this friend to be present because she was familiar and comfortable with childbirth and Lea was fond of her. They trusted her ability to relate sensitively to Lea and to help her cope with the loss of her baby brother. For about three hours, the Sheltons rocked Collin, held him close, and Steven sang to him. They gave their boy all the love they knew how to show him under the circumstances. "I wanted to do those things that I would never have another chance to do," Steven told Donahue and his audience. "I tried to get as much done as I could in the short time that we had."

"Coming away from it," Naomi went on, "I felt it had been the better of my two births. People look at me as if I'm strange when I say that. The outcome was terribly painful, yet I felt that I had been more in control of the process than with my first birth in the hospital. I also felt comforted that I had provided a birthplace for Collin where he could be received, loved, and honored; that I had done all that I could do for him."

Many people, including some medical professionals, who ought to know better, would look at the Sheltons rocking their dead baby and Steven singing to him and decide that this couple was in need of psychiatric help! Much of what looks hysterical to persons who are not knowledgeable about bereavement is simply a normal and necessary release of emotion.

Steven and Naomi had yearned to have a second child, *this* child, a son. Before they could go forward, comforted by the hope that someday another baby would join their family, it was necessary fully to mourn the loss of the child who was with them only briefly. "I wanted to do this well," said Steven, "because I didn't want my grief to follow me around for the rest of my life."

RITUALS AND SYMBOLIC ACTS

Many people have reported to me a continuing sadness and regret that things weren't done the "right way" when a loved one died. Often mourners are left feeling incomplete because one or more of the following events occurred:

- ☐ Certain important relatives, friends, or work associates failed to visit the funeral home or family.
- ☐ There weren't any or enough flowers, gifts of food, or persons offering help.
- ☐ The funeral or burial ceremony was too quick or failed adequately to honor the person.
- ☐ A proper and accurate obituary did not appear in the newspaper.
- ☐ There were no printed funeral cards or memorial service programs with the deceased person's name and dates of birth and death.
- ☐ Not enough relatives or friends of the person who died were present at the funeral or memorial service properly to pay respect and recognize the person's passing.
- ☐ The clergyperson wasn't sufficiently informed about family relationships or the personality or life situation of the one who died to make his/her remarks and prayers meaningful to the family.
- ☐ There was not an appropriate plaque or burial marker at the gravesite.
- ☐ Too few friends and work associates sent written condolences or were willing to talk openly about the loss.

In addition, as a report of the National Academy of Sciences, reviewed by Daniel Goleman, states, "rituals such as the Roman Catholic wake and the Jewish custom of sitting shiva are increasingly important in modern society. The rootlessness of contemporary life, the report points out, leaves little time or place for the expression of the deep feelings that mourning brings. The old rituals, however, signal that the feelings of grief have their rightful place in life."[1]

The Sheltons took pictures of their baby, named him, and had memorial and burial services. They acknowledged to themselves and others Collin's importance in their lives and the fact that a real member of their family had died. Naomi cross-stitched a birth sampler for the baby, framed one of his pictures, and placed these mementos next to the photographs of other family members on the bedroom dresser. Collin's baby clothes and bassinet sat at the end of the couple's bed for a period. "Rather than being a painful reminder of our loss," explained Naomi, "the baby furniture and clothes were a daily sign of hope to me that one day another little child would come live with us and use them."

Not every couple would choose to photograph a stillborn baby, display the photograph, and keep the baby's things in a conspicuous place. Many people would find it more painful than helpful to have these constant reminders of parental yearning. It isn't necessary for every bereaved person to follow the lead of what was meaningful and helpful to someone else. It is important only that each individual carefully select those rituals, symbolic actions, and memorials that are meaningful and comforting to him or her.

Cemetery or columbarium visits and grave-tending activities can be a meaningful way to remember a loved person after the death and for years thereafter and are psychologically healthy activities, if one continues building a new life. For some people, however, cemetery visits can interfere with ongoing life, such as when the mourner goes to the gravesite nearly every day for longer than a few days or weeks, or so often over the years that the visits become an obligation or preoccupation.

The same is true of nursing home visits to a family member or friend whose mental faculties have failed so dramatically that the person is no longer aware of his or her identity or the identity of loved ones. Remembering and honoring such a person is important, but being consumed with an almost daily obligation to visit the person and thereby crippling one's own life is not of benefit to anyone.

MAKING A LEAP OF FAITH

The Sheltons would have adopted a child instead of having another pregnancy had they felt their chances were high of having another child with major abnormalities. Since an autopsy was not performed, the genetic counselor whose advice they sought could not assess and predict with certainty their chances of having another child with a defective set of chromosomes. After talking with the genetic counselor, searching out medical books for further probability estimates, and allowing for almost a one-year mourning period, Steven and Naomi decided to have another child.

"Having a successful next birth would be a real source of healing for us," explains Steven. "We felt we had to risk it but we wouldn't have taken the chance if the probability estimates had been anywhere near fifty-fifty that things would go wrong again."

The Sheltons made a careful and thoughtful decision. Morally opposed to abortion, they knew they would carry any pregnancy to full term and therefore did not avail themselves of amniocentesis, a medical procedure which can diagnose chromosomal and certain other fetal problems. Steven and Naomi wanted another baby and decided they would love and care for any child who was born to them. It took courage to make that choice, because the loss of Collin was devastating and there were no guarantees against a second such loss. In spite of the knowledge that such feelings were irrational, the Sheltons struggled with the feeling that they were somehow defective persons because they had produced an abnormal child.

A daughter, and a sister for Lea, was born to Steven and Naomi twenty months after Collin's stillbirth. "I look at Jessica a hundred times a day," says Naomi, "and am so grateful to have her. She's so healthy and perfectly beautiful. After losing Collin, it seemed impossible that I would ever have a healthy, whole baby again. She's a real affirmation to me."

"Having Jessica was an obvious leap of faith, statement of hope, and act of healing," says Steven. "For a long time before she was born, we tried to spend time near the water. I dug and built many sandcastles, but I continued to have difficulty when seeing little children, especially boys the age that Collin would have been. At each step my strategy was the same: Face the pain, let it wash over me, honor him in the ways we could, share our story with others, and get going. Now I look at how much I love Jessica and realize we would not have her had he lived."

Steven's desire and ability to talk about Collin's death with close friends and work associates, and in several sessions with a bereavement therapist, contributed significantly to his healing. In her master's thesis, Sister Marilyn A. Carpenter, O.S.B., found that "ritualization itself did not achieve grief resolution" in the events of miscarriage, stillbirth, or newborn death. "However, persons who also had the opportunity to talk about the loss in their lives, in addition to participation in rituals, experienced greater resolution of grief."[2]

THE USE OF POETRY

Naomi found herself writing poetry as a way to honor her son. On the day after Collin's birth she wrote a poem entitled "For Collin":

> *This Mother's Day I have two children.*
> *One I have never heard cry,*
> *nor bathed, nor nursed, nor rocked to sleep.*
> *I have never comforted him, nor sung to him.*
> *The most I could do was to carry him inside me,*

warm and protected
till his need for even that was gone.
And I could give birth to his still little body
in the bed where he was conceived.
into the arms of those who love him.[3]

A year and eight months later, shortly after the birth of Jessica, Naomi felt compelled to write about Collin again:

The family portrait
will always be incomplete.
There's a little ghost child
who walks among our hearts.
He never came to live with us,
but claims our love
the same as if he had.

We hear his baby laughter faintly
and wonder who he would have been.
We have a blurred and hazy image of his face,
and wonder how he would have looked.
We have brief records of his presence
in our lives,
but no picture of the way it should have been.[4]

Sometime later Naomi and Steven visited the cemetery with their daughters. It was the first time Jessica saw Collin's grave, and it prompted Naomi to sit down and write:

Jessica,
you are here with us
because he is not.

How can I make sense
of that fact?
Because I want you
both.

To have to give you up
to have him back
would be impossible.
Because I want you both.

I want you both
here with me.
To hold and care for
To comfort and caress.

Jessica,
I watch you run
through the grass.
You pat his stone
and babble in delight,
not understanding
how much I want you both.[5]

THE USE OF A SIMPLE PRAYER

One young woman I counseled told me that she and her brother were kneeling at her murdered sister's casket, weeping, and about to say a prayer for their lost sister. Another surviving sister, quite uncomfortable with the intense emotion in evidence, rushed up to my client and her brother and urged them to rise. "All this emotion isn't good for you two," the sister said, pulling them up from their knees.

"I never got to say that prayer for my murdered sister," the young woman mournfully explained.

"Could you say the prayer now with me?" I asked. "Could you pray aloud the words you wanted to speak then?"

My client's prayer came six months after losing her sister. It could have come six years later and still have helped her in saying goodbye.

For a variety of reasons, many persons are unable to say the words that need to be said or otherwise to pay their respects soon after a loved one's death. It may be necessary to find ways to say goodbye over a period of several months or years. When confronting a major loss, people need to feel a sense of closure.

THE USE OF A SMALL CEREMONY

Karen Brownstein in *Brainstorm* remembers the odd little man who came to her hospital room to shave her head. To diagnose what was probably a malignant brain tumor, causing a buildup of fluid around the brain, she would be taken to the operating room. There a burr hole would be drilled in her skull, a delicate medical procedure. She recalls in her book:

"I'm-a gonna give you the haircut, missy," the man said cheerfully. His name was Salvatore, he said, "but . . . you could just call me 'Sal.' . . ."

"I asked him if I could go to the bathroom before he began," writes Brownstein.

"Why not?" he said. "You gonna throw up?"

"No. I just have to go to the bathroom," she replied. "Do a lot of people get sick over this?"

"Some," he answered. "Mostly the ladies."

"I crossed the hall to the small bathroom provided for patients whose sparse accommodations did not include private facilities," writes Brownstein. "I didn't need the toilet; I needed the large mirror. I was not about to suffer this parting in public; if I was going to be without my hair for however long this heinous journey lasted, I wanted a private farewell."

"I stood in front of the mirror," she continues, "and ran my hands through my hair like a lover. I piled all its chestnut thickness on top of my head and watched my eyes brim. I pulled it hard away from my face and began to braid it. I pulled apart the braid and made a French twist. Oh, God, I said to the longhaired woman in the cloudy mirror, I'll miss you. Hurry back!"[6]

ANTICIPATORY THOUGHTS AND ACTIONS

Karen Brownstein's "private farewell," fond goodbyes said while embracing and caressing her hair in front of a bathroom mirror, helped her. It happened, however, that the farewell ritual was said prematurely. Brownstein was thrilled to discover that the medical procedure for which she was scheduled required only a shaving of her hair at the base of her skull.

In the weeks that followed, the presence of a malignant, inoperable brain tumor was confirmed. As Brownstein faced radiation therapy, the brief goodbye ceremony held earlier somehow made more bearable the approaching loss of her lovely hair.

Accompanied by a close friend, Brownstein sought out a good wig manufacturer and ordered a year's supply of fine-quality wigs. Together they visited an exclusive department store and selected several huge, beautiful scarves "displayed as turbans on mannequins in the hat department."[7] Brownstein's baldness and the spots of purple dye which she knew would be the aftermath of radiation therapy would be hidden, she decided, as attractively as possible.

Anticipating a loss and ways of coping with the loss makes it less difficult to say goodbye. As Steven and Naomi utilized the week before their son's stillbirth to plan for his birth and funeral, others (like Karen Brownstein) prepare themselves mentally by attending to practical matters or by taking actions which render the approaching loss more bearable.

PUTTING WORDS ON PAPER

People all over the country have described to me a variety of situations in which the writing of a letter seemed to complete one or another stage of a mourning process. A widowed Native American in New Mexico told me that writing a loving goodbye letter to her deceased husband had helped her to release various regrets. A nun in Maryland typed and photocopied an eloquent two-page letter to the sisters in her order. She declared her love for them, gave her reasons for leaving religious life, and bade her sisters farewell. A newly pregnant woman in Colorado, young and unmarried, wrote a long letter to the fetus explaining why she felt emotionally and financially incapable of carrying a baby to term. Before the arrangements were made for a therapeutic abortion, a spontaneous miscarriage occurred which the young woman interpreted as acquiescence on the part of the fetus.

A pharmacist approached me after a lecture I presented in Indiana. The man told me about a letter that he had felt compelled to write in order to end an old friendship—a friendship with alcohol. His compulsive drinking had been a threat to his marriage, career, and health. He said that the words he had committed to paper had helped him to follow a new path in life after spending nine months in a treatment center for alcoholism.

"Dear Friend," wrote the pharmacist, "I know I must now bid you farewell forever. I remember the good times and I bear no malice toward you. I don't know when you turned on me. I only know that the friendship is over. If I allow you back, you surely will finish the job and I will never be free to live my life in the way that I can. Sincerely, Merv."

A woman in Colorado told me the touching story of saying goodbye to a cherished part of herself following surgery for cancer. Several months after having a mastectomy, the thirty-eight-year-old woman wrote a letter to her lost breast. She thanked her breast for the pleasures it had given her in lovemaking and for contributing to her good feelings about herself as a female. On paper she also expressed intense feelings of loss.

There are many women who undergo a mastectomy, especially younger women, for whom it is a profoundly traumatic and difficult loss. Some even entertain the idea that they would have preferred death to what they experience as mutilation. For most women the loss of a breast results in a prolonged period of depression and mourning. Finding meaningful ways to say goodbye can be an aid to healing.

Writing a letter to a living or deceased parent, child, sibling, spouse, lover, or other significant person can affirm the powerful emotions of love, longing, and gratitude. Such a letter can also release feelings of sorrow, anger, regret, and guilt.

One psychologist asked the parents of a child who died of cancer to write a letter to the child saying some of the things the parents felt that they should have said when the child was alive.[8] Another mother, Paula D'Arcy, completed a whole series of letters to her daughter Sarah and published them in a little book entitled *Song for Sarah*. The letters began shortly after the child was conceived and continued for several years after the car accident that killed her, at the age of two, along with her father.

In many cases it is the writing more than the mailing of a letter that results in a sense of completion. Angry or guilt-inducing written communications, letters that burn bridges instead of building them, are best burned themselves instead of posted.

I myself have written goodbye letters to my former husband, to a psychiatrist approaching retirement who helped me greatly, and to another therapist who probably did more damage than good. I have telephoned or written letters of appreciation to a number of my teachers from grade school through graduate school and to others who remain important influences and contributors to my life. I have written long letters to several friends with a life-threatening illness, having seen too much regret not to say what needs to be said.

HAVING A VIVID CONVERSATION

The Reverend Gordon Spencer of Tulsa, Oklahoma, a well-trained pastoral counselor who was my minister years ago, helps people of all ages say goodbye through the use of a technique called the Gestalt approach. He learned the technique from Dr. Robert and Mary Gouldings at the Western Institute for Group and Family Therapy in Watsonville, California.

Once Reverend Spencer helped an unhappy third grader say farewell to her favorite school friends after moving away to a new community. The little girl, extremely upset about the family's relocation and suffering from stomachaches, was brought to Reverend Spencer's office by her recently divorced mother.

After they talked awhile together, Reverend Spencer asked the little girl to name the friends she missed the most. When she named five other children, the minister brought in five small chairs from a Sunday School room. He asked the youngster to imagine that her five friends were present, sitting in their chairs. "I want you to see Sally, Jimmy, Sarah, Tommy, and Amy's faces, the clothes each of them is wearing, and talk to them one at a time," he explained.

Following Reverend Spencer's directions, the little girl described Sally's appearance to her minister. She began to address Sally directly, calling her by name as if the child were actually present.

"Tell Sally what you like about her and tell her about the fun you've had together," Reverend Spencer counseled, pointing to the designated empty chair. "No gossiping," he continued, smiling. "I want you to talk directly to Sally."

After the little girl had spoken her feelings of appreciation, Reverend Spencer asked her if she would also tell Sally about any unhappy memories. "Well, I got angry with you that day when you didn't skip rope and play with me," she told Sally.

Speaking individually to each of her five best friends, the youngster expressed her appreciation and resentments. Then, with Reverend Spencer's guidance, the little girl said, "Goodbye, Sally. Goodbye, Jimmy. Goodbye, Sarah. Goodbye,

Tommy. Goodbye, Amy. I liked you and I miss you. But some things I didn't like so much."

Reverend Spencer asked his young parishioner to imagine that the chairs were now occupied by boys and girls she had recently met at her new school. She described the facial features and physical appearance of each of the new friends and vividly imagined them present. "Say hello to your new friends," Reverend Spencer counseled. "One by one, call them by name, say what you like about them, and tell them that you're looking forward to having them as your friend."

The divorced mother and her daughter have continued to attend the large city church where Reverend Spencer is on the staff. The mother never brought the little girl back for more counseling, so he assumes that things have gone well for the child. Says Reverend Spencer, "The little girl probably remembered her old friends with some sadness, but I suspect that her stomachaches went away and she went on to enjoy her new school."

Many can benefit from the exercise of vividly imagining someone or something that has been lost and conversing with the lost person or thing. A lost or ailing relationship, marriage, or part of one's body can be addressed. It is possible to converse with a lost job, dream, or opportunity, one's home, innocence, feeling of safety, or sense of purpose. The exercise can be particularly helpful in talking with a person who has left home, is severely ill, is drug or alcohol addicted, or is otherwise unapproachable in actual life.

Since many losses are not replaceable in the way that the third grader's friends were replaceable, it is not necessary to conduct a conversation beyond the speaking of appreciation, resentments, and regrets. Once meaningful goodbyes are said, saying hello to new opportunities and relationships in life usually follows automatically.

THE CURFMANS: DEALING WITH A VIOLENT LOSS

Hope and George Curfman's firstborn of five children was the kind of young woman actively involved in trying to make life better for other people. Fluent in Spanish, in her early twenties Claudia worked with impoverished Hispanic people in a California slum and taught English to Spanish-speaking students in Bogotá, Colombia. From her college years forward, many of her activities were on behalf of world peace and expanded opportunities for poor people, women, and minorities. She lived by the ethic of the ancient Athenian lawgiver Solon, whose words faced her daily: "Justice can be secured," read the quote on her desk, "only if those who are not injured feel as indignant as those who are."

Born and reared in Denver, Claudia was drawn to the vitality of New York City and went there for a master's degree in education. "I'm not going to give up my freedom to fear," she vowed, speaking of the risks of living in Manhattan. Not one to dwell on horror stories or headlines about violence, she lived in the city for a decade, during which time she completed her degree at Columbia University, fell in love, and married. She taught Spanish at a private school and looked forward to the day when she and her husband could start a family.

At noon on a Sunday in August 1977, Claudia was brutally murdered at the bottom of a subway stairway near Lincoln Center. This innocent young woman was heard pleading, "Leave me alone, please leave me alone!" The savage stranger who stabbed her repeatedly, supposedly with robbery as a motive, left the knife and the belongings from Claudia's purse scattered on the concrete. The tickets she had just purchased for a Mostly Mozart concert were still in her purse, and her wallet was left behind.

"When you have to live with something senseless and wasteful," explains Claudia's mother, speaking softly, "you have to go through it and agonize. You don't know *how* you're going to bear the pain; you just have to get through it the best that you can."

Claudia was thirty-three years old, the Curfmans' only daughter. How could it be possible, I wondered, for this couple adequately to say goodbye to their bright, loving, giving, and much-cherished daughter?

SAYING EARLY GOODBYES

After receiving the devastating news of Claudia's death in a phone call from their profoundly distressed son-in-law, Hope and George notified their other children and took a plane to New York. They were able to function rather well and make decisions, perhaps because both were in a state of shock.

George, with Claudia's husband, went to the city morgue to identify his daughter's body. He felt that he had to see her for himself and also for Hope, who wanted him to answer a question that was plaguing her. Hope felt she had to know whether or not Claudia's face had been stabbed. George came back and said that their daughter's face had not been cut but that she didn't look like herself.

Claudia had been a dedicated, caring, and beloved teacher at the private primary and secondary school where she taught Spanish. Two hundred mourners attended the memorial service at Kings Chapel of Union Theological Seminary, where two and a half years earlier Claudia and her husband had been happily wed. At the service the minister who had married them read several quotes from Claudia's desk, including Solon's words about how important it is for those who aren't victimized to care about those who are.

A quotation by Oliver Wendell Holmes was also meaningful to the family. "Life is action and passion," said the renowned Supreme Court justice in an 1884 address. "It is required of a man that he should share the passion and action of his time at peril of being judged not to have lived."

Immediately after the memorial service, Hope and George and their son-in-law were driven to the airport. They carried with them Claudia's ashes because her husband wanted her burial to take place in Denver.

The next day more than seven hundred mourners were present at the memorial service in Claudia's hometown. The family was held in high regard in Denver, and she was remembered with fondness. According to Alan Cunningham of *The Rocky Mountain News*, the minister said that Claudia "lived a life of love more than she talked about it" and "learned the secret: that it is in giving and loving that one receives. The circle of her love," he said, "grew and grew and grew." After speaking these words, the Reverend Kenneth Barley "commended the soul of Claudia into the hands of God, giving thanks that someone who had refused to be afraid of living had been granted the gift of life, with its action and passion, for even a little while."[9]

Shortly after this second memorial service all seven family members—Claudia's parents, husband, and four brothers—climbed into the family station wagon and headed to the mountains where in the wintertime the family liked to ski. Together they hiked up to an old lean-to, resting in an area where the family had skied with Claudia. "The seven of us were together physically that afternoon," says Hope, "but I've never been so isolated. It was displayed in our way of walking on our own lonely paths after sitting in a circle and eating together."

Two of the Curfman sons would be returning to the cross-country ski area to work there the following winter. After the first big snow they would honor their sister, they decided, by cutting a trail and calling it "Claudia's Trail."

In the early weeks, months, and years it would be important for the family to find many ways to honor Claudia and her life. She was their beloved daughter, wife, sister, and companion. They also cherished her contributions as a teacher and social activist and wanted her legacy to live on.

So many painful goodbyes remain to be said when one's

child dies or a loved person is lost through suicide or homicide. As it gradually becomes clearer how our loved one's influence continues and presence remains with us, the goodbyes become more bearable.

TRIBUTES THAT ENDURE

In lieu of flowers, Claudia's family asked that donations be made to a memorial fund at the school in Manhattan where she had taught. Over five hundred contributions poured in from Claudia's friends, colleagues, her students' parents, and friends of the family. In addition, the school gave money, and Claudia's parents, husband, and in-laws contributed, as did her brothers and other relatives. The fund was so large that over the years the annual interest it earned would support numerous projects deemed a fitting memorial to Claudia's memory.

Claudia's violent and senseless death was a haunting reality. Contributing money and actively serving on the committee that administered the memorial fund would help Hope, George, and their son-in-law not to be consumed by feelings of rage and despair. In Claudia's name, aid would be provided at her school to minority students and students traveling abroad. Needy youngsters would be enabled to participate in school ski trips and trips to Washington, D.C. Films and curriculum materials would be purchased, and projects would be sponsored that encompassed Claudia's interests in Spanish language and culture, Central America, women's issues, and the education of children.

"How do you do this?" Hope asked a friend whose son had been killed in a mountain climbing accident three days before he was to graduate from medical school. "We're not sure we can live to the next day."

Eight years had passed since the death of the friend's son and six years since the death by heart attack of the friend's fifty-two-year-old husband. "I don't know how I did it, but here I am," the friend replied.

The day after Claudia's memorial service, the friend talked with Hope. "You have to keep track of these flowers, gifts, letters, and condolence cards. Let me make a card file for you." Not everyone would be helped by a friend's effort to organize the outpouring of concern. For Hope and George, however, answering condolences would become an important way of dealing with their anguish and honoring their precious daughter. Their sons answered letters, too, helping in their own grief.

On Monday, eight days after his daughter's death, George went back to his work as an internist with a primary interest in cancer. One of his patients, a member of their church who had been present at the memorial service, got off the table after her physical exam. Standing in a paper gown, she spoke directly about Claudia, acknowledged George's sorrow, and hugged her doctor. They shed tears together.

While many persons in a professional role would have been unable to receive such an intimate offering of love at the workplace, George had already established a warm relationship with his patients. "It helped that my patients talked about my daughter," George explains. "This is where I learned not to hesitate to bring things up, that it's helpful to talk." It irritated George that many people who knew them well "absolutely have neglected to talk about Claudia." Speaking freely and frequently about their daughter, early in their mourning process and years later, was a way of paying her tribute.

As the painful days and weeks went by, Hope and George handwrote thirteen hundred letters of appreciation to those who offered condolences or sent contributions to Claudia's memorial fund. There were letters to answer from hundreds of family, friends, work associates present and past, people who had known and loved Claudia, and strangers who had read about the tragedy in a New York or Denver newspaper. The Curfmans wrote personal letters rather than simply signing a printed card. They wrote Alan Cunningham of *The Rocky Mountain News* to thank him for his touching newspaper story.

Writing was a meaningful mode of self-expression and sharing for Hope and George and a way to honor Claudia. The letters they exchanged led to a feeling of being loved and supported in their grief. It took the couple from August until Christmas to answer each letter personally.

Claudia was the second person whose ashes were interred at the columbarium which had been established a year prior to her death. The columbarium is a burial yard and garden outside the Curfmans' church, where those who choose cremation can bury the ashes of their loved ones. In keeping with the cycle of life and the biblical phrase "from dust to dust and ashes to ashes we shall return," Hope believed deeply that an alternative was needed to the traditional practice of embalming and cemetery interment. A columbarium is the present-day equivalent of being buried in the churchyard, and the Curfmans liked the idea of "having the church be responsible for the totality of human existence from birth to death and eternal life."

Claudia's plaque at the columbarium was affixed to a stone fence with her birth and death dates inscribed. When the Curfmans took their son-in-law to see the plaque, his continuing anger was apparent. "What a waste!" he said sadly. Subsequently Claudia's husband had a wrought-iron fence built on top of the stone wall to prevent inappropriate intrusion, one of his ways of honoring Claudia.

A biblical quote inscribed in granite at the center of the burial garden comforts the Curfmans: "Neither life nor death, nor depths, nor heights can separate us from the love of God." In the summers Hope and George, along with others who are bereaved, weed the columbarium, choose trees for planting, and work with the flowers. Continuing an involvement with things that grow has comforted them. Over time they have been helped to experience the life and death cycle with an increasing sense of peace.

REENACTING LAST STEPS

Many grieving people have come up to me after a lecture or have approached me in counseling with an urgent need to go to the place where their loved one lived his or her last moments. People seem to need permission, often the encouragement of a respected professional, to know that it's all right that they need to do that.

One woman happened to be walking by a dining room where I was lecturing to hospital volunteers. The luncheon was being held at a country club and the woman had just come off the golf course. She overheard me talking about the importance of saying goodbye and sat down in the hallway to hear my lecture. "My son drowned seventeen years ago," she told me later, "and I've never been back to that lake. Do you think it would help me to go there?"

I asked the woman if *she* felt that returning to the place where her son's life had been lost would enable her to say goodbye to him in a way that had not yet been possible. To this day I don't know what she decided to do. When I briefly saw the woman again, about a year later, we were both wearing golf clothes and she greeted me warmly. She told me my presentation that day had been a help to her.

Two years after losing their daughter, Hope and George reenacted Claudia's last subway ride. They retraced her steps. They went to a little church near Lincoln Center which Claudia occasionally had visited, checked the guest register to see if she had signed it that day, and talked to a custodian to inquire whether he had seen her. Obtaining no evidence that Claudia had been there in her last hours, they went to Lincoln Center, where she had bought Mozart tickets, and walked down the steps to the place where she must have died.

"It helped us," Hope explains. "We had to know where our daughter died. We had to accompany her on that last subway ride and to Lincoln Center. We felt that she died so alone, that hers was the ultimate loneliness at the time of her death.

We saw it as the parents' responsibility and privilege to share what we could, and we did it together. We retraced her steps to accompany her, to be with her at the time of her death. It was something we *had* to do."

Claudia's husband has never ridden the subway again. He continues to live in New York City, has said his own anguished goodbyes, and has made his own enduring tributes to the woman he loved. He has remained close to the family but knows the reality that Claudia is gone. Half of his life remains to be lived; he has to look ahead.

Each person must say goodbye in the way that feels appropriate. A reenacting of last steps can aid healing; a completion of something in the past often makes it possible for one to go forward. It's not what everybody needs to do.

Claudia's case number, 93-10-20, remains in the files of the New York Police Department. Numerous times over the years George called Detective Lopez, the officer in charge of the case, to see if any progress had been made in finding the despicable killer. The last time George called he learned that Detective Lopez had been transferred. In effect the case is closed, and nothing seems to diminish the "considerable amount of hostility and anger" which George says he continues to feel. It is lastingly difficult for anyone to live with the horror and rage that result from violence.

REACHING OUT TO HELP OTHERS

Over the years Hope and George have found themselves writing letters to other parents who have suffered the loss of a child. George wrote to the parents of a young soldier stationed locally who had been shot to death by some people trying to steal his motorcycle. He wrote to the parents of a young boy murdered in New York, and to a psychiatrist whose daughter had been murdered there. "The letters in return have been deeply moving," George says. Claudia lives on in acts of caring such as these.

In Hope's letters to grieving people whom she has read or heard about, she acknowledges, "No one knows the grief of another." Hope may then go on to say, "Since the death of Claudia we have some understanding of the loneliness, despair, and senselessness that you may be experiencing." If the person is a religious person, she might say, "Our love and prayers are with you," consciously avoiding the expressions, "It was God's will" or "She's better off in heaven." Hope and George feel they have learned from the letters they received which words of comfort are meant well but aren't likely to be experienced as helpful.

Before mailing a letter, Hope or George review what the other has written and discuss ways of improving the wording or content. They share a genuine concern to help people who are hurting. Usually when initiating a correspondence, Hope or George will tell the grieving person to expect a telephone call within the coming weeks. They make it a point to follow through.

The Curfmans have also organized and participated in conferences where both professionals and lay people are educated to help themselves and others with loss and grief situations. Hope had been a school social worker consulting with autistic children and counseling their troubled parents. Thirteen months after her daughter's death, she joined a support group to aid her own healing and later trained as a bereavement group leader. She has since served as fund-raiser, treasurer, and president of the Grief Education Institute in Denver.

While he had always been a sensitive man and a caring physician, George found that his loss heightened that sensitivity and made his work with bereaved families and dying patients more skillful and empathic. Other professionals, too, have been helped by sharing their grief with Claudia's parents. One nurse, when George was making rounds, told George that she had been divorced and left with two young children.

One day while she was making cookies, somehow a fire had started and both children had perished. "Becoming recipients of such privileged information was somehow a strength and comfort," explains George. "The realization that you are not alone," he adds, "minimizes that awful isolation." Some people would not have been able to receive comfort from others sharing their pain in this way.

Every year for seven consecutive years, Hope and George traveled back to New York to meet with the committee that makes decisions on behalf of the memorial fund in their daughter's name. In the eighth year they decided it was time to continue this work from their home in Denver.

"The existence of the living memorial fund," explains Hope, "with goals, life, a direction of its own, and a value system we like has helped us in the momentum of looking ahead instead of back."

MAKING THE ULTIMATE TRIBUTE

Saying goodbye to someone you greatly love—as her parents, husband, and brothers loved Claudia—is both something impossible to do and something that must be done. A paradox, but people have to go on with their lives.

Having honored well the memory of someone we love, we are free to perform the ultimate tribute: We go forward in the living of satisfying and productive lives.

All four of his sons came to George's hospital retirement party and presented their dad with a group photograph. The eight-by-eleven silver frame was engraved: "Grateful appreciation and love from Claudia, George, Jim, Bob, and Paul." Remembering that Claudia was the one who had always had the thoughtful idea, the boys asked if their parents wanted a picture of Claudia superimposed on the photo. George and Hope agreed that no, this was a gift from their sons, that

Claudia had died eight years earlier, and that it was important to live fully in the present.

Recently George was diagnosed as having cancer and underwent chemotherapy. He is in remission now. "Because we know time is limited," says George, "we're having a lot of fun together. We see things with greater color, such as the paintings in an art museum. We're traveling and spending time with family. We were already living life fully in this way because of Claudia."

"We know that, having lived through the violent loss of our daughter, we can live through anything," adds Hope. "Out of the seemingly dead bulbs emerge daffodils and tulips in the spring," she affirms. "Human resilience is boundless. Our capacity for new life is never ending."

SEEING THAT LIVES ARE NOT WASTED

"A senseless, wrongful death presents a real obstacle for people in their healing," said Steven Shelton. We were speaking of the violence and waste wrought by homicide, suicide, terrorist acts, and certain military situations in a discussion of the Curfmans' story with Steven and Naomi. Immediately the couple was struck by a major difference in their loss of Collin and the Curfmans' loss of Claudia.

"I always felt that Collin's death was a rightful death," Naomi explained. "Collin died because he couldn't have lived with his many abnormalities. Nature meant him not to survive.

"I felt that losing our baby was unfair because I had done everything I knew to do to have a healthy pregnancy—no smoking or drinking, a careful diet, that sort of thing. Yet violence was not done to us [as it was done to Claudia and those who loved her]. We weren't done to by others. I truly don't look at my experience with bitterness or regret, although

I still miss my little boy very much. I have always felt he is where he needs to be and is perfectly okay.

"It takes a greater amount of effort and more intentional ways of memorializing a loved person who dies a wrongful death," Naomi continued. She spoke with tenderness, reverence, and respect for Hope and George Curfman's monumental struggle. She sensed their great, abiding pain and long effort to redeem a terrible loss. "You must have to do an enormous amount of things to have any peace after a loss so unredeemable," she said.

"Hope and George and the rest of their family found comfort in loving and honoring some of the things that Claudia loved," said Steven. "Similarly, sometimes I think of the laughter and playfulness Collin would have enjoyed had he lived. I really like having fun with the girls. If I weren't a good dad to them, I wouldn't have been to him either.

"My worry when we lost Collin," continued Steven, "was that somehow I would lose the rest of my life. I was afraid I would be forever ruined by becoming a hardened person just to survive it. Now I know I was *wishing* I'd become hardened in order not to hurt.

"It's so important that a loved one's life not have been wasted," Steven said. "My tribute to Collin is not to become a deadened, unfeeling person. If I had become a person with a hardened heart, then Collin's life and the idea of his life would have been senseless. Anniversary times or holidays when we stop by the cemetery create for me times of asking whether I'm living up to my potential as a person, achieving what I deserve in life and what his memory deserves. I want Collin's death to be real to me in the productive and positive way that I live out my life."

"I can say now," adds Naomi, "that Collin's life and death have been a vehicle through which I have helped others whom I otherwise wouldn't have been able to help. I have learned that I have a strength and will to go on that I didn't know was as indomitable as I've discovered. To become nonfunctional seemed disrespectful to Collin's memory. I believe people are meant to survive these things."

The Sheltons have said that appearing with me on Donahue's nationally syndicated television show made them feel they were "making a contribution, creating something worthy and beautiful out of something tragic, painful, and wasted."

Like the Curfmans, Steven and Naomi have taken part in bereavement planning groups and public discussions. They have shared their experiences in panel discussions at medical schools, in hospitals, and at childbirth classes. Once Steven was called to their local hospital to comfort a father whose baby died and to aid the staff in working with the distraught man. "Giving to others," Steven summarizes, "balances our own sense of neediness and emptiness. And the decision to live, to redeem my own life, not to waste what I have left— is a decision made repeatedly, not once."

A theme that emerged in the life of person after person interviewed for this book was that one's own healing was profoundly aided by helping others in pain or by improving people's and institutions' responses to human suffering. Whether an individual's loss was grossly wrongful, cruel, and unjust or was somehow in keeping with the order of nature, the triumphant survivor made a decision that a loved one's life would not be wasted and that one's own life would not be destroyed.

HONORING MY "GRANNY"

When my grandmother died, I went back to the rural community of Thomas, Oklahoma, where I was born. The familiar billboard outside of town, near the skyscraper-sized grain elevator, greeted me once again with "1200 Friendly People Welcome You to Thomas."

The town was almost as I had left it many years before, except that the movie house and roller rink had closed and a storefront library had opened up on Main Street. Also the farmers, who still wore bib overalls, had exchanged their wide-brimmed hats for baseball caps with emblems advertising farm implements. Pickup trucks and an occasional car still parked diagonally on the street. People were still friendly and trusting. If you wanted to pay for something in a store, there was a stack of blank checkbooks on the counter by the cash register. You could fill out the check on one of the two banks in town. There was usually somebody around who knew you or one of your relatives, so there was no need for identification.

There were people here who still remembered my childhood visits to Granny and Grampa's house, remembered my mother with beautiful black hair in long braids, my father as a college student. Not many more years of life remained for most of these people, I sadly realized, and with them would pass away their treasure of memories.

I took a room at the local motel and drove my rental car to the funeral home. The purpose of my sentimental journey across the country was to reminisce, to pay tribute to the wonderful lady we called "Granny," and to mourn the approaching end of an era when the undertaker greeted you in a Western tie and black cowboy boots.

It pleased me that although I had the greatest distance to travel, I was the first family member to arrive at the funeral home. I wanted to be alone with my grandmother just one more time.

Entering the viewing room, I smiled at the pink casket. It would have pleased her, and it delighted me that somebody in the family had had the good sense to choose it. Closing the door behind me, I knew that I wanted to spend several hours with Granny. The flowers and prayer cards that had already come from my friends in Michigan and Maryland made it easier to be there.

"Granny," I said aloud, approaching her pretty casket, "I've always loved you and I always will." I stroked her cheeks, temples, and forehead with my young, tanned fingertips and patted her dear brown-spotted, wrinkled old hands. Finally my right hand rested on the knotted, arthritic joints of her fingers and the wide gold wedding band from a fifty-year marriage. She had been nearly ninety, and it struck me that I had never heard her complain about the arthritis that had disfigured her hands.

"I'm so glad that you aren't suffering anymore," I went on, beginning to cry. "It hurt me so to see you these last years, locked up in your body, not remembering us, incontinent, and pitiful."

My grandmother had had only an eighth-grade education, yet she had read all of the Great Books, liked to sign her letters in Latin, and had published short stories and poems in farm magazines. At the age of sixty-nine, when she lived with me, she took courses in college, and we lived and traveled together in Europe for a year when she was seventy-five. At the nursing home where she had passed her last years and died, I once told the young employees what a proud, intelligent, personable, humorous, well-traveled, dignified lady she used to be. Older employees remembered Granny from another day: At the age of about eighty-four, when she was still in good health and of sound mind, she used to come regularly to the nursing home, as she put it, "to visit the old people."

I thanked Granny for faithfully remembering Christmas and my birthdays for as long as she was mentally capable and for sending all those twenty-five-dollar gift checks over the years. Once, after helping me finance a summer of study in the Middle East and giving my sister a piano, she had given each of her other grandchildren the equivalent in money, to be fair to them.

Remembering the one-dollar checks she liked to enclose in my letters made me smile and weep at the same time. Instructions were always written on the checks: "Treat" or "For Ice Cream." Never mind that I was thirty-four, still exchanging those checks for dollar bills: I loved it. The woman at the payroll window on the college campus where I'm on the faculty always got a kick out of cashing Granny's checks, too.

After several hours with Granny at the funeral home, I left her side, saying, "See you later, Granny, I'm going after a hamburger." I liked talking to her one last time in this routine way.

At the local fast food drive-in, a hallowed spot, I watched cowboys get in and out of their hay-loaded trucks and remembered countless meals and soft ice cream cones shared in a red Ford with Granny. The park where our family had had picnics and feasted on watermelon was in full view here too. Later at the florist I chose long-stemmed blue asters, one of my favorites, for Granny, and visited on the street with people who recognized me and offered condolences. A sentimental soul, I went to the old-fashioned local drug store, where they still give you a milkshake in a metal cylinder. I must have tasted at least a hundred thousand chocolate milkshakes there with Granny over the years, and now I had one more in her honor along with a few more tears.

I drove out to spend some time parked near one of my grandparents' wheat fields and remembered the tornado that had taken the barn. I stopped by the cemetery and sat awhile by the ground that had already been broken for her grave. Grampa and Granny's gray marble tombstone was there, engraved with both names twenty years earlier. There had been visits with Granny to this place, I recalled, when we had brought flowers for Grampa. Leaving the cemetery, I drove back to town to retrace the streets where Granny had lived in various houses with my grandfather or alone, all the years of my life.

Determined that my remarkable and loving grandmother have the tribute she deserved, I returned to the motel to write the eulogy for her funeral service and a longer piece for Thomas's weekly newspaper. Later I saw to it that the minister knew the things about our Granny that we all cherished. It was important that he get acquainted with the person he was going to help us bury.

Our grandmother had traveled in a covered wagon across the Dakota and Nebraska territories, I told the minister. She had been orphaned, married young, and homesteaded with our grandfather in Oklahoma shortly after statehood. At her death, I said, she should be celebrated as a Pioneer Woman.

I remembered the mesmerizing stories Granny loved to tell of those turn-of-the-century days. The pioneer tales were so captivating that even late into my twenties I'd lie on her couch with my head cozily against a pillow on her lap. She would put her wrinkled hand on my shoulder and, like a young child, I would ask her to tell me about the long-ago days "just once more."

Now, with flowers in hand, I went to the nursing home to thank the staff there for taking care of my Granny, to ask about the circumstances of her final hours, to explain one more time why she was so dear to us all, and sadly to pack up her things. It pleased me to learn from one of the nurses that despite the ravages, indignities, and pitifulness of advanced Alzheimer's disease, a little piece of Granny's original, lively, spiritual self remained with her to the end. Her mind was gone to the point that she no longer recognized any of her relatives by name. A few days before her death, however, she was heard singing softly and tenderly from her bed. Clearly recognizable, the song she sang was "God Bless America."

Among Granny's modest belongings I found the beginnings of several letters written to me in the days when she still had partial memory but couldn't complete the tasks she began. Her letters were precious discoveries. I was especially glad that the envelopes were addressed to "Dr.," because that meant she knew, before losing her mental faculties entirely, that I had finished the long-pursued education she had encouraged and aided.

It was a sweet goodbye that I had both with my Granny and in her honor those two days in Thomas, Oklahoma. Years later I continue to hold cherished images in my mind of stroking her dear old wrinkled hands and telling her how much I loved her. The goodbyes that were said overlooking the family wheatfield, by the homes where she lived, at the cemetery, the nursing home, the drug store, the fast food drive-in, the funeral home, and elsewhere have made it possible for me to feel a sense of peace about my grandmother.

Granny had been dead for four years when my mother and I, on a trip together, decided to leave the interstate route and go out of our way a bit for a visit to the Thomas cemetery. On the narrow, slightly graveled road adjacent to my grandparents' tombstone, I parked the car facing the gravesite. My mother and I sat awhile without speaking, holding hands. Eventually we got out of the car, spoke of Granny and of life and death in general, and moved about the marble marker, tidying up some dusty and faded artificial flowers. As we slowly walked back to our open car doors, I looked over my shoulder and said aloud something I'd almost forgotten. "Granny," I said with excitement, "I finally got a publisher for my first book!"

My mother, responding immediately, smiled warmly. "Oh, Ann," she said, "I think she already knows." We linked our arms and continued on toward the car.

I have felt Granny's loving presence at the milestone events of my life: buying a home, publishing my writings, becoming a mother. She is also present each day as someone whose love continues to warm, cheer, and encourage me. I feel she is whole again, no longer imprisoned by illness or frailty, and free to love us from where she is now.

Many people misunderstand "goodbye behavior." They wrongly interpret others' grief reactions as morbid, excessively emotional or hysterical, even indicative of serious mental disturbance. Certain behaviors unquestionably promote healing, such as Steven and Naomi's tender goodbyes with Collin, mine with my grandmother, the woman bidding goodbye to her cancerous breast, the man saying adieu to his drug of choice, and the Curfmans' many contributions to others as a living memorial to their daughter.

It has been my experience and the finding of my studies that those who are able most completely to say goodbye, either soon after a loss or over the years that follow, are the persons most likely to reclaim their lives.

GUIDELINES

Saying goodbye to a particular individual or lost part of ourselves helps to make room for the emergence of new life. The more completion you can bring to things past, the more attention you can direct to things present and future.

By their example, people who have made good recoveries from a personal crisis offer the following advice:

Goodbyes in General

If a marriage or other important relationship has ended, if your home has been destroyed, if your good health or a part of your body has been lost, a dream shattered, or another major crisis event has occurred—talk about your loss with people who listen well. Put into spoken or written words both your fond and unhappy memories.

Write a goodbye letter or speak out loud to the cherished person or thing that you've lost. Put your feelings of longing, love, appreciation, sorrow, anger, regret, or guilt into words. Listen to your own words as you speak or read them aloud. Do you sound like

The Death of a Person

If a loved one has died or is dying, don't hesitate to linger at the person's bedside, at places holding sentimental value in your relationship, near the casket at the funeral home, at the cemetery or columbarium.

As you meditate in silence, pray, or speak aloud your feelings, ask yourself what needs to be said to or about your loved one. What words would honor the person, express your regrets, complete something unfinished, or otherwise help you to feel more at peace?

Use the rituals and rites of your religious tradition as fully as pos-

Goodbyes in General

you mean what you say? If not, say the words again until your appreciation, resentment, or regret is spoken with genuineness.

The Death of a Person

sible, or get whatever help you need to write your own memorial service to mark the passing of your loved one. If a funeral or memorial service in the past was not of your choosing or was somehow inadequate, you can still arrange a private service with the help of a priest, minister, rabbi, or friend. The rituals or rites selected should feel right to you and bring comfort and a sense of completion. Allow your clergyperson or friend to help you find the words that need to be said, read, or sung.

As the months and years go by, follow what feels comfortable regarding visits to the burial site, the saying of prayers, or conversations with the person who has died. You alone know the expressions of love, appreciation, anger, regret, guilt, apology, or sorrow that will enable you to go forward with your life. Vividly imagining the person's presence, say what you feel with the intensity that you feel it.

When you find yourself really stuck, spending weeks and months feeling emotionally down without gaining any ground, ask yourself, "Have I said goodbye so that I can grieve and go on with my life?"

If close friends or family members ask how you're doing, tell them honestly, "I'm not doing so well right now," or "I've been feeling really sad and depressed," or "I'm having a tough day." Then say,

"I won't always have to feel this bad and you don't have to make me feel better. This is just the way I have to feel right now."

Tell others that you are going to grieve but that you will not be distraught forever.

Share your struggle and healing process in letters to a friend, or strike up a correspondence with someone who has suffered a similar loss. Let the purpose of your sharing be to promote healing.

Decide "I will take care of myself" by arranging to be with others on holidays, on anniversaries, and at other difficult times, instead of remaining miserable or alone.

Decide "I will always have my memories, but the time will come when I will be ready to live in the present and for the future."

Make a verbal or written "contract," shared with somebody important to you, committing yourself to take some action on behalf of your own growth.

Decide to stop hassling yourself with statements or questions that begin with the words, "If only," "why," or "what if."[10]

Make a contribution of time, money, or both to an appropriate cause or charity so that some concrete good can result from your personal crisis.

Goodbyes in General

If your suffering has resulted from a disease, accident, social ill, or evil, consider how you can help fight the problem, disease, or condition in society. Perhaps you can prevent others from suffering a similar crisis.

The Death of a Person

If a person was lost, a cause he or she believed in can be aided and supported. Certain interests which the deceased person held in life can be continued at death. You can contribute to a worthy cause in the person's memory on anniversaries, birthdays, or other occasions that remind you of him or her.

Make a contract that reads "I promise that no matter how bad I feel, I will not destroy myself by driving fast, taking drugs, shooting myself, or using any other means of self-destruction. I will go see a doctor or do whatever I have to do in order to feel better and heal." Share this contract with a respected person other than a family member—a clergyperson, teacher, counselor, or physician.

Set up a living memorial to honor your special love by planting a tree, initiating a scholarship, or donating a book, painting, musical instrument, flower garden, plaque, or other long-lasting memorial to an appropriate institution.

Make a list of specific ways that the cherished person or thing that you've lost has positively influenced or aided your life and will always remain with you.

Rearrange your home, room, and personal effects as a symbol of the change that has taken place in your life.[11]

Consider what you have gained from others' compassion in your time of crisis. Ask yourself, "In what ways can I pass on what has been given to me?"

Outline a plan for the rest of your life and share this plan with a trusted person outside of the family.[12]

Ask God to strengthen you each day with permission to enjoy the day and to share joy with others.[13]

When the time is right for it, prepare a lovely dinner and invite the people who have stood by you in your mourning, cared for you, listened to your troubled feelings, or otherwise have provided moral support. Thank each of them for their help and announce that you are beginning to move on now. Say that you still need their love and friendship but that you don't need them in the same way that you needed them earlier. Say that you want to go forward in life and want to share your growth and new life with them. Clink your glasses in a toast, hug each other, or distribute small gifts as a celebration of friendship and growth.[14]

Resolve to learn from your pain something of benefit to others. Who especially are you now in a position better to understand and help?

THE PEOPLE | 7
WHO HELP |

*It is the quality of sustained
relationships with important people
that shapes our future.*

PARAPHRASED FROM
GEORGE VAILLANT,
ADAPTATION TO LIFE

S ome years ago I heard a comment made by Anne Morrow
Lindbergh in a television interview with Dick Cavett which
I expect will stay with me for many years to come. Clearly
taken by Mrs. Lindbergh's graciousness, obvious strength,
wisdom, and gift for poetic expression, Cavett asked the famous writer and wife of Charles Lindbergh where she got her
strength. Making an implicit reference to the infamous and
tragic kidnapping death of her infant son and the pain she
experienced when her husband fell from hero status into widespread and angry disfavor in the country for his support of
Hitler, Cavett asked Mrs. Lindbergh if her strength had come
from suffering.

The exact wording of Anne Morrow Lindbergh's reply has
left me, but the meaning of her response is still perfectly clear.
"Oh, my dear," Mrs. Lindbergh replied, "traumatic experiences only break people down. What builds us up, what
strengthens, is the love and caring we receive while we are
broken."

"Close relationships . . . shape our adaptive resources," wrote George Vaillant in his classic work *Adaptation to Life*.[1] In a famous study funded by the National Institute of Mental Health, ninety-five men were scientifically selected from an original group of 268 Harvard students initially chosen because they were sturdy individuals, boys "able to paddle their own canoe." The study followed these men for thirty-five years, telling the story of "How the Best and the Brightest Came of Age." Vaillant's study described successful and unsuccessful, healthy and unhealthy adaptive styles and coping mechanisms. Like Anne Morrow Lindbergh, Vaillant concluded that character is molded not by traumatic events but by the people with whom we are involved in close and abiding relationships.[2]

Gerald Caplan, Professor of Psychiatry at Hadassah University Hospitals in Jerusalem and a Harvard Medical School professor emeritus, has for three decades studied how people respond to stressful life circumstances. His research has shown that those with a strong social support system are "less vulnerable to stress" and that people "without social support suffer from three to ten times the mental or physical illness" following a stressful situation than do people "who have the personality traits that maintain support for themselves."[3]

One Harvard study reported by Caplan found that among men who had prostate surgery, those who maintained a good human support network were far less likely to suffer impotence afterwards than were those without a well-functioning social support system. In hospitals where patients had elective surgery, men and women requested pain medication less often and recovered earlier when supportive friends or family members were on hand. Children undergoing tonsillectomies had less fever elevation, less vomiting, less crying, and less disturbed sleep after surgery when a supportive network stood by. When "a matrix of interpersonal support" is present, Caplan concluded, people of all ages are aided in "the extent of the burden they can bear."[4] This support can include family, friends, a clergyperson, a teacher, a scout leader, an employer, school or work associates, a student nurse or other hospital visitor.

In another National Institute of Mental Health study, reported in 1986 by author/educators Charles Basch and Theresa Kersch, it was said that "nonsupportive social environments" may be one of the most important factors in determining why "adolescents are the only age group for which mortality rates have increased in the recent past" and why there exists in this age group "disproportionate rates of anxiety, illness, accidents, suicide, homicide, and unwanted pregnancy."[5]

Support from people who care about us is something that few of us can live well without. In times of transition, crisis, or loss, we definitely need the people who help. Virtually every triumphant survivor I interviewed for this book said that recovery was the result, in large measure, of the presence of supportive friends, family, or others of personal importance.

"While friends and family are buffers against stress," however, "they are fallible ones," according to a recent report given by James C. Coyne at a meeting of the American Psychological Association in Los Angeles. Dr. Coyne explained that family members can be "overly invested" in the well-being of a loved one who is suffering "an intensely distressful life change, such as recovering from a heart attack." Such problems can also occur with "a concerned parent and a troubled child." Family members can be guilty of unhelpful efforts to help in other situations as well, Dr. Coyne said, citing that in "one study of obese women trying to lose weight, more than 90 percent of the husbands said they fully supported their wives in the attempt" yet "made frequent offers of food to their wives and criticized the wives' efforts at dieting twelve times more often than they praised them." Seriously depressed individuals such as cancer patients, too, can be made to feel worse by their family members' reactions and friends' efforts to help. When ill people are "babied" on the one hand or, on the other hand, are made to feel "an obligation to stop feeling sad" for the benefit of others in the family, their depression can intensify, according to another study that was cited.[6]

On a morning television show with a live audience in Seattle, Washington, I told the story of the woman who had written a goodbye letter to her breast following a mastectomy, as described in the preceding chapter, "Saying Complete Goodbyes." In the audience was a lady of retirement age who had probably witnessed many tragic events in her life. "That's the silliest thing I've ever heard," said the gray-haired lady emphatically. "A mastectomy is not the worst thing that can happen to a person," she continued. "That woman who wrote the letter to her breast should be thankful that she didn't suffer a greater loss!"

"I'm glad that you've spoken your mind," I said, answering the woman in the audience. "A lot of people in America think as you do." Many persons feel quite genuinely, I went on, that the way to help someone in pain is to remind them of the greater losses of others. In life it's almost always true that things could have been worse; unfortunately, the knowledge of this reality rarely diminishes one's pain. "Telling a friend," I explained, "that 'things could be worse' will probably cause your friend to stop confiding in you her feelings of sadness. Such feelings don't just go away."

We minimize another's loss when reminding him or her that others suffer, too. If such persons take our words to heart, they are apt to grow more depressed as a result of being ashamed of their sadness, feeling judged and misunderstood.

It is important to choose well those friends, family members, and others whom we seek out as confidants or whom we approach for advice, encouragement, compassion, and understanding. In this chapter, in an effort to clarify which kinds of persons and what kind of help were most useful, I will describe how the triumphant survivors I interviewed were helped.

CHILDREN AND ADULTS WHO REMEMBER
OUR LOSS

About a year after Jan and Ed lost their seven-year-old son, they were greatly comforted by a thoughtful act on the part of the principal at Mark's school. Sister Juanita asked all the children who had been in Mark's class at the time of his death to write down their thoughts and feelings about losing their friend and classmate. After the boys and girls completed the assignment, "Sister Juanita brought us the papers they wrote," Jan remembered warmly. "What a gift!" she exclaimed.

Each second-grader vividly recalled the day or the event of Mark's death in the first grade and their sadness because he had died. Their papers were written in the honest, forthright, and touching way that children speak: "I wish he didn't die because we shared our lunches," wrote one little boy. "I new [sic] his mom and his brother. They were nice people," wrote another child. "I am sad right now that I can't see you again," said another, speaking to Mark. "He was my best friend," said nearly everyone in the class.

Jan and Ed found that nearly all of the children's papers brought them comfort and a smile. One of the most tender and touching papers was inscribed, in the upper right-hand corner, "Jenny, Oct. 14, English":

Mark

Mark was nice and shared his pencil, and I felt happy that he's up in heaven. Write now I feel happy because he might be having fun wright now. And I'll just bet you Mark and God are reading stories. And I wish Mark didn't die antill he was about 9 years old. Mark always got a star on spelling, math, English, and other papers. And he was a nice friend to everybody. And when ever I fell down Mark would always help me up. I wish Mark would of never died so he could make his first comminoin and his first connfeshion. Mark was my very best friend I ever Had. Then all the others.

Sister Juanita's loving gift not only contributed to the on-going healing process of Mark's grieving parents but undoubtedly helped the children with their grief as well. It is important to both adults and children who have suffered a traumatic loss to know that others have not forgotten their sadness and have not forgotten the lost person they cared about.

Jan and Ed also told me they were grateful for continuing expressions of love from their friends and family members. Their friends Karen and Bob had long been undecided about having children. About a year after Mark's death the friends told Jan and Ed of a decision they had made and the role Mark's death had played in the decision. "We felt if you loved Mark that much and it hurt that terribly to lose a child," Karen explained, "then how precious it must be to have one." A little daughter, Meredith, was born to Karen and Bob the following September. The event added another important piece of meaning to what Jan and Ed saw as the inherently meaningless event of losing a child. Also cherished is the friendship in which such feelings and decisions can be shared openly.

Karen and Bob have been good about remembering Mark as the years have passed, said Jan. They still make a long-distance phone call to Jan and Ed every year on Mark's birthday.

Three years after Mark died, Ed's brother and his wife sent a contribution in Mark's name to aid hungry children in Africa. It meant so much to Jan and Ed that years later Mark would be remembered in this way, perhaps preventing another child's death.

Jan's sister Patty faithfully remembers Mark, especially on special occasions. She feels the loss of Mark very deeply because she and her husband lived with Jan and Ed and young Mark in the first several years of the boy's life. Once Patty wrote a note that said, "I love you Jan and Ed" and enclosed it with a poem she had written four years after her nephew's death:

March 11, 1986

> *A tenderness rushes*
> *through me sharp like*
> *when I remember the backyard*
> *and planting for tomorrow's dreams.*
>
> *I am so happy Mark was born,*
> *that his spirit lives on in me.*
> *But this does not heal my broken heart*
> *when I face the overwhelming and*
> *impossible truth . . .*
> *that we continue to grow,*
> *that we continue to live*
> *without him here and now.*
>
> *I will never forget.*
> *I will never stop loving.*

—Patty

"Our closest friends," said Jan, "absolutely realize that Mark is as much a part of our lives now as he was then. He is never gone. We think about him all the time." It is very important to this couple that Mark's ongoing presence be realized and that their friends and family should never hesitate to talk about him. They go on with their lives, yet, as is true for all of us when we love someone, Jan and Ed want to keep Mark's memory alive.

RACHEL: BEING HELPED AND HELPING OTHERS

Rachel is among the one in eleven American women who get breast cancer. Her cancer necessitated a mastectomy. After surgery she had chemotherapy treatments every other week for a year. She continued her part-time job at a hospital but chose Monday as her treatment day so that she could get over any nausea and sickness episodes in time to enjoy the weekends. On weekends her sons came home from college, Rachel and her fourteen-year-old daughter painted, and everybody worked on their newly built shore house. "That place has been a haven for us," she says. "We go for walks or canoe rides or just sit out and watch the sunset over the water. Life seems good. After my surgery, we spent an extended time there, and those times helped all of us, including the children."

"It was definitely my family from which I got the greatest strength," acknowledges Rachel. "It wasn't hard for me to be myself on the weekends. I really felt happy at the shore. The kids went out of their way to make light of my surgery, yet we did talk about it a lot and the word cancer was often mentioned. My family kept giving me the message that everything was going to be all right. I never felt I was alone, facing this by myself. I felt all of us were in this together and I was going to be okay."

With her husband, Josh, there were sensitive talks and many long walks. "He can cry easily, which is one of the things I love about him," Rachel says. "He's strong and we've always leaned on him and yet he can cry." They talked about how lucky they felt to have had a really wonderful life. They talked about investments, what would happen with the children if one or both of them died. They decided to update their will, which they thought they should be doing in any case. Josh listened to Rachel talk about being afraid to die.

Memories flooded back of a crisis that had occurred when their daughter, at age three, had come down with a dangerous bacterial infection of the trachea. They had rushed the child to the hospital for a tracheotomy, and the physicians had told them to prepare themselves to lose her. They were so sure their daughter was going to die that they had been crying and saying things like "We'll get over this." Now, eleven years later, as Rachel and Josh faced the fear of her possible cancer recurrence, they agreed, "We'll get through this, too."

Rachel had grown up in a family where people were unable to share their feelings. They had never said "I love you" to each other, and Rachel had felt unable to say those three words to her friends. After the surgery a transformation occurred. At the age of forty-eight Rachel began openly expressing loving feelings to her friends and family.

"I didn't say to myself, 'Life is short. I'm going to show people that I love them.' It just oozed out of me. It started when I was writing thank-you notes. I was really writing in a different way."

Learning how to have a deeper level of open closeness, both with her family and with others, has been a key factor in Rachel's recovery. Rachel discovered that, like many of us, she could live with somebody a long, long time and really love the person and feel she was communicating and yet hold back and not say certain things. After the surgery she and her husband felt so much closer that it was safe to share even negative thoughts that they had been afraid to express. She told him that whenever they were with friends, he monopolized the conversation and embarrassed her because he always had to get the last word in. He told her that he didn't like the way she clammed up instead of arguing. They remembered arguments they had had when they were younger, and they laughed about them.

Another key factor in Rachel's recovery was the fact that her relationship with her husband always made her feel like a whole woman, who was still lovable. She never considered breast reconstruction, which some women find very helpful after a mastectomy, because she didn't feel she needed it. Their relationship, which had begun with physical attraction thirty-one years before, when they were both seventeen, had grown into a mature, abiding, holistic love. She knew her husband loved many aspects of their relationship and saw her as his companion and partner through many facets of life. They had always shared a lot of activities and interests. He talked to her about his work as a cardiologist, about politics, and about a wide range of other topics, and they had a mutual intellectual stimulation.

Also, as a cardiologist, he was not disturbed by the changes in Rachel's body the surgery had wrought. It was he who first looked at her when tenderly and lovingly he changed the bandages at the site of her lost breast.

Rachel had perhaps chosen to marry a man like Josh because he was like her father in one important way: he valued her as a person. "Way back I think a lot of it had to do with my father, who really gave me a sense of being in his eyes a whole person," Rachel says. "Even though we didn't spend that much time together, he made me feel that I was bright. He wasn't educated, but he would talk to me about elections and the candidates and he made me feel that I had something to contribute even when I was in elementary school. He made me feel really important."

Having recovered so successfully with her family's support, Rachel herself was able to become a helping person. While she was in the hospital, she was visited by a woman from Reach for Recovery. The woman said she had had a mastectomy twelve years earlier. "When I heard it was twelve years," recalls Rachel, "I thought that was just great. Seeing someone in person who had recovered was such a lift." Two years after her own surgery, Rachel started visiting women following their mastectomies and has made more than a hundred such visits. She knows how it helps when she says it's been six or seven years since her own mastectomy.

Rachel has also had occasion to be a helper closer to home. A year after her surgery, during her last month of chemotherapy, it was determined that her husband needed major heart surgery. As a cardiologist, he had recognized his own symptoms of heart disease for many months, but he had been denying these symptoms so he could cope with his wife's cancer. Now it was Rachel's turn to set aside her fears for her own life and to be strong for her husband.

Rachel and Josh talked openly about the dire circumstances.

They made contingency plans—if such and such happened, they would do so and so. They determined what relatives and friends to call on and what sort of arrangements would be made for the children.

The months after Josh's bypass surgery were difficult, but they gave Rachael a new sense of purpose, she says. "It forced me to turn off what I was feeling and concentrate on something else. Focusing on somebody else really helps."

LYNN: A CLUSTER OF PEOPLE HELPED HER TRIUMPH

In her senior year of high school Lynn was diagnosed as having Crohn's disease, an illness in which ulcerations and lesions in the intestines become infected and cause damage to the lining of the intestine. For a time she took steroids and her violent stomach cramps and fever subsided. Throughout college her illness remained in remission without medication. After college she married her high school sweetheart, Rodney, and began teaching to help pay his way through pharmacy school.

In their first five years of marriage she was very ill about once a year. Nevertheless, Rodney, a self-centered, vain man, started to claim that she was sick all the time. Lynn feared becoming ill enough to necessitate an ostomy, a procedure in which the large and small intestines are surgically disconnected and the rectum is closed. When she was twenty-seven years old, her fears were realized and the ostomy was performed. She was fitted with a small bag for waste products, which is worn close to the body and must be emptied several times daily.

Shortly after her surgery someone from the Ostomy Foundation came to visit her in the hospital. The visitor, a beautiful, articulate woman, was upbeat in her attitude and brought comfort and encouragement to Lynn. The woman said that she herself had had an ostomy and that it hadn't stopped her from living an active and fulfilling life. To Lynn the woman did not look different from any other woman. "I made up my mind," she said, "that the ostomy wasn't going to stop me either."

There were major setbacks. Lynn went home after fifty-six days in the hospital to a strained marital relationship. Rodney, preoccupied with satisfying his own needs, was grumpy and emotionally unavailable. He went off on a week-long holiday with a buddy.

Two months later Lynn, critically ill, was hospitalized for another long stay. Her husband rarely came to see her. She didn't know that Rodney had asked her father and stepmother for the key to their summer vacation home, claiming to be worried about Lynn's condition and needing time away. Actually, he was having an affair with another woman there.

Two weeks after Rodney graduated from pharmacy school and shortly after Lynn came home from the hospital, he announced to Lynn that he was leaving her. He admitted to having been unfaithful many times, including during her hospital stay. He took their expensive cameras and new car, leaving behind an old car that wouldn't start. The next day he came back, but only to discuss what Lynn would need in order to live without him. He made promises that he would fail to fulfill. Rodney told his ill wife, "It's not that I don't like you, but you're a vegetable and how can I love a vegetable?"

HAVING A FAMILY THAT RALLIES AROUND

Lynn was devastated. She called her father and stepmother. "Daddy," she said, and then she started to cry. Her father had figured out what had happened. "We'll come get you," he said. He and his wife, Doris, came to Lynn's apartment and took her to their house. "I saw no reason to live," Lynn remembers. "I was depressed. I slept all the time. I didn't want to talk to people. I felt I was a vegetable. I felt sick and stopped eating—a form of suicide. I started seeing a psychologist, but I was too bad off physically for her to be able to do me any good."

The woman with whom Rodney was having an affair was an acquaintance of Lynn's. She had come to the hospital with Rodney to visit and had given Lynn a haircut. Lynn remembered that her husband had kept saying how nice it was of this woman not to charge anything for the haircut! Lynn was furious.

"I was angry at the disease, angry at the ostomy, angry that I had put him through school and lived with all his promises that we were going to have a house and a family. I was angry that he saw me as a vegetable and that he was having an affair with this woman who came to the hospital and cut my hair.

"I shared with my mom, dad, and sister the despairing times. I told them I was ugly, a freak, that I had nothing to live for. They said 'You're not ugly. You're not a freak.' And dear old Dad said that someday Rodney would realize he had made a mistake."

In the months after Rodney left her, Lynn grew more and more emotionally upset. Her physical condition deteriorated on her meager diet. Shortly after seeing an attorney to start divorce proceedings, Lynn began to bleed rectally and was hospitalized again.

"There was a long period when I was pitying myself," she recalls. "I hated myself and felt hopeless. My parents, who were divorced, each let me have my feelings of anger for about one month. Then my Dad said, 'Knock it off, this is ridiculous!' " Lynn's father later told her that he didn't mean to be angry with her but he felt it was time for her to start working on getting it together because they loved her and cared about her.

Lynn's mother said the same thing in a gentler way. "It's time to start getting better," she said.

Lynn realized that she was "tearing up her family" by refusing to eat and by giving up on herself. She was shocked by her father's harsh words yet touched by his tender ones, and she knew that both themes came from his caring. They were words she needed to hear. Lynn remembered the woman from the Ostomy Foundation who had talked with her about wearing bathing suits and sexy nightgowns, even after her ostomy. Lynn decided, "I'm going to be like her." She began to assume a new attitude.

Lynn received support and caring from her relatives, her fellow teachers, and her high school special education students. Through twelve major and minor surgeries (ten in two years) Lynn's father, her mother (his first wife), and Doris (his second wife) put aside any differences between them and pulled together to give Lynn the emotional support she needed. The three sat together, at first feeling strained and uncomfortable with each other, and focused on the problem they all shared. Since then they have remained civil and decent toward each other. They get in touch with each other when someone in the family is sick or in trouble. They also attend birthday parties for their grandchildren. Lynn sees it as a real declaration of their love for their children that they stand together for both sad and happy occasions. Their unselfish devotion to their children, which overrode their personal differences, was an important source of support for Lynn.

Lynn and her sister have also become very close. Even though her sister is four years younger, Lynn says, "She's very motherly to me. It's sweet and sometimes amuses me. She has a heart that is humungous. I don't think I have any secrets from her." They are now best friends as well as sisters.

Early in Lynn's recovery, her sister arranged a blind date for her. Lynn repeated over and over that she had no interest in dating. Her self-esteem was very low. She was still feeling battered from the assault of Rodney's harsh words and cruel behavior. Nevertheless, she finally did accept the blind date. He was a nice guy, and Lynn married him three years later.

"When I go to see someone who has had an ostomy," says

Lynn, "I wear something close to my body, tight-fitting clothes. I tell them I teach full time, swim and water-ski in the summer, work out at Nautilus, play racquetball, and write school curriculums. I explain that I have a nice social life, that I give talks about special education. Then I tell them I've had an ostomy, and sometimes I lift my clothes and show them the bag."

Lynn was fortunate in having at her school a principal who was understanding and supportive through her periods of illness and the various hospitalizations, which required absences from teaching as long as six months and one year. He telephoned Lynn's dad and said, "Tell her not to worry. She'll come back here. No one else will take her room and no one else will take her position. I will be sure of that." Knowing that the job she loved awaited her and that her principal was so supportive was a great source of comfort and strength to Lynn. She later became a department head at her school and is continuing in the position made secure by her principal's promise. She was chosen by an honor society as one of ten "Outstanding Women in America" for 1985. Those sharing in her award, as Lynn sees it, are the following helpful persons: an upbeat, positive-speaking woman who had had ostomy surgery and who visited Lynn in the hospital, parents and a stepmother who were able to place their children's and grandchildren's welfare ahead of any conflicts or grievances among themselves, a loving sister and husband, and a boss and coworkers who gave Lynn their full support.

Because of recent medical advances, there is now a possibility of doctors' reversing the ostomy. Her husband says, "That's wonderful, and I think you should go for it. But it's fine if they can't do it. I've never known you any other way. I look at you as someone who is my wife and someone who is very special and someone I love."

ENCOUNTERS THAT AFFIRM SELF-WORTH

In *Hiroshima Maidens*, Rodney Barker tells the courageous story of twenty-five atom bomb victims, young women who were terribly scarred facially and elsewhere by the "grisly way (their) burns had healed."[7] All in their early teens when Hiroshima was destroyed in 1945, these survivors suffered in "a society that placed such great emphasis upon aesthetic presentation and losing face in every sense" that it "offered no place for their kind. . . . Employers refused to hire them because, they said, it would be too demoralizing to have them around, and marriage was out of the question because it was roundly believed that they would give birth to a generation of genetic monstrosities."[8]

It was not until three years after the bomb fell that these girls were brought together in a support group organized by Reverend Kiyoshi Tanimoto. Reverend Tanimoto, who later was a moving force in getting them medical help, enabled the scarred girls to find fellowship with each other and "gave them a chance to experience a unity of spirit."[9] He also worked hard to get them jobs (in a dormitory for blind children, where the girls could do such things as teach sewing classes), because he realized that they needed to feel useful and to be able to manage their own lives if they were ever to develop feelings of self-worth.

Their story, as Barker movingly describes it, tells of "the healing power of feeling important, wanted, needed and accepted" when one has severe deformities and lives in a world that has been brutal, rejecting, cruel, and unfriendly. In order to avail themselves of what would become their most important source of healing, the "maidens" would have to learn to trust the very enemy who had wrought destruction and great suffering. In 1955, after initial U.S. State Department objections by officials who feared that these young women's presence might embarrass the United States and be turned into propaganda, arrangements were made to bring the girls to America for medical treatment. They stayed with Quaker families, who accepted them as family members. Their new experiences seemed to bring as much healing as did the many operations they would have. One of the girls, before being wheeled into the operating room, sent a message to her doctor: "I know my scars are very, very bad and I know he is worried because he thinks I may expect that I will be as I once was. I know this is impossible but it does not matter because something has already healed here inside."[10] Whether the Quaker families' warm reception and full acceptance were based on guilt about the atom bomb or were simply a humanitarian response to their suffering, the young women saw that "their general treatment in America was more positive than it had been in their own country." The realization offered a powerful cure. [11]

These women share a "bond of loyalty" with each other as proud people who have survived incredible experiences. Barker writes, "Today they do not refer to one another as Hiroshima Maidens, but as members of the *Satsukikai*. *Kai* is Japanese for "association"; *satsuki* is the word for azalea. It's the way they view their lives: like a gathering of flowers that bloom in May, the month they arrived in America."[12]

A NETWORK OF SUPPORT

Alex, who lost 150 pounds and maintained this dramatic weight loss over many years, looked for reinforcement early in his struggle to lose weight. "Everywhere I turned, encouragement was there," he recalled. "I received all kinds of support." Working on a staff of more than one hundred people in a secondary school system, Alex lost all that weight in their presence. The approval of the other teachers, administrators, and school counselors was so enthusiastically expressed and so important to him in the first eighteen months that it was one of the reasons he didn't gain back the weight. He didn't want to let down all those supportive, good people.

"For me somebody had to be there not as much while I was losing the weight as when I landed on the other side," says Alex. He looked around for help and got it, from friends, and from a close group of about thirty co-workers, including school psychologists and social workers. "Different people supplied different things," he recalls. Casual acquaintances complimented him on his appearance and accomplishment. Several close friends spent hours sharing his fears, anxieties, and hopes while he was uncertain whether or not he really wanted to remain at 175 pounds. "Because of their compassion, I made it," Alex acknowledges. "I don't know how people can make it unless they feel that other people care about their welfare."

People need support when going through a major change such as Alex's profound change in self. Many old issues surface for the recovering obese person, alcoholic, drug- or tobacco-addicted person, and person grieving a major illness, death, or other significant loss. These issues have to be dealt with. People may ask themselves, "Am I a good person?" "Can I live without depending on my old coping mechanisms?" "Will people like me as I am now?" "Do I deserve to be happy? (sober? thin? healthy?)" In Alex's words, "If I didn't have friends who made me feel normal and accepted, I don't think I could have made it. These friends were with me when I was heavy, while I lost weight, and after. They helped me through the transitions."

The people who help don't have to be universally supportive or give us unqualified love. It would be a mistake, in fact, to think that any one person could provide for us all the support and understanding that is needed. We are much more likely to find ourselves feeling supported and upheld if we look for a certain type of encouragement from one person, a particular quality of good listening from another, practical help from another, an example of how we can survive from another, assistance with spiritual, medical, or legal problems from someone else, and simple companionship from others.

"The balance between asking others for help, not being a

burden, yet not being a martyr," a friend told me, "is difficult to achieve." It becomes easier to rely on others and determine how we can comfortably count on each person when our attachments are spread out in a network of support.

OTHERS WHO HAVE BEEN THERE, TOO

A camaraderie arises among people who have shared a particular loss and who understand firsthand its anguish. The community spirit shared by Londoners after the Blitz is found in hundreds of support groups that have been established in this country. Groups are available for bereaved parents and siblings; widows and widowers; cancer patients and their families; victims of incest, rape, and spouse beating; alcoholics and their family members; single parents; infertile couples; people with illnesses or special problems of various kinds such as arthritis, lupus, anorexia nervosa and bulimia, ostomies, and others; survivors of suicide or homicide; people with aging or mentally ill loved ones unable to care for themselves any longer; and many more.

It has been my experience in more than twenty years of helping people that support groups such as these offer a healing balm which often is more curative than any other type of support, including professional counseling.

If you live within driving distance of a metropolitan area and are suffering from one of the losses or problems described above, you can look in the phone book or newspaper or ask your clergyperson, physician, teacher, or a friend if they know of support groups in your area for people like you. Most local hospitals have a chaplaincy, community service, or patient advocacy office also knowledgeable about sources of support.

If you are a parent who has lost a child, I would urge you to find out where and when the nearest Compassionate Friends or other group for bereaved parents meets. You can at least get on the group's mailing list so that you can hear or read what other parents say about losing a daughter or son and what helps them. Even if you yourself are unable to put into words your feelings or struggle, hearing others will help you to clarify troublesome feelings and to feel that your feelings are normal under the circumstances. It is not necessary in a support group of this kind to talk or share openly. You can benefit as much from listening to others as from sharing. You will learn that you are not alone and will receive practical advice on coping with your specific problems.

Sometimes a combination or cluster of helpful groups and individuals is needed. Marlo, a woman I interviewed for this book, was an incest victim. Because she was sexually abused during a vulnerable period in her life—from the years of three to ten—a comprehensive, long-term healing regime was needed. Marlo had more than two years of intensive psychotherapy with a gentle woman psychologist who saw her on a weekly basis. She was also in a college creative writing class with a small group of supportive women and a sensitive, caring teacher. Marlo wrote about her experiences and feelings and was able to share some of her writings in this intimate setting where other women shared deeply personal and difficult experiences. For several years Marlo participated in a survivor's group for incest victims which was led by a trained social worker. This specialist in the treatment of incest victims aided the group members in sharing, letter-writing, and role-playing activities.

Marlo needed all of these supports to work through the traumatic events of her childhood. Now she herself is helping to lead support groups for women who have been victimized by incest, rape, or other domestic violence. She also serves in her community as a resource person, panelist, and speaker, educating the public about sexual and other violent crimes and about programs available to aid victims.

Journalist Amy DePaul reports that "the imprint of help-lessness left by sexual assault can linger, haunt and debilitate victims long after the attack, sometimes stalling recovery in-definitely." For this reason several "wilderness therapy" programs have been established in cities such as Denver and Santa Fe, specifically to aid assault victims. Rigorous outdoor activities which build confidence are provided to help rape and incest victims "confront—and overcome—their often crippling sense of powerlessness."[13]

Carolyn Agosta is therapist and co-director of Ending Violence Effectively (EVE), a Denver program similar to the Outward Bound nonprofit outdoors organization. The EVE program, she says, "forces women into physically demanding situations that evoke the same feelings of helplessness experienced during the rape, and then provides a chance to conquer them, by crossing the river, scaling the rock or simply hiking the hill."[14]

Not every type of therapy or support suits the needs and personality of every person. By being open to investigating various treatment opportunities, looking into support groups, and checking the credentials of a wide variety of helping professionals, the needed kinds of support can be found.

Jennifer Barr, a rape victim who tells her story in *Within a Dark Wood*, has articulately expressed what she needed from others in her time of crisis: "I needed to be assured I wasn't alone. . . . I knew I was terrorized, but I didn't know if other people would view the assault as a disaster or a mishap. I wanted to be assured that there was nothing to be upset about, yet just as urgently, I wanted to be assured that I was not overreacting to something minor."[15]

In the aftermath of a shocking, traumatic, humiliating, frightening, or painful event, all of us need to know that others take our crisis seriously. We need the assurance that we will not be destroyed by what has happened to us, but we also need to know that our overwhelming feelings of grief, rage, or terror are completely understandable and appropriate in the situation in which we find ourselves. Other people can help most by not being alarmed over our intense reactions. What we need from others is simply to have them get into the boat with us and ride out the turbulent seas.

Often in my life I've looked for help. Reading has been one of the best sources of help for me—reading about grief when I was mourning, searching for information about family problems, learning about weight control, and even finding out how to improve my public speaking abilities. Reading books about the sleep disturbances and developmental stages of infants and children has been a big help to me as a mother. Before I became a mother I read avidly on the subject of adoption. Survivors look for help and find it in the ways that speak to them. For some people private help is found in books, while others openly talk over a problem with a trusted confidant or like-minded friend.

REMEMBERING EARLY PARENTAL MESSAGES

Prisoner of war Robbie Risner describes himself as having been a "runt" during his growing-up years, but he wrestled on junior high and high school teams. Robbie's father was an Oklahoma sharecropper with ten children to feed during the Depression. His favorite saying was, "Son, you can't whip a man that won't quit."

Robbie and his dad were close. His father was not a demonstrative man, yet when young Rob left home to join the Air Force, his father cried and cried. Robbie cherishes boyhood memories of their riding into town together to swap horses. When he was only seven or eight years old, Robbie was allowed to drive the horses and wagon home, sitting in the spring seat at the front of the wagon while his dad slept, leaning against the sideboards, in the back.

His dad's confidence in him and encouragement from childhood offered strength when he was in prison. Once a former All-American football player challenged Robbie's directives and authority as the ranking officer in captivity. The other officer easily outweighed Robbie by fifty pounds and was claiming to outrank him.

"Well, we'll have it out," Robbie told the big guy. "You may whip me four or five times but eventually, some way, I'm going to whip you. I'll fight you before I'll change any of my decisions or relinquish command."

There is authority in a person's voice when he or she is absolutely convinced. The other officer backed down.

At other critical times during the ordeal of his imprisonment, Robbie determined that he was going to win. "If you won't quit, you can't lose," he says. "It's a good feeling to know that."

Often in crisis counseling, I'll ask an individual to tell me the name of someone during childhood who had faith in him or her and offered encouragement, and I'll ask what that individual's favorite saying was. Commonly the answer will come, "No one, there was nobody like that available for me."

"Well, I don't believe you," I'll reply. "If your life is so impoverished that nobody ever had confidence in you and urged you on, then you wouldn't be here with me. You wouldn't have a job or be in college or have the strength to seek counseling. You'd be in a jail someplace or living on the streets.

"Come on," I'll say, pushing, "tell me who was a support for you—a teacher, a relative, a friend's parent, somebody from your church or synagogue, a scout leader?"

Usually the person will recall the name of at least one significant individual. A memorable sentence or set of specific supportive words spoken years before will bring encouragement again. People from the past, including persons who have long since died, can be a powerful strength to us.

Robbie Risner, years after his release from captivity, told me about an important message he received from his mother. It still strengthens him.

In 1974 Risner received a telephone call in Texas from the White House and was asked if he could be there at ten o'clock the next morning. He took a fighter jet, because a commercial airliner would not get him there in time. "No one knew why I had been called to the president's office," he said, "but when

I got there President Nixon had a copy of my book, *The Passing of the Night*, and wanted me to sign it."

"The president," Risner went on, "was embroiled in the Watergate controversy." He was so obviously aged in his appearance and so troubled that Risner felt sorry for him. "It came to me," Risner remembered, "that I'd feel honored if I could just loan him some strength.

"Mr. President," Robbie began, "when things were the toughest when I was a prisoner of war in Hanoi, I remembered something my mother said. She told me, 'When you've done all you can to stand—then stand!' "

There were "big old tears that rolled down his cheeks," said Robbie, recalling Mr. Nixon's response, "so it must have touched him."

What his mother's words have meant to him in every tough time in his adult life, Robbie Risner explained, is that "when you've used all your resources, don't give up. You've equipped yourself the best that you can. You're going to make it."

". . . there is no way that we can divide and give back to the world more than we are ourselves until we have first taken other people inside," wrote George Vaillant in *Adaptation to Life*. "To reach full maturity we must first rediscover our parents so that, now internalized and immortal, they become a source of fresh strength. Second, we must acquire new people to care for faster than they die or move away. In other words, to internalize and to identify is to grow."[16]

*Misfortune is great,
but human beings are
even greater than misfortune.*

RABINDRANATH TAGORE

"A survivor is a person who, when knocked down, somehow knows to stay down until the count of nine and then to get up differently," said Dr. Joy Joffe, a psychiatrist who was on the faculty at Johns Hopkins Hospital in Baltimore. "The nonsurvivor," she went on, "gets up right away and gets hit again."

What it means to "stay down until the count of nine" is to plan ahead how to handle the next blows before they come. When even the best-laid plans are undermined or sabotaged, those who triumph plan for the triumph and move on that course of action.

When I knew that my marriage was over, I made a declaration to myself to continue my education and go for a doctor's degree. There were obstacles and setbacks of various kinds. It would be seven years before I completed my educational goal. The mental preparations I made for my future during this long period of mourning often sustained me. By the time my grief was mostly resolved, I had begun another life with new opportunities, an upgraded income, and new challenges. While we are hurting, it isn't easy to envision in concrete and specific ways the achievement of a satisfying, happy life. Such vision, however, is imperative for making the new life possible.

Many people have planned this way as they look ahead to old age. Instead of waiting until one spouse dies or becomes infirm, these people decide to move to a single-story house, to an apartment or retirement community, or to a location near relatives. In reasonably good health, they make a major move while it is still not an overwhelming task. They are able to make decisions before the onset of a crisis that would impair their judgment and add stress to the move.

Two of my friends of retirement age, Norma and Jack, broke up their family home to move to an apartment. It was hard to leave the house where they once lived with two of their three children and where they had watched six grandchildren play and grow. While feelings of nostalgia at times made them feel terrible about their decision to move, they knew that if tragedy immobilized one of them, the other would have to do all this work alone. "Later on," said Jack, "even if we have to leave our new apartment for a nursing home, it won't be as traumatic because nothing will be as difficult as dismantling this home place."

Of course, after examining their circumstances and alternatives, many persons in retirement decide that the right decision for them is to stay put. Yet by thinking ahead, without morbidly dwelling on misfortunes that may never occur, they are able to anticipate many problems and their solutions. People who look to the future usually have more options. There is also the advantage of being in charge. "We would rather make the decisions ourselves than have them made for us," said Jack.

It is often not possible, of course, to anticipate that a particular adversity will come our way or even to know precisely what difficulties we will face following a crisis. We can prepare ourselves for whatever difficulties await us in life by studying the traits that are typical of survivors and by nurturing and incorporating more of these qualities into our own personalities.

LUKE: POSSESSING THE WISDOM TO PLAN AHEAD

The moment you walk into Luke and Sarah's home, you are struck by how regular their family life is. Except for one thing: These people seem happier than the average family. You sit there and watch them. You try to figure out how everybody is so happy when Luke, the head of the family, has chronic progressive multiple sclerosis. He is thirty-five years old and a construction worker. He has not been able to work for most of seven years since his diagnosis.

Luke describes how the type of M.S. that he has slowly progresses. "Generally you just go downhill," he says. "You kind of deteriorate." It started with a weakness in his legs at the age of twenty-eight, when his wife was pregnant with their second child. "I was going downhill real fast, was practically confined to a chair," Luke explains. He responded to high doses of prednisone given intravenously and for a period got back on his feet with the help of a cane. These days he mostly maneuvers about the house in a motorized wheelchair. He walks very short distances with Canadian crutches, which are metal canes with support devices for his upper arms. All of his remaining strength is in his upper body, and he is starting to lose some strength there.

Luke's mother had the same illness for twenty-six years. At the beginning she walked with a cane and dragged one leg. Eventually she needed a wheelchair but still had the use of her hands. Gradually she lost the use of her hands as well, about fifteen years before she died.

Everywhere in Luke and Sarah's house you see beautiful things, revealing Luke's giftedness as a craftsman. A handsome cherry grandfather clock, which he made before he became ill, ticks proudly away near the stairs in the living room. It chimes regally, slightly ahead of a magnificent, mahogany-stained wall clock hanging in the dining room. Another large wall clock with a box face chimes noticeably later nearby.

In the house where Luke has spent much of his time for the past several years and where time seems to pass too quickly, lovely stained-glass pieces are mounted in every room. He has made most of these pieces since becoming ill. A huge mirror is trimmed with green and caramel opalescent glass, a large white flower with green leaves decorating one side. It dominates and beautifies its wall. Reminiscent of Luke's hunting days, a multicolored glass pheasant hangs in the expansive bay window, adding to the room the rich hues of yellow, red, and green. The living room walls are finished by Luke in rough-cut western red cedar.

It's hard to tell, as you talk with Luke and watch his wife and young daughters come in and out of the room, whether the warmth is coming from the wood-burning stove near Luke's chair and footstool or from the people who live here. An unusual kind of warm, lively energy permeates the entire house. It is something of an understatement to describe the people who live here as upbeat. Even extended family members who come and go seem full of humor and liveliness—Luke's father, his uncle Rollie, his sister and brother-in-law. There is a good deal of teasing back and forth and pleasure in the company of each other. You believe Luke when he tells you, "I'm very happy. I think the whole family is. That doesn't mean we don't have things to be concerned about."

"I can get terribly moody sometimes," he continues. "It must be unbearable. Sarah just puts up with it until I come around. She is very tolerant. I get in a bad mood where everything seems to irritate me. It lasts a day or a few hours. Sometimes it's something very small like the children irritating me by just not listening to things I tell them to do."

Most of his life, Luke was an outdoorsman who liked to

hunt and fish and who enjoyed working outside in his construction job. He sometimes gets depressed because his life is so different now. His moods occur because "I can't get out much now and am pretty much stuck in the house." When the weather is bad and the ground is wet, it's tough to move across the lawn in his motorized wheelchair and difficult for him to get in and out of the van. In better weather he spends more time in the yard.

Although he is not a man to brood or dwell on the negative side of things, there are times when Luke can't avoid looking toward the future and worrying about what kind of condition he'll be in a year from now or further down the road. He is concerned about who would take care of him if anything happened to Sarah even for a short time. "Even if she had to be away a few days," he says, "I wonder what would happen to me, because that's how much I depend on her."

When she sees that her husband is feeling down or depressed and observes him being inactive, Sarah will say, "Get to work! This isn't right, sitting around feeling sorry for yourself!"

Luke smiles as he speaks of Sarah's nonpatronizing way with him. "She has so many projects lined up for me to do that I don't even want to think about it," he says, laughing. "She wants the kitchen painted and papered and wants me to get to work helping to choose the paint color and the paper. She also is after me to make her a stained-glass lamp, which is a project I haven't attempted yet. She can't stand it when I just sit around and is constantly on me to keep busy."

ASSUMING A PRACTICAL, PROBLEM-SOLVING APPROACH TO CRISIS

Luke's moods are usually not related to thinking about the future or his deteriorating physical capabilities. In fact, "I try to think as far ahead as I can," Luke says. "It just doesn't get me in a bad mood thinking about it. Foreseeing how I'm going to handle different problems, *that* gives me a lot of peace of mind."

Like many who live well with difficult life circumstances, Luke gets comfort and a sense of power from planning in advance how he will cope with the still greater difficulties that lie ahead. Sometimes Sarah tells him she's worried about his illness. Frequently the subject of her concern is something he has been thinking about also. "If she is noticing I'm having trouble getting up and down the stairs," he explains, "she'll come to me and say, 'What are we going to do?' I had been thinking and thinking about it. I just hadn't said anything to her." In this case Luke called the M.S. Society and learned that a chair lift was available for loan. The couple was relieved to discover that they could obtain one in this way. Installation would cost about five hundred dollars—only one-fourth the cost of purchase.

"When Sarah has something really bothering her, we sit down and talk about it. She gets a lot of consolation from talking about what is bothering her, whether it's a big problem or a small one. Sometimes she'll be worried about the kids, whether they're doing well in school. She'll worry if there is money for this or that. I just have to show her on paper what the situation is, that we do have money for this or we don't have it for that."

For several years part of Luke's planning ahead has included the careful management of money. When he worked part time, they were able to save some money. Even with their Social Security income, they maintain a modest savings plan. Sarah does not work outside the home. Luke is planning a downstairs addition to the house so that he'll have a bathroom with grab bars and a door wide enough and sink and countertop low enough for a wheelchair. He is to provide the materials, and his father-in-law and uncle Rollie are going to build it. He always makes detailed preparations for future eventualities, arranging alternatives for those times when his mobility might be greatly diminished.

"When I was diagnosed," Luke explains, "it was a big shock. But this disease gets on you a little at a time. You have an impairment and you adapt to it, you find another way to get into the bathroom and maybe don't even notice that you can no longer do something easily. In that way it's really good that it gets you gradually. You don't all of a sudden wake up and find you can't move your legs. I can see how that could be really traumatic, being in an accident and all of a sudden you can't move."

After the initial shock, Luke modified the way he worked. For several years he worked on his stained-glass projects in a basement workshop while his daughters and their friends played with their toys in the same room. What would take somebody else eight hours to do might take Luke sixteen hours because of difficulties getting around to the different machines. By carefully planning ahead, he could reduce the time his work would take. The same was true when he approached an odd job upstairs. "If I was fixing the dimmer switch in the dining room, I couldn't run downstairs to get a screwdriver and then come back up and realize then that I left the wire nuts and go back down again. Just for a simple job there is a lot more thinking to do." Because it is becoming harder and harder for Luke to get downstairs and because his hands are weakening, Sarah helps him by arranging some of his materials upstairs before she leaves the house on errands. One Christmas he received a glass cutter designed for those who have diminished hand strength.

He had been the kind of kid who took things apart and put them back together, and he's that kind of adult, too. The first time I visited Luke, he had his motorized wheelchair turned upside down, having pulled it apart to investigate a problem. He was on the phone trying to find out if the warranty still covered the seven-month-old mobile chair. (It didn't, and he was amazingly good humored about it, I thought.) With a positive way of approaching things, Luke is always searching for alternatives, looking for solutions to problems, and exploring the resources available to him. As far ahead of time as possible, he makes plans for how he will adjust to limitations. Survivors do this.

REFUSING TO BE A COMPLAINER

Luke has many of the personality traits that seem to characterize one who can handle life's difficulties. He is not a complainer. "I really don't have a lot of reason to complain," Luke contends. "I get what I need. The kids haven't suffered. They get to go to a lot of places with my sister and brother-in-law and even have a pony to ride at my sister's place. They're really active girls who like to do everything—gymnastics, ice skating, swimming. There are a lot of relatives giving to the children, and they don't want for anything. They get to do what they want to do. I think we've handled this pretty well.

"A lot of people like to whine and complain," Luke continues, "but it doesn't do any good and people don't want to hear you complain. I don't really feel that I'm doing such a great job with being strong. It's just the situation I'm in. I'm doing what I have to do. I'm just living. I'm not doing anything special. I'm living like I normally would, except that I don't go to work every day."

People tend to feel comfortable with someone whose life seems so normal. The people I interviewed come from all sorts of life situations ranging from significant disability or life-threatening illness to infertility, the death of a loved one, an alcoholic relative, the anguish of prison life, or the end of a marriage. In every case these survivors live their daily lives in a way that makes pity the last thing one would feel for them. Although each has undoubtedly waged a painful battle, it just wouldn't occur to anyone to think of them as frail souls.

ASKING FOR HELP AND TREATING WELL THOSE WHO RESPOND

Luke's personality and approach to others have made him the kind of person you want to help. He learned a lot from his mother. "Ten years ago I didn't appreciate my mother's attitude, but now I do. She was responsible for running a house and taking care of two children. I admired her. She had a lot of courage. During her last fifteen years she was completely dependent on other people for everything yet had no trouble because of the way she treated people," Luke explains.

Luke's mother often complimented her husband. "What a pretty head of lettuce," she would say. "That's a beautifully done roast beef." Her positive outlook expressed a genuine appreciation to those around her for the nice things in life. She loved and enjoyed her husband and children. She was a lot of fun to be with, an avid baseball fan, a woman who loved music and people, a person well informed about politics and daily world events. It was said that everyone who knew Violet loved her and that you wouldn't hear anybody say a criticial word about her.

"When you have to ask somebody for everything you want, it's an imposition on everybody. Her personality was such that there were always people there to help her," says Luke. "My father was great with her; he did everything he could. Neighbors, friends, and her sister regularly came to see my mother."

Many people in times of personal crisis feel isolated and alone with a bitterness toward the world because human caring and support appear unavailable. It may help to remember how Luke and his mother won the helpfulness and loyalty of virtually everyone around them. While having much to complain about, they didn't make a habit of complaining. They handled their disabilities with a dignity that comes from having a normal life in the ways they knew how. Perhaps most important, they showed others sincere warmth and appreciation.

They also had the ability to empathize with others. "If I had my choice," says Luke, "I'd rather be the person sick than the one taking care. I think Sarah has more pressure and responsibility than I do."

Those who can ask others for help and who are genuinely appreciative of this help usually receive the assistance they need, especially if they can sympathize with others' difficulties. If you show an abiding interest in the problems of others, most people will respond with an abiding interest in you.

HAVING AN INSPIRATIONAL ROLE MODEL

Luke has been able to handle his illness positively because he saw the way his parents handled his mother's illness and he watched his mother's graciousness and ongoing ability to live a quality life. He knows it is possible for him to live a fulfilling life despite major obstacles and disability because he had the advantage of a role model who lived fully and well. He doesn't have trouble with dependency because his mother so comfortably received what others did for her.

His mother, over the decades of her deterioration, had the advantage of a husband who was so loving and selfless that their friends would constantly remark about it. "When Albert dies," they'd say, "that man ought to go right straight up to heaven. Up like a rocket!"

In the days before hydraulic lifts were available, he fixed up a van so that her wheelchair could be bolted into the passenger side, and he took her for long Sunday drives in the country. She followed the children's events at school because she never said "I can't go" and he always agreed to take her. They visited friends for dinner and he fed her with a matter-of-factness that made everybody comfortable. Their friends never heard them complain, "This is so hard" or "Why me?" They shared happy times with their friends and frequently enjoyed a good laugh. One lifelong friend said, "Some of the best times that my husband and I have ever had in all our forty-five years of marriage have been in their kitchen when Violet was in a wheelchair. Now that says something."

Sarah says about her mother-in-law, "I thought this woman was a remarkable person. We'd sit and talk to her and you'd always forget something was different about her. It's the same thing with Luke. We try to treat him like that."

Luke was eight years old when his mother began having problems. "I grew up seeing her cope really well," he said. "This has made it a lot easier for me. The disease isn't so strange to me. A lot of the symptoms I have are symptoms she had. The problems in trying to take care of the house are also similar. I just grew up with my mother in a wheelchair. It was not a big deal to me."

As Luke's father used to take his mother for rides in the van, Sarah now takes Luke to his favorite store, a huge hardware and building supply store. They go in the same orange van that his parents used, now more weathered-looking.

Luke is fortunate in that he has a strong sense of his usefulness and place. He is confident in the knowledge that he will continue to be the head of the family. As it was his mother's role when Luke was growing up, it is his role and responsibility now to be chief advisor and decision maker. Luke's firmly embedded personal attitudes of optimism and positive self-regard clearly seem related to the sense of belonging and to the responsibility he feels in maintaining the family. No matter how physically disabled he becomes, he knows that disability will not prevent him from being an important support person for Sarah and the children. Luke says he has learned that he can help most by being a good listener, so he does less talking and more listening when helping to solve a family problem. When advice is needed, he is able to come forth with it. He is also a thoughtful, warm, engaging, appreciative receiver.

DESIRING TO LEARN AND GROW

Another trait of survivors is a craving for growth and learning. They resolve to grow wise enough not merely to cope with the crisis but to be in charge of its impact on their attitudes toward life.

Gloria Back, whose struggle with her younger son's homosexuality was described in earlier chapters, reached a level of acceptance she would not have thought possible six years earlier. It had not been easy. "I spent years trying to understand my reactions: the blow to my ego, the hurt, the confusion," she remembers in her book. Gloria wanted to grow in her understanding of what it meant to be gay and to be the mother of someone who was gay. She also wanted to understand why so much social hostility and revulsion exist toward homosexuality and homosexuals.[1]

"My mother was the kind of person," says Ken, "who was going to deal with my being gay. Although it might take some years to work out her feelings, she wasn't going to lose me. She would learn whatever she needed to learn in order to remain close to her family."

Gloria built an impressive library on the subject of homosexuality and opened herself to new learning. She sought professional counseling, engaged in long talks with her gay son, and met his straight and gay friends. She allowed herself to get acquainted with Ken's early lover Clem, with Clem's parents, and some years later to get to know Sam and his family. Through it all, Gloria made herself an eager student at an age in life when many of her contemporaries were no longer actively pursuing new learning. She stretched her mind to absorb fresh ways of looking at family life and basic values despite the fact that these renovated perspectives were initially extremely uncomfortable and unpopular in society.

Enrolling at Fordham University at the age of fifty-three, Gloria set out to find her niche. Over several years she completed her bachelor's degree, started on a master's, and gravitated toward social work. Then "one day," she explains, "when I was given an open-topic research assignment, a light bulb lit up in my head. It could be possible," she realized, "to further my own growth by studying other parents of gay people. Sharing experiences and feelings, we would arrive at a positive understanding of our children."[2]

Gloria placed an ad for parents of gays in *The New York Times*, assuring them of anonymity, asking them to take part in an academic study. In the weeks that followed she met with the many mothers and fathers who called her, conducting interviews in coffee shops and other meeting places throughout Manhattan. Sometimes the parents were so scared to discuss this taboo subject, they would request meetings in parking lots or subway stations! Gloria sympathized, recalling her own devastation when first dealing with the subject.

A LESSON FOR PARENTS: ALLOWING OTHERS TO BE THEMSELVES

Gloria learned that there are as many reactions to having a gay child as there are types of human beings and varieties of human circumstances. Several threads ran throughout the pattern, however. "The parents who reacted violently—even brutally—to their gay sons and daughters, with rare exceptions, lost them."[3] Those who were close to their children and enjoyed communicating with them before learning the child was gay tended to come through the crisis with the family intact. "If you love your son as a heterosexual," explained one person involved in the study, "it's hard not to love him as a homosexual."

Many of the parents, Gloria observed, were struggling with injured egos: They believed their gay son or daughter reflected badly on them, and they felt diminished in their worthiness as human beings. Having lived vicariously through their children, in many cases these parents had counted on their children to make up for their own deficiencies or to bring them credit by achieving fame, fortune, and social recognition. When the child went his or her own way in life, the parents saw the behavior as rebellion and were outraged. Their hopes were shattered. They wanted an adult child who would follow in their footsteps and go beyond to what society would applaud as a "better life."

Gloria couldn't help seeing herself in the stories she heard and in the narcissism of some of these parents. It was instructive to hear the tales of rejection and to witness the suffering that resulted from their trying to live a life through their children. "I began to see Kenny as an individual," she says, "not as a person whose job on earth was to live up to my expectations."[4]

The wisdom of Kahlil Gibran's famous poem in *The Prophet* began to strike home:

> *And a woman who held a babe against her bosom said, Speak to us of Children.*
> *And he said:*
> *Your children are not your children.*
> *They are the sons and daughters of Life's longing for itself.*
> *They come through you but not from you,*
> *And though they are with you yet they belong not to you.*
>
> *You may give them your love but not your thoughts,*
> *For they have their own thoughts.*
> *You may house their bodies but not their souls,*
> *For their souls dwell in the house of tomorrow, which you cannot visit, not even in your dreams.*
> *You may strive to be like them, but seek not to make them like you.*
> *For life goes not backward nor tarries with yesterday.*
> *You are the bows from which your children as living arrows are sent forth.*
> *The archer sees the mark upon the path of the infinite, and*

> *He bends you with His might that His arrows may go*
> *swift and far.*
> *Let your bending in the archer's hand be for gladness;*
> *For even as He loves the arrow that flies, so He loves also the*
> *bow that is stable.* [5]

As Gloria learned, many people must mourn the loss of their dreams for their children. Dreams can be shattered when a child chooses not to enter the family business, converts to a different religion, moves out of state, or marries someone of another culture. It is seen as a loss to many parents when their children do not provide grandchildren. Dreams are most certainly shattered when a child becomes mentally ill or addicted to alcohol or drugs. Parents mourn when a beloved son or daughter engages in criminal activities, drops out of school, or fails at work. In each of these situations, a desire to learn and grow can eventually lead to understanding and acceptance, as it did for Gloria.

Not all losses are dramatic. Sometimes a loss is a slow realization over the years that one's expectations will not be fulfilled. One of my friends has a talented and intellectually gifted nineteen-year-old daughter. When the daughter was growing up, my friend thought her child was headed for special accomplishments in life. In the mother's mind, her child would become a member of the National Honor Society, cheerleader, and class valedictorian and eventually would study to become a doctor, lawyer, or psychologist. As the years passed, the daughter found her own path. A mother's hope for academic excellence had to be exchanged for the modest expectation that the girl would at least stay in school long enough to earn a high school diploma. When it was clear her daughter would not graduate, the mother hoped the girl would obtain her high school equivalency certificate. Now that the daughter is employed as a waitress in California, the mother hopes simply that she will be able to function in life well enough to take care of herself.

Often there is nothing that a parent can do to ensure happiness, security, or prosperity for a beloved offspring. Without the ability to be flexible when it becomes evident that one's fondest parental dreams and expectations will not be met, my friend and others like her probably would lose the relationship that still is possible with their young adult or adult child.

ACCEPTING PERSONAL RESPONSIBILITY

In one of her last books, anthropologist Margaret Mead said that personal responsibility is the greatest evolution of humankind. She also said that the idea that we are all the products of our environment is our greatest sin.

A dozen years ago a nurse named Katherine came to me for counseling. She had explored the feelings of hurt and anger which she long had harbored toward her alcoholic father. She was in a good marriage and enjoyed mothering several children but knew she could be much happier. Having written about Katherine in my first book, I made a point of contacting my former client to follow her progress while I was interviewing people for *Coming Back*. I asked her to summarize her journey.

"Little seeds were growing for a long time," Katherine remembered, "and finally, about eight years after my father died, I decided to lose my continuous anger and grief over him and his alcoholism. I made a decision to resolve those old feelings, and that's when I sought counseling."

For much of her adult life, Katherine explained, "I think I used my father as an excuse for my not being able to achieve what I thought I should have achieved. I would say to myself, 'Well, you know, I came from this chaos.' "

She had had an opportunity to go to the University of Minnesota on a scholarship to get a nursing degree, but her father believed college was for boys and wouldn't allow his daughter to accept the scholarship. Years later, while she was in nursing school and pregnant with her third child, her father died of leukemia. Katherine dropped out of school and said, "See, there he goes again," concluding that her father once again had deprived her of something precious.

What Katherine had learned in counseling was to express anger and allow her children to express it. "Although I could never show Daddy anger all those years," she told me, "I learned I could release those old feelings and not be stymied by them any longer. Dealing with anger was a big part of going forward." She was also able to remember a number of the forgotten good times once shared with her dad, and she made peace with many regrets concerning their relationship.

In her late thirties Katherine went back to her nursing studies and became a registered nurse. The new skills for handling feelings which she learned in therapy have been valuable in her career, she says. "I'm more direct with people now. I have been able to do a lot more since I am no longer intimidated by persons in authority such as the physicians with whom I work. We have a nice, egalitarian relationship instead of my feeling and acting like the nurse handmaiden."

Most important, Katherine explains, "I got to the place where I'm willing to take risks and take the responsibility for the outcome." Recently she returned to school in preparation for switching to another nursing specialty. "I'll never know what I can achieve unless I'm willing to take risks," she goes on. She now can pursue the career opportunities she wants to pursue because she has accepted the responsibility for the direction of her own life. "I've stopped using my alcoholic father and other things as excuses," she says proudly.

Often it is easy to blame events or persons outside ourselves for our personal suffering or missed opportunities. We can attribute our misfortunes to the actions of our parents, our spouse or ex-spouse, our in-laws, a loved one's premature death, an unwanted or ill-timed pregnancy, an illness, accident, assault, robbery, fire, flood, being fired at work or being mistakenly accused of a crime, being medically misdiagnosed or mistreated, or being born with a handicap or genetic predisposition to some illness. Some blame God, the military or a particular war, the government, or a happenstance event, and they give the perceived villain credit for having irreversibly changed the course of their lives. As long as one relinquishes the center of power and control in this way, the person likely will remain a nonsurvivor.

All of us feel powerless at times because we are human beings. Triumphant survivors, however, trade in the position of helplessness for a decision to take charge and search for options.

I know a psychologist who has been having some problems in her personal relationships. She will probably become more and more unhappy and frustrated with the people she cares most about, because her way of accepting personal responsibility is also a way of denying that she is in charge. Once the psychologist labels a problem by saying, for example, "I'm not receptive to therapy" or "I'm this kind of person" or "I'm that kind of person," she figures she is off the hook. It is a characteristic of nonsurvivors, people who cope poorly with the day-to-day stresses and special crises of life, to conclude that one is as one will always be and therefore to make no attempt to change.

DEVELOPING A COMPREHENSIVE COPING STRATEGY

Triumphant survivors take charge of their lives even when a clear case can be made that one has a biological predisposition or strong tendency toward a certain problem. Diabetes, clinical depression, alcoholism, obesity, heart disease, and many types of cancer have all been shown to run in families. While a person might rightly argue that many factors work against self-care and the ability to oversee the course of one's health or fate, the triumphant survivor often behaves as if his or her life is within the realm of personal control. Even when clearly not to blame for a problem or only partially responsible, survivors take charge. These sturdy individuals focus on the personal power it is possible for one to have. They establish small, winnable goals and cheer their achievement as victories of significance.

When I interviewed Alex, this remarkable, formerly obese man, I looked for underlying character traits which might explain his continuing achievement.

In high school and earlier, Alex told me, it had been difficult to think of himself as having *any* strengths. His parents had made him feel as though it were a weakness of character that made him unsuccessful in his dieting efforts. He kept pointing to his 300-pound cousins. Even in adolescence Alex suspected that many people battle a weight problem because their physiological makeup is simply different from that of normal people. He knew how difficult dieting was and he knew normal people were barking up the wrong tree when yapping endlessly about their own eating habits and how he'd have no weight problem if only he would eat what they ate. Studies following the adopted children of obese biological parents appear to confirm what Alex's body told him years ago: It is probably the case that heredity more than environment influences the development of obesity.[6]

Fighting against unfavorable odds and a formidable enemy, Alex at twenty-three knew that he needed a comprehensive weight loss and maintenance plan and that the plan needed to be established in advance. Those who have been successful in overcoming crisis situations and problems of many types typically demonstrate this characteristic of planning ahead. People who quit smoking, alcoholics who recover and remain sober, those who endure a divorce or death in the family, even people who face a terminal illness—in each of these difficult situations, having a specific and well-developed coping plan makes triumph possible.

Alex was aware that it was critically important for him to abandon his normal patterns. Social situations always involved eating. Times shared with friends or family, lunch meetings at work, parties and holidays, all were associated with food. In order to lose weight, Alex isolated himself for several months from these situations. While his co-workers ate lunch, Alex ran or played racquetball. After his weight loss, he felt he should learn how to watch others eat and still remain in control. His plan involved drinking a lot of water, filling his plate with vegetables, and staying away from sweets and fats. He now participates fully in social aspects of holidays and other gatherings of friends and family but with a plan to avoid dips and chips and other calorie-laden snacks and to count calories faithfully. He has also become "addicted" to exercise, a trait of virtually all weight loss maintainers, according to the research of Drs. Colvin and Olson in their book *Keeping It Off*. And, as is also typical of successful maintainers Colvin and Olson studied, by trial and error Alex has developed and pursues his own personalized maintenance plan. He has discovered the system that best suits his personality and needs.

Fourteen years after losing 150 pounds, Alex proudly explains, "I've gotten this down to a science. I can tell you it's four-thirty in the afternoon and I've had 730 calories today, and I can tell you what I can eat the rest of the day." Calorie counting is almost automatic and unconscious, as less of his time now goes into thinking about calories. "I've set up rules and regulations for myself, and it gives me satisfaction to follow them. It's satisfying to leave my job for Christmas vacation and come back a week later no more than two pounds heavier. Everybody knows that losing two pounds is a snap and losing ten is very difficult."

Alex does not do what many Americans do at Thanksgiving, which is to consume five thousand calories in a single meal. He socializes with his family, but he watches what he eats, filling up his plate with low-calorie foods such as raw or steamed vegetables and going very light on desserts. If he knows he's going out with his wife to his favorite restaurant on a Saturday night, he cuts back four days ahead of time. At a party he never eats in the first half hour, when everyone starts to eat. Then he puts broccoli and other vegetables on his plate and walks around, visiting with people and filling himself with vegetables. He intentionally focuses on the people and an enjoyment of socializing instead of focusing on food. "You can do it without bringing notice on yourself," laughs Alex. "There really is going to be food for you if you don't get into the first frenzy—honest to God—they're not going to pick all the meat off that animal! You can rest assured there will be enough there to meet your nutritional needs and to achieve your overriding goal, which is the maintenance of your weight.

"When you are formerly obese," Alex continues, "you cannot live in that world of dips and salad dressings that are so dense with fat and calories that you can just see the pounds. I don't believe you can eat those things. And if you do make a mistake for one night, you have to rein yourself in the next day. You can't give in to that luxury more than one day at a time. I have learned to smell the brownies and enjoy watching other people eat them, to break off a little piece and walk away. I know that half an hour later it won't have been worth it to eat more. I know the consequences. To accept that challenge of living under a different set of rules gives me a profound sense of satisfaction and control."

When he goes to the movies he doesn't eat at all. He'll drink a large diet Coke with ice in it. If he wants something more he takes apples and carrots. He has learned to enjoy eating both raw and plain cooked vegetables. He never puts butter or salt on corn on the cob. He has found he doesn't need to dip lobster into whole butter. "Habits gain strength with time," Alex explains. "Over time my tastes have changed. Whole milk tastes like cream. It's now very natural for me to eat bananas, apples, and broccoli. I've learned what fish is all about, and lemon, pepper, mustard, and tomato-based dressings and spices instead of things with cheese or mayonnaise. You can go a long way with oil and vinegar on a salad, light on the oil, heavy on the vinegar. For formerly overweight people, Roquefort and French is just not the way to live.

"I don't believe that normal-weight people need to discriminate in their diet but I believe heavy people need to develop an acute sense of discrimination," he says. Alex has developed a comprehensive, new way of thinking and a different way of looking at food—something that he has taught himself. Because he so loved steak and potatoes, sodas, brownies, and cakes, it was a difficult transition to make.

Part of Alex's plan for success involved timing. For beginning the diet, Alex chose a low-stress time in his life. He remembered that he had lost a hundred pounds during a summer vacation in college, only to gain it back once the pressures of his college studies resumed. This time when he dieted, he was at the end of working on his master's degree. The anxiety of achieving was no longer present. Although he had a new job, it was an interesting, exciting job that he loved. To the surprise of everyone, including his parents, he had done well in college and graduate school and was now on the first step of the professional ladder. He was proud of himself even before he started dieting. It was a good, low-pressure time to take on the challenge.

I finally gave up cigarettes some years ago, after having been a heavy smoker for nineteen years and after many unsuccessful attempts. I utilized many of the behavioral change principles pursued by Alex. My plan involved choosing a low-stress time, taking time off from work, using sports as a physical release, avoiding for some time my old smoking buddies and the activities such as card playing where I had smoked the most. When I went through my marital separation, I similarly avoided certain places and persons for an extended period of time. Withdrawing and making changes in our lives can be a big help, particularly early on, as we try to build a new life.

Whether one is dieting, giving up an addiction to a drug, grieving the loss of someone or something dearly loved, or

endeavoring to cope with excruciating mental or physical pain—
it is important to determine and pursue whatever is necessary
in order to triumph one day at a time, achieve one small goal
at a time.

ANCHOR POINTS

It is said that fighter pilots have an extra amount of self-
confidence. "If a hundred go up and ninety-nine get shot down,
I'm the guy coming back," confirmed POW Robbie Risner,
explaining his mental set and that of most of the other fighter
pilots he has known.

Becoming a prisoner of war changes things, however. "You
don't have a chance of winning the way you do when it's your
airplane and you're in control. In prison they have control
over everything you do."

Robbie knew that he couldn't comply with prison regulations because it would mean aiding the enemy in their propaganda efforts by making confessions and false statements. He
also couldn't comply because of his commitment to the military
code, which required him to continue his duties as the senior
ranking officer. Both by requirement and by choice he would
continue to give directives to the other men. Noncompliance
being his stance, he reminded himself, "You're going to get
hurt, and it's not going to get better as long as you're here."

He realized early in his captivity as a prisoner of the North
Vietnamese that "a different kind of courage, a conviction,
would be necessary." He says, "You have to believe in something bigger than yourself. We knew God was going to bless
us and watch over our loved ones."

A belief in something bigger than self seems to typify the
triumphant survivor. In Robbie Risner's words, "You have to
have an anchor point or points, a beacon, a candle in the
window—something that won't ever change, that you can vis-
ualize or hold on to."

Robbie Risner's candle in the window was his love for family, faith in God, belief in the purpose of the war, and confidence in America's leaders. He also believed in high aspirations.

His second-grade teacher had told Risner he could be anything he wanted to be. "If it's not an absolute, ridiculous impossibility," says Robbie, "I learned to go for it. Sometimes I wear a golden bumble bee on my lapel. The bumble bee is not supposed to be able to fly because his body is too big for his wings, and the pin reminds me that I can be whatever I want to be."

Many POWs were justifiably concerned that years of imprisonment would shorten their lives. One man who had read about American POWs in the Korean War said that nutritional deficiencies and other hardships could shave off as much as one third of a life span.

"I remember saying," says Risner, " 'Hey guys, I'm not going to lose any years!' " He felt certain that God either would make what time he did have so rich as to make up for lost years or would extend his life until he lived out all the years he otherwise would have lived.

"I'm a born optimist," explains Risner. "I'm not a fanatic, but I choose to look on the bright side of life, always have." Robbie Risner's healthy combination of a strong religious faith, an optimistic outlook, and positive actions worked together to produce results.

DETERMINING YOUR OWN PERSPECTIVE

Robbie Risner had been in prison for seven years when the North Vietnamese presented him with a recent copy of *The Christian Science Monitor*. Circled in ink, the headline read: "POWs Family Split on Politics." The article spoke of Risner's eldest son, Rob, who was working on behalf of Senator McGovern's campaign for the presidency.

Deeply loyal to President Nixon, Robbie was "shocked and a little sick" to think of his son campaigning for McGovern. Robbie had great confidence in Nixon's leadership and was unfalteringly devoted to the president's policies.

Finally, after searching his heart, Robbie decided that he loved his son too much to condemn him. "I respected Rob," his father explained, "and I knew that anything that he was doing had my best interests at heart. He was doing his level best to get me out of prison. I couldn't do anything but love him more for it."[7]

The prison guards showed Robbie the article with the aim of demoralizing him. They knew well the extent of his patriotism.

Robbie refused to be demoralized. He would not allow himself to perceive his beloved son's actions in such a way as to undermine the love they shared. Unlike many parents during this period, Robbie did not place himself in the situation of having to choose betweeen a respectful relationship with his son and his fierce loyalty to official American policies regarding the war.

In a time of crisis it is difficult to remain in charge of our own attitudes and perspectives. The alternative, however, can be a view of things that robs us of the support to which we are entitled and which is readily available to us.

"I had always wanted my boys to stand on their own two feet," continues Robbie, "to make their own decisions. Rob had done that for sure. I respected him even more to think that he would go against the tide to do something that he felt very strongly about."[8]

MAINTAINING PHYSICAL AND MENTAL FITNESS

There were times when Robbie Risner's vigorous program of physical exercise while in prison was an activity of desperation, a means of coping with overwhelming stress, a way to survive. Robbie's push-ups, sit-ups, and running activities were a way of keeping physically fit in order to strengthen himself emotionally during his seven and a half years of imprisonment. In boyhood Robbie had discovered the sustaining and healing benefits of athletic activities including wrestling, racquet sports, various ball games, and rodeo performance. His long-established need for physical activity was like a faithful old dog accompanying him through the best and worst of times.

As the senior ranking officer, Robbie sent out a policy through the tap code urging the other POWs to exercise regularly and, where two or more were together, to conduct classes. "You don't want to go home a vegetable," he directed, sometimes writing on pieces of toilet paper with a handmade pencil. "You want to go home with strong minds and bodies; you need to do that to be a good daddy and husband when you get back." Robbie knew what he needed to do to return in the best possible condition. He derived from that the policies he sent out.

Robbie's belief that he and his compatriots were going to return home motivated him to keep physically and mentally fit. He continued that positive assumption even when he learned that several of the POWs had lost their lives in captivity. Calling it "living off the camel's hump of memory," Robbie explains how the POWs "lived back through their stored memories" for intellectual stimulation and mental fitness. They developed pastimes, studied languages, and remembered aloud books they had read and movies they had seen, communicating secretly from their separate cells. Every Saturday evening a couple of great dramatists described a movie while all the POWs within hearing range lay on the concrete floor of their cells with their ears to the crack under the door. The dramatists were so good that they took two hours to tell *Doctor Zhivago* even though they had never seen the movie!

Survivors in various situations of duress or sorrow make it a point to figure things out. They go inside themselves in

order to determine which coping strategies and which strength-
and morale-building activities will help them to fare better.

"Support from others is important to all people," wrote
George Vaillant in *Adaptation to Life*, "but there is much that
humans must do for themselves."[9] Robbie Risner helped
himself by devising a physical and mental fitness plan. Alex
established a new attitude toward food and a new behavior
pattern for handling social situations where food was present;
he also took up racquetball and jogging to further ensure his
diet's success. Lynn, who had an ostomy, subsequently discovered that her husband was having an affair and took up a
regimen of regular workouts at a Nautilus center after her
strength returned. She also bought herself a sexy swimsuit
that would conceal the bag that was attached to her body for
waste products. Others buy attractive wigs or hairpieces after
losing their hair to radiation or chemotherapy, find a support
group of persons who are dealing with similar losses, or take
books out of the library to learn more about the type of loss
they are experiencing and how to come to terms with it.

RAY BEVANS: A MAN WITH MOXIE AND AN ENVIABLE GOLF HANDICAP

According to the dictionary, "moxie" is a slang expression for
"energy" or "courage." It's a word aptly descriptive of a stranger
with whom I ended up playing golf. He's a fourteen handi-
capper, which means he plays thirteen or fourteen strokes over
par, which puts him in the top 10 or 15 percent of all amateurs.

My friend Norma and I were in our golf cart waiting for a
man in front of us to tee off. He was tall, slender, and athletic-
looking, had gray hair, and hit an impressive drive—maybe
260 yards.

"Nice shot," I said to myself, watching the silvery ball fly off into the sky. It formed a magnificent arc and sailed over the center of the fairway.

"How about that?" I commented to Norma, when the golfer turned toward us and walked to his cart. "Downright amazing," I said, suddenly realizing that the golfer had only one arm.

"Hi, I'm a writer," I told the stranger, presumptuously leaping from my three-wheeler and approaching his cart. "I wrote a book called *Living Through Personal Crisis*, and my next book is about people like you."

"I'd be glad to talk to you," the ruddy-faced outdoorsman replied, pulling out his wallet and removing a business card. "You may be surprised," he went on, "by some of the things I have to say. Would you ladies like to go along with me?" he asked, inviting us to play golf. Not having seen us play, the stranger was already showing his courage. Furthermore, as many women golfers will agree, the invitation was somewhat uncustomary since chauvinism reigns supreme on most golf courses.

Norma and I had pretty good golf scores that day. As we went along, however, it was clear that our male companion was in a league of his own, in more ways than one.

I sat with Ray Bevans in his law office for my first interview. Golf memorabilia and appropriate diplomas covered his desk and walls. Especially eye-catching was a prominently displayed golf scorecard. It documented the first day Bevans broke eighty, a hallmark of good golfing coveted by most amateurs. He has achieved this golfing feat on five or six occasions, he told me. His best score was a remarkable seventy-four.

Ray was six years old when he lost his arm. The youngest kid in the neighborhood, he was playing baseball with the bigger boys in a back lot that they called "the orchards." His mother had told him to stay in his own yard. Some of the kids were stealing cherries off a tree when suddenly one boy yelled, "Here comes the caretaker!" The boys scattered, including little Ray, who stumbled over a trash pile, fell into chicken wire, and landed on a broken bottle, severely lacerating his right arm.

The accident took place at the back of a doctor's estate, and the trash pile contained the doctor's dirty, discarded dressings. Within a week gangrene set in and there was no choice but amputation in order to save the boy's life. There was never a lawsuit related to the accident—a fact that years later Bevans said probably contributed to his becoming an attorney.

"I guess I was tolerated at first by the kids in the neighborhood," Bevans recalls. "Marbles were the thing and my mother said the boys were letting me play with them but that they were taking advantage of me. I just kept working at the various games we played until finally I was competitive."

Bevans learned to field a baseball barehanded in order to play catch and later developed a smooth technique for catching the ball with his baseball glove, quickly throwing ball and glove in the air, catching the ball, and speedily tossing it. He learned to handle a basketball by skillfully cupping his hand to shoot baskets and to pull the basketball toward his body in order to catch it. Many long hours of practice were necessary to develop competence in these activities.

Right-handed until he lost his right arm, it took Ray until about the age of thirteen to overcome significant troubles with penmanship and until the age of fifteen to establish himself as a "pretty good athlete."

His dad would play the catcher's position for young Bevans. "Dad taught me to throw a curve ball, and my buddy Frank would come over and we'd pitch a whole ball game, calling balls and strikes and working on the curve ball." The boy *loved* baseball.

Earlier Ray's mother had sent him on excursions sponsored by the Maryland League for the Handicapped. When he went on various day trips with other children and adults who were blind or had polio, said Ray, "I felt I didn't belong there because they were handicapped and I wasn't. I decided I wanted to be somebody, to be accounted for—in soccer, volleyball, and bowling. I wanted to play organized baseball. I wanted to be a class officer."

A DRIVE TO EXCEL

In junior high school, Ray had been "a hot pot," as he puts it. Highly defensive about his lost arm, he was provoked easily and often got in fights when the inevitable childhood name-calling incidents occurred and on other occasions. He had a reputation as a "sorehead" and as "too combative." He wanted to be liked and he wanted to make something of himself, so in high school he decided to change the image people had of him by changing himself.

Ray worked hard at learning to get along with people, and he practiced his sporting activities endlessly in order to become competitive. "My reputation changed," he explains, "and I made varsity baseball, made varsity soccer, was invited into a fraternity, and played with a championship city baseball team for sixteen- to eighteen-year-olds." He became president of the student body and national president of his high school fraternity.

His buddy, Frank, was a tremendous help to Ray by never making concessions to him and by accepting him as a regular guy. About the time the boys started being interested in girls, Ray used to try to walk on the inside lane of the sidewalk, putting Frank on the outside so that the fact of Ray's missing arm would not be apparent. "Frank would haul off and punch me or push me to the other side," Ray remembers. "He wouldn't let me hide." Years later it was never necessary for Bevans to ask the woman who would be his wife if she would always love him as he was.

By the time young Bevans went to Loyola College on an academic and athletic scholarship, a famous one-armed major leaguer named Pete Gray was playing baseball for the St. Louis Browns. Bevans played the outfield at Loyola and also pitched for the team, sometimes doing some of each in the same game. Even when he pitched, he could field the ball well with a calloused bare hand and with body blocks to stop the bouncing grounders. In 1945, when he was a nineteen-year-old college sophomore, *The Athletic Journal* published an article about him. He had a .273 batting average and was described as having a physical "strength well beyond what would be normal for a boy of his age and build." In the journal article the sportswriter Craig E. Taylor also said that Bevans was "very fast" as a retriever and called him the "Pete Gray of college ball."[10]

Bevans's mother also played an important role in his early development and accomplishments. By not being overprotective when she saw young Ray playing rough sports, she gave him a gift, he feels. He remembers only one time when she cried after watching him play and shrieked, "You're going to get hurt!"

"Most of the time," Bevans says, "my mother just bit her lip, and eventually she saw that I could hold my own." Both parents were proud of their son and liked to attend his sporting events. He was on a variety of teams in high school and college, played in a fast-pitch softball league for three years, and was part of a semiprofessional baseball league for nearly nineteen years after high school, as well as playing semipro soccer. At the age of thirty-nine, Bevans decided he was getting too old for baseball and soccer and took up golf, playing successfully in numerous professional-amateur tournaments.

"Ray, because of your arm you have to do things with your brain," his mother repeatedly had told him, emphasizing from his elementary school days the importance of a good education.

"Mom, I'm going to do it both ways," he replied, determined to have his athletic adventures in addition to academics. He was a prelaw student and studied hard while at the same time loving sports. "I was given the opportunity to perform, and I welcomed the opportunity. I just looked forward to it," he remembers.

"I didn't ask for anything. I never felt it was necessary for anybody to give me special treatment, because I didn't consider myself any less [than anybody else]. Sometimes I considered myself better. At any rate, I didn't take a back seat."

Ray is moved when he sees a person accomplishing something special. It touches him to see others excel, he supposes, "because I have a drive to excel and I'm so glad it was not frustrated in my youth."

Ray Bevans and his wife of thirty-six years live in Baltimore, where he does general practice law and "continuously works and practices" at his golf game. "To this day," he says, "the only time I know I have one arm is when I go swimming and people seem especially to notice." At the golf course he sees people watching him, but it doesn't bother him at all to be stared at. In fact Bevans rather likes to tee up the ball and perform.

"Amputee YES, handicapped NO," wrote Bob Ibach in a 1977 Golf Column of *The Baltimore Evening Sun*. "I'm telling you the truth," Bevans was quoted as saying. "I don't *know* I have a handicap." When golfing friends call him a "one-armed bandit," he takes it as a compliment.

"You can't *wish* things to change," Bevans told me. "You've got to develop a positive approach and work hard in life to develop your abilities."

"Just like anyone else," wrote Ibach. "That's how Bevans views himself, a normal human being, a competitor, a hard worker."[11]

In the words of Ted Kennedy, Jr., who lost a leg to cancer at the age of twelve, "There are people out there who don't regard their disabilities as a burden."[12] Ray Bevans is that kind of person.

Bevans has a feeling of pride and pleasure in living a memorable life. Like most of us, Bevans knows he won't reach *all* of his goals. Although he is a successful attorney, he'd like to have been as extraordinary an attorney as he was an athlete, he says. He has also long held the dream of a judicial appointment. In addition to being held in esteem by many others, however, Bevans realizes that he has something that many people lack: self-respect.

DETERMINATION

Major losses hold back many people from life. Almost everyone has known the survivor of a tragedy who, as the years go by, seems to lack the desire to triumph over it. Such a person appears to grieve forever and never goes forward to build a new life. The triumphant survivors I interviewed had the character trait of determination. These people *wanted* to triumph over the pain or loss in their lives. And they have gone forward.

Luke, in dealing with multiple sclerosis, is determined to follow his mother's example and fully receives the support and help which his partner in marriage freely offers. He plans ahead and sets his mind on living life as fully and normally as possible despite his disabilities.

Gloria had always thought of homosexual men as ". . . ridiculous caricatures of women: sissified, effeminate, weak, comic, [and] tragic."[13] Her perception changed after she got to know her son, his lover, and their gay friends. She saw that most, like her son and Sam, were "not discernibly gay."[14] They were ordinary people, ". . . people who want what we all want: love, intimacy, acceptance, a home, friendship, and success."[15] The old stereotypes began to disappear. "I began to challenge bigoted views on life," Gloria explains in her book. "I began to think for myself."[16]

She was determined to grow enough not to lose a beloved son. "Gradually at holiday times Kenny and his gay friends blended into our family celebrations. As my awareness of the gay world expanded," Gloria continues, "my anger became redirected: I was no longer angry at Kenny, but at the heterosexual society that sneers at and rejects homosexuality."[17]

Katherine, the nurse I once counseled, made the permanent decision (with a wide-reaching impact) not to continue to blame her alcoholic, long-deceased father or anyone else for present problems in her life or for dreams unfulfilled.

Alex is determined to remain slim and athletically fit and to leave behind forever the unhappy obese person he once was and whose photograph he no longer carries in his wallet.

Robbie Risner had the determination of a man devoted to God, country, and family and the confidence that his long prison ordeal would eventually end. He was anchored by deeply held convictions.

Ray Bevans made an early decision that the loss of a limb would not interfere with his desire to excel in sports. He was determined to work hard in life, to develop his abilities, and not to waste his energies wishing things somehow magically to change.

THE ABILITY TO LAUGH, ENJOY, AND SEE HUMOR

When the British edition of my first book came out, I was upset to see the book jacket that my London publisher had chosen for *Living Through Personal Crisis*. It had a drawing of a curious-looking little dog and a broken vase which the little dog seemed to be examining quizzically. I felt that the cartoonlike sketch trivialized my work, and I complained about it in a long transatlantic telephone conversation with my London agent. "I have received hundreds of letters from people suffering grievous losses," I told her, "such as bereaved parents. I want hurting people to know that this is a serious book."

"I see why it's upsetting to you," the literary agent replied, "but you have to see the book jacket as the British see it. The British don't take things straight on," she explained. "It's too much for us." Humor is an important coping and survival mechanism for the British people, even in dire circumstances. And the fact that it was a solid white book cover with only stark black ink presenting the title, author, and sketch, the agent explained, made it clear that *Living Through Personal Crisis* was a serious work.

I decided not to make any further fuss about the way my book was being presented to the British people. Approaching crisis from an oblique rather than a head-on stance is an effective way for many people to soften the blows and bear up in a wearisome battle, I remembered. Humor is the saving grace of many persons even in situations utterly grave, serious, or painful.

Among the triumphant survivors I interviewed or studied in the literature, humor emerged repeatedly as a weapon of survival. "Humor has helped me not to take myself so seriously all the time," said Alex, discussing his weight loss. "The focus of my humor, however, has changed. When I was heavy my humor was thinly veiled hostility because of my own sense of inadequacy. Now I laugh at the human condition. The things that we humans do are funny."

Alex sees the absurdity, he explains, of the commercials on television "where they still ring a bell and say 'come and get it' and all the people stampede toward the food." Says Alex, "It's that be-quick-and-eat-it thing that is funny to me. It's also humorous to hear people say we should clean our plates because there are people starving in Africa and India. We're in a land of plenty and stuffing ourselves won't give the food to the world's people who are hungry." Alex also gets a kick out of "people at exercise class who work out for one hour, then sit around and eat carrot snacks and drink high-calorie exotic fruit drinks." The men who go out and exercise and then drink three or four beers also strike him as humorous. "The wildness of the way groups of people eat is very funny," Alex says, "but when I see obese kids at fast food places being fed milkshakes and cheeseburgers by overweight parents, it's not funny to me."

When Karen Brownstein was hospitalized with what would be diagnosed as a malignant brain tumor, her longtime and dear friend Barbara flew eight hundred miles to be with her in the hospital. Karen said, "Oh damn it, Barbara, I don't want to die!" and they cried together. Then they talked about Karen's concern for her children's welfare, Karen's hopes that her husband would remarry after she died, and the need for a will. Then, manifesting the magnificent wit that would un-falteringly sustain her in the ordeal yet ahead, Karen turned to another subject. Their conversation is recorded in her book *Brainstorm*.

" 'Okay, Barbara, if I die, I want you to swear to me, right here and now, that you will not allow Neill to choose the children's clothes! Under no circumstances is he to decide what they wear.'

" 'Are you serious?' [Barbara] asked, trying to stifle her laughter and failing.

" 'I am, you should excuse the expression, deadly serious! The man has no fashion sense whatsoever! If I find out that my adorable children are walking around like schleppers I will roll over in my grave and point directly at you. Understand?'

"We laughed until we were rolling on the beds," wrote Brownstein.[18]

In mourning someone, we frequently laugh at the things they once did or said. We are comforted by the laughter that rolls into tears. Many times during Jewish shiva calls or Christian wakes or in eulogies at funerals, comfort comes from quoting funny things said by or funny incidents involving the deceased person.

Jan and Ed like to remember an incident that took place when Mark, the son they lost at the age of seven, first saw his aunt Mary nursing her new baby. Although Mark had many times seen his mother nurse his younger brother, the event filled the little boy with questions about new babies. Having once been told by his mother—who carefully used the phys-iologically correct language—that his own brother had come out of his mother's tummy through the vagina, Mark was curious about Mary's baby. He went over, kissed the baby on her forehead, looked at Mary, and asked, "Did she slide out your lasagna?" It is a story that Jan and Ed fondly tell again and again.

Manny Lawton says in his book *Some Survived: An Epic Account of Japanese Captivity During World War II* that those who survived the infamous Bataan Death March in the Philippines rode like animals in crowded railroad cars to a prison camp. One American soldier who survived the ordeal reported, "With conditions as they were, always bad, it would have been easy to become depressed. To prevent this, I made it a point to cultivate the friendship of optimistic and humorous men. . . . Optimists always believed there would be a tomorrow with better opportunities, whereas a pessimist was fully convinced we would never make it and, if you took him seriously, could assure you there was no use in trying."[19] Here's somebody who is a prisoner of war in a railroad car cultivating the friendship of humorous men!

*M*A*S*H* (the book, movie, and popular TV show) is based on dark humor in the operating room during the Korean War. Such banter is common in all hospitals. Although humor in such a life and death setting may sound callous, it is necessary to relieve tension. Professionals in helping roles and caregivers in the family often feel the necessity for jocularity and for the support and stress reduction it provides.

Laughing at ourselves can also be useful. For many the healing power of laughter relieves the sting of a serious loss.

I know a man who has an artificial plastic eye, and he often speaks of it with good humor. "You can tell which is the artificial eye," Terry quips, "because it's the one with the glint of human kindness." He also likes to tell the story of the woman he once dated who wasn't very bright. "Why didn't you get a glass eye," she asked, "so you could see through it?"

Geri Jewell, a comedienne who has often been seen on television, has cerebral palsy, a frequent subject of her performance humor. In this situation a person brings her condition into the open and gives everyone permission to laugh at it, including herself. There is a powerful therapeutic benefit.

A person who has one of the most marvelous senses of humor I've come across is the popular radio and television personality Elane Stein, known as "The Franchise" at WBAL radio in Baltimore. Several times I have had the opportunity to appear on this delightful, talented woman's show. Fascinated by her wit, I made certain to interview Ms. Stein for *Coming Back*.

In my everyday life I don't come across many women who are taller than I am, so during the interview I was aware of Elane Stein's commanding presence as an attractive, stylishly dressed and coiffed person slightly more than six feet tall. While her personality is warm, engaging, and personable, the striking physical appearance of this pretty, middle-aged woman is almost regal in the way she carries herself. It wasn't always so, she told me. Growing up as an exceptionally tall female and as a youngster who felt like a "freak," she did not begin to learn self-confidence or know how to use her appearance to advantage until she went to New York as a photographer's model at the age of twenty. Later she would deal with her height as well as with a variety of painful realities including family problems, open-heart surgery for Marfan's syndrome (a disease of the connective tissues which partly accounts for her unusual height), and the end of her marriage—all with a life-saving sense of humor.

"I liked to use my kitchen stove as a file cabinet," she quipped, explaining to Stephen Wigler of *The Baltimore Sun* why her marriage broke up. "At the divorce proceedings, my ex-husband complained that I hadn't cooked a meal in eight years. I told him that if he had been hungry he should have gone to a restaurant."[20]

Elane Stein is inherently funny. Her timing is perfect, and her sharp wit and funny delivery made me enjoy my interview with her enormously.

Many people who incorporate good humor into a way of making their living are Jewish, as is Ms. Stein. Many comedians have come from minority groups who have felt the sting of discrimination or are from poor or deprived backgrounds—at one time Jews (mainly from the Lower East Side in New York), and then Blacks and Hispanics. Not only is humor often an outlet for pain, but in some cases it was also a way out of the ghetto. Among those who make up part of the enormous percentage of comedians who are Jewish are Woody Allen, Jack Benny, David Brenner, Mel Brooks, Lenny Bruce, George Burns, Eddie Cantor, Rodney Dangerfield, the Three Stooges, the Marx Brothers, Buddy Hackett, Sam Levinson, Jerry Lewis, Jackie Mason, Nichols and May, Don Rickles, the Ritz Brothers, Joan Rivers, Soupy Sales, Phil Silvers, Ed Wynn, Henny Youngman, and many others. *Seinfeld*

HELPFUL VERSUS HURTFUL HUMOR

Rachel told me that after her mastectomy there was often an atmosphere of teasing and joking in the immediate family. The children wanted their mom to feel they weren't worried and wanted her to feel not so serious about the loss she had suffered. At one point there was a family talk about swimming suits and one of the kids said, "Mom won't need the whole set, so hers won't be so expensive." Another time they all took a trip to the beach. They had just gotten everything into place when the heavens opened up. They ran and ended up in a place called Rachel's Restaurant. Together they bought a red shirt with the word "Rachel's" over the left breast. It was the left breast that Rachel had lost. Her daughter said, "Mom, it should be over the right breast to be yours."

With her children she could laugh and find humor. "I was a part of it, too," Rachel said. "Maybe I started it. We were all trying to help each other in that same way.

"When my kids were all at home and we had dinner together, we made puns," she continued. "Let's all pass Mom the breast of the chicken. I like your single-breasted suit. You have to keep abreast of the times. It all went around and around with the groans." With her immediate family, Rachel wasn't just tolerating a humorous approach to her profound loss, she was enjoying it.

Humor sometimes extends to close friends. "One friend is very, very large-breasted," says Rachel, "and for years has thought of breast reduction surgery. She joked with me about how she'd like to give me a transplant and we laughed about that."

Not all humor is helpful. Whenever humor is a put-down which does not include the grieving person in the joke or when humor trivializes a person's loss, the effort to be funny is hurtful and in bad taste. Usually those who have the "right" to joke about a loss are the loved ones closest to the grieving person, those who most fully share the anguish of the loss.

In Rachel's case, someone outside the family, a physician who ought to have known better, made a tasteless joke after her mastectomy about "three is too many and one not enough." A hospital visitor not well known to Rachel drew a stick drawing and termed it "two fellas walking a breast." These jokes were not funny, and they intensified Rachel's emotional pain.

SURVIVOR PERSONALITIES

The personality characteristic of "being flexible and adaptable, more than anything else, is central to being a survivor," writes Professor Al Siebert of Portland State University. "People who are best at surviving life's difficulties and who gain strength from adversity," Siebert's research has shown, have "a variety of responses available" for handling life's unexpected circumstances, uncertainty, and chaos.[21]

Siebert believes that the human flexibility he has observed "is derived from the survivors' paradoxical personality traits.

Instead of trying to live their lives being 'either one way or another,' [survivors] are comfortable being 'both this way and that.' They are bold and shy, tough and sensitive, analytic and metaphoric, etc."[22] Survivors do not always respond to a situation in the same way.

"People with survivor personalities," Siebert's studies indicate, "have a need to have things work well" both for themselves and for others. Presenting selected items from the published work of psychologist Abraham Maslow (best known for having defined and described "self-actualizing" people), Siebert explains that survivors have "a need for synergy."[23] In other words, those who triumph in adversity yearn for people and events to work together harmoniously:

☐ [Survivors] seem to like happy endings, good completions.

☐ They try to set things right, to clean up bad situations.

☐ They manage somehow simultaneously to love the world as it is and try to improve it.

☐ [They have] some hope that people and nature and society [can] be improved.

☐ They change to improve the situation. . . . They enjoy improving things.

☐ They enjoy bringing about law and order in the chaotic situation, or in the messy or confused situation, or in the dirty and unclean situation.

☐ They like doing things well, "doing a good job," "to do well what needs doing."

☐ They enjoy greater efficiency, making [things] more neat, compact, simple, faster, more foolproof, safer, more "elegant," less laborious.[24]

"People with survivor personalities," continues Siebert, "are foul-weather friends." Partly because others' pain hurts them, survivors "volunteer to help out when there is trouble." While they may drift away from friends and family in good times, survivors often reappear when needed.[25]

"A few people are born survivors. They are the natural athletes in the game of life," Professor Siebert explains. "Just as some people are born musicians, writers, artists or singers, some people are gifted at coping well. This ability is so strongly inborn in a few children that even the most adverse home conditions and neighborhoods cannot break them." Most of us, however, have to "learn how to take control" of our lives, how to develop into people who can cope well.[26]

Three additional traits characterize the survivor's personality, according to Siebert: "getting smarter (wiser) and enjoying life more as one gets older; falling back to and successfully relying on inner resources in disruptive, chaotic circumstances; and having a talent for serendipity, being able to convert accidents or what others would regard as misfortune into good luck."[27] For people experiencing true tragedies, of course, to say that one is turning misfortune into "good luck" is putting it too strongly. The survivor in this case simply changes misfortune into something that produces growth or somehow benefits others.

TRAITS OF THE SURVIVOR: A SUMMARY

Survivors have many characteristics in common that are described and detailed throughout *Coming Back* in addition to those mentioned in this chapter. You may find it helpful to take a notepad and jot down the dozens of traits that appear from the beginning of this book to its end. In this particular chapter I have identified some of the most important qualities and attitudes. While no single person will have all of the following characteristics, those who are in a position to cope well and who are well equipped to overcome adversity will have many of these traits:

1. They plan ahead whenever possible in order to be prepared for a loss, crisis, or major transition. The preparations are practical and offer a way to solve potential problems.

2. They often examine the traits of strong and resourceful people and learn from them when it is not possible to plan ahead.

3. They are not habitual complainers, although they may feel sorry for themselves at times. They examine and express and find a way to release negative, nonproductive feelings.

4. They are resourceful within themselves, yet can ask for others' help and support when needed. They have learned genuineness in expressing warmth, love, and appreciation.

5. They often have identified inspirational role models from childhood or adult life and draw strength, wisdom, or insight from their example.

6. They have a desire to learn and grow. Most don't begin with the wisdom and skill sufficient to handle what life has given them to deal with, but they manage to learn what they need to know.

7. They accept the responsibility for making their own lives livable and rewarding. Blame may be assigned to others as part of a mourning process, but blaming others, God, or fate for one's misfortune does not become a way of life or an excuse for personal unhappiness. They work to overcome their environment or background or whatever impairs them.

8. They often develop a comprehensive coping strategy. Many often consciously plan how it will be possible to

prevail over a particular crisis or loss situation, and they pursue that course of action.

9. They become anchored in a belief in God or belief system outside themselves—a loyalty to one's country or to one's citizenship in the world; a belief in the dignity and worth of human life or in the family of humankind; a respect for nature, the earth, and its creatures!

10. At heart they are optimists who struggle to maintain a positive attitude in the aftermath of the most difficult of human circumstances.

11. They can enjoy life at times, even while hurting. There is the ability to see humor in a situation or laugh at themselves.

12. They find a way to gain from misfortune something of benefit to themselves and others.

13. They have determination, lots of it, and they work hard on behalf of their own recovery.

14. They learn to be flexible and adaptable in order to work out their own happy endings.

15. They set about improving things, setting things right, doing things well.

16. They are not faint-hearted; they find the energy and courage to fight for a comeback.

SURVIVOR | 9
ATTITUDES |

*Developing your psychological
strength is just like developing physical
abilities. The more you exercise, the
stronger you become.*

HAROLD BLOOMFIELD AND LEONARD FELDER,
THE ACHILLES SYNDROME[1]

Some triumphant survivors are extraordinary individuals and have unusual strengths; most aren't. Most of the people I studied were regular human beings with the usual frailties and vulnerabilities. Those who have made comebacks, however, do show certain ways of thinking which set them apart. Similarly, people who are defeated by adversity often are predictable in regard to the content of their thinking.

In this chapter, each heading is set in quotation marks and represents an attitude typical of survivors. While not every person who overcomes a life crisis thinks in the manner of each of these quotes, each of us can strengthen ourselves psychologically by adapting to our own situations the perspectives that follow.

"*I WILL VIVIDLY EXAMINE THE FUTURE*"

I once sat in on a psychology professor's class[2] in order to make a routine teaching evaluation of a colleague. I didn't expect the presentation that day to hit me right between the eyes.

Professor Papantonio first explained psychoanalyst Erik Erikson's notion of how some people despair in old age instead of feeling a sense of integrity about the lives they've lived. For these individuals there is deep regret over life-shaping choices, decisions, and a lifestyle it is too late to change. It is possible, said the teacher, to avoid that type of despair by carefully examining our priorities and values at a younger age and living our lives accordingly.

The professor asked each of us to close our eyes and engage in a fantasy exercise—one that turned out to be extremely meaningful to me. Each was asked to imagine vividly his or her own aging process in five-year increments. We were to reflect on a series of questions at each five-year interval. I found the exercise quite provocative.

"However old you are now," said Papantonio, realizing that his students ranged in age from nineteen to sixty, "imagine that you're five years older now. Observe your physical appearance and any changes that have occurred."

"Now that you're a little older," the professor continued, "what are you doing with your life? Who is there with you, what goals have you accomplished, and how happy are you with how things are going?"

Forty-one years old then, I imagined myself at forty-six. I figured I looked pretty much the same except for having more gray hair and wearing glasses full time. I saw my daughter entering the first grade and imagined having a second daughter, also adopted from India, still a toddler at home. I felt happy about having a family. Two little brown-eyed girls at the supper table seemed to be just what I had always wanted.

"If you think you won't be alive in five years," directed the professor, "raise your hand." Since my eyes were closed I didn't see a nineteen-year-old student raise his hand. It surprised me when my colleague later told me about him. As for myself, I planned on being alive into old age.

The professor led us through the next progressions—five years passed, five more, five more, another five. We moved through the decades, imagining our changing physical appearance and the substance of our lives. My children were in elementary school, high school, and out on their own. They had birthday parties, we went to Disneyland, they preferred outrageous clothing. I wasn't crazy about their music. They drove an old Volvo. Things continued to feel good to me, except that golf and tennis didn't prevent my body from aging and aging still more.

"In what ways are you discontent? In what ways are you satisfied with your life?" continued the professor.

I found it remarkable, loving what I do for a living, that twenty years of fantasizing went by before my work entered the picture. How good it is, I realized after two decades, that I enjoy writing books. When the time comes to let go, having worthwhile work to do will help me allow my children to finish growing up!

Finally, I figured, those nineteen years of smoking when I was young would get me. In my middle seventies I raised my hand to the question about death and sat reflecting on the exercise. The professor led others in the quiet classroom to the conclusion of their lives.

"I want you to let that old wise person give a message of wisdom now to the younger person," the professor said. "What can you learn from him or her about ego integrity versus despair? Can you avoid despair in later life and instead stand with a sense of personal integrity? Can you say when it's over that you lived your life as you'd live it again?"

"The joys of professional success can be fleeting," said my wise old woman to the forty-one-year-old. "What will make you happy is having and enjoying a family."

It was a valuable, important, and surprising message for somebody whose first book had just become a national bestseller. "You'll be happy," continued the wise one, "if you don't let a successful career mean too much to you, if you maintain perspective. Going to the kids' school plays, helping with their homework, traveling together, and having their friends enjoy visiting your home is what you'll remember most at the end."

Whatever it is that you the reader will most remember at the end of your life, it is something that you can vividly imagine now. We can all make an effort to alter certain ways of thinking and take specific actions which will enable us to be at peace with ourselves as the years go by.

JOHN LILLER: "I WILL NOT BE DEFEATED"

Construction foreman John Liller, in addition to being a highly paid builder, was a skin diver and a daredevil. He was tough too. Once, when working on a bridge with his crew, he fell forty feet to the ground—and walked away without injury. He had played baseball and softball and run cross-country track in high school, and as an adult he played minor league baseball. Then, when he was twenty-two years old, he had another accident, this one with serious consequences.

While deer hunting in the marshlands of Maryland's Eastern Shore early one morning, John climbed to a tree stand on the property he had leased especially for hunting. Seven or eight deer approached the stand—all of them females, off limits to hunters in that region and season. John was surprised and furious when a shot rang out, missing the herd completely but scattering the deer. "I knew that shot had scared everything in my area for at least the whole morning," John remembers. "So I slipped my gun sling over my shoulder and decided to come down from the tree. I wanted to look for the jerk who shot off his rifle."

As he was coming down the tree, the gun slipped off John's

shoulder. He reached for it, lost his balance, and grabbed a branch, but it wasn't strong enough to hold him, and he fell about twenty feet.

John was a former rescue squad volunteer, so he realized that his back was broken. He yelled for his father and brothers. John told them he was paralyzed and explained how they should move him onto a stretcher. "Going the two miles to get out of the swampland to where the ambulance could meet us was difficult, so I organized the rescue," he remembers. "We got within a hundred yards of the ambulance when the stretcher broke and I fell again. Then I started bleeding from my mouth."

John heard the examining physician at the local hospital say to his father, "I'm sorry to tell you that your son has a severe broken back. He won't make it through the night." The physician gave the name of a specialist at Johns Hopkins Hospital, three hours away, to see "if anybody can help him."

They raced in an ambulance led and followed by police cars, John lying flat with his father at his side. When the ambulance reached the apex of the tall, majestic Chesapeake Bay Bridge, remembers John, "I put my arms behind me, raised myself up, and looked through the ambulance window, out over the span of the bridge."

"What are you doing?" yelled an alarmed ambulance driver. It had now been fourteen hours since the accident, and John's condition was grave.

"I heard the doctor say that I'm going to die," John replied. "If I'm getting wiped out at twenty-two, then I'm going to look at the Chesapeake Bay one more time." Even as a young man, John was the kind of guy who loved beauty in nature and would squeeze out of life every bit of goodness and energy it offered him.

"MY GOD, I'M LUCKY"

John was in a coma for several days and spent the next two years in a rehabilitation hospital for paraplegics and quadriplegics. He saw that many of the patients, most of them men, could move only their heads or had brain damage. "I thanked God that I had my two arms and a good brain to use," John says. "I really don't remember getting down on myself or asking God 'Why me?' "

The father of one of John's best friends had lost the use of his legs in World War II. Though the man was confined to a wheelchair, John had watched him carry on a normal life for many years. Partly because of the older man's example, John realized that he, too, could make a good life for himself.

John was visited in the rehabilitation center by his bride of one year, his parents, and three younger brothers, who ranged in age from ten to nineteen. "Some patients," John remembers, "would have no company whatsoever, but my mother made it a point to see me at least three or four times a week, and she saw to it that my brothers came, too. We were in rooms with other patients, and my mother talked to everybody in the room." Just as he considered himself lucky not to have been killed or injured more severely, John compared himself with others and felt fortunate that he had a family who cared about him.

In keeping with a characteristic almost universal among triumphant survivors, John found he could best help himself by offering strength, help, and encouragement to others. From a striker frame in which he remained in traction for nine months, John helped initiate a peer support group in which he and the other young men could talk over their situations. "The group was made up of me and a little clique of guys," John recalls. "Twice a week we'd get the nurse to push each of us down the hall in our striker frames so we could gather in one place. The guys would ask me about sex because they knew I was married; we'd talk about religion and in general just talk over whatever was on our minds."

After some months went by, explains John, "the nurses started bringing me the guys who were really down and wanted to die. But I started telling them there was a lot they could do even though they were disabled."

Determined to regain as much upper body strength as possible, John started lifting weights the last month he was in traction. He built himself up to the point where he was strong enough, from his wheelchair, to push three or four men in a line down the hospital hallways to the concerts in the auditorium. "The average person couldn't do anything for himself," John remembers. "There were only so many volunteers, too few in the evenings especially. There were places to go and things to do but you had to have a way to get there."

John kept asking the doctors if he would still be able to function sexually; it was a question that at that time (twenty-one years ago) few medical people seemed to know how to answer. It was not commonly known then that many men with spinal cord injuries are able to have erections and/or to experience climax and that virtually all men with such injuries maintain a healthy interest in sex and would enjoy creative lovemaking activities. As for John, "I had always been very sexually motivated," he says, "and I wanted answers to my questions."

Even when John's wife said she couldn't handle his disability any longer and left him, ten months after the accident, John was determined "to live life almost the way I lived it before." He mourned his wife's abandonment yet continued to push himself around the hospital to visit other patients whom he saw as physically or emotionally "in a worse situation than I was."

A few weeks after his wife left him, says John, "I went home for a night at my parents' house with sex the uppermost thing on my mind. I called up a girl, Maggie, someone whom I had known all of my life and who had a reputation for sleeping around with a lot of guys. We had played together and been friends since the age of three, although we had never dated. I dialed the phone and said to her, 'Maggie, if you care about me at all, there's something I want you to do for me. I've really got sex on my mind, and I need to see what I can still do about it. Would you come over?' " John, laughing, recalls, "Maggie was at my parents' doorstep twenty minutes later."

John pulled out the catheter that he wore regularly at that time and enjoyed several hours of playful intimacy with Maggie. His parents were aware of what was going on in the bedroom on the first floor since John was ecstatic and not one to be quiet in moments of delight. The next day his father and mother had John's brother take him back to the hospital because they felt too embarrassed to drive him themselves. Still, John's parents must have sensed how deeply his wife's abandonment had hurt him, or they had seen his intense need to feel whole again. He never felt that his parents judged or condemned him.

John began to cause havoc among the nurses by wheeling himself out of the hospital and down a long distance to a local bar. There he met various women who would come to the hospital to visit him and with whom he would lie on a blanket on the hospital lawn! He became a symbol of hope and a cause for smiles and laughter as stories about John's escapades filtered through the hospital gossip channels to the other patients.

"I WILL TAKE ADVANTAGE OF THE AVAILABLE OPPORTUNITIES"

"I saw more baseball, basketball, and hockey games when I was in the rehab center," John says, "than I ever saw in my life. If you could transfer without assistance, meaning get yourself out of a wheelchair and into a vehicle, you could go.

I admired those people who donated their time to the Red Cross to drive us places. I could transfer, so I went a lot."

He began to establish a tender and mutually caring relationship with a physical therapist, a woman with whom he enjoyed long talks in the hospital. Their relationship remained on a friendship basis until John was no longer her patient. Then he pursued her and they dated frequently.

After John was released from the rehabilitation hospital, he was often asked to come talk with various patients who were feeling hopeless or disheartened. For about eighteen months he returned there many times, driving his own car. It was an opportunity to help people in great need and, at the same time, to grow in self-esteem as a person who is "handi-capable," as John likes to put it.

On the advice of his vocational rehabilitation counselor, John studied engineering drafting and related mathematics at an engineering institute. He had decided to prepare for a career that would keep him in contact with the work he had done as a construction foreman. It had become financially impossible for his parents to take care of him, and he had used up his savings. "An individual has to have motivation in his life not to become a vegetable," he says. "I'm glad that I *had* to get out and work."

Many persons always blame other people or events outside themselves for their inability to get or keep a job. This has been confirmed by Rick and Kay Lamplugh, professionals who work on behalf of unemployed people, many of them injured workers, in an economically depressed region of Oregon. Many of those who remain out of work despite available opportunities, Kay explains, are "yes butters"—they always have excuses. Those who succeed, on the other hand, recognize that the power is within themselves to work hard at finding and keeping a job. "When you give your power away," says Kay, "you set yourself up for failure."

John's attitude is what made the opportunities that came to him plentiful. " 'No' and 'I can't do it' are words just not in my vocabulary," says John. "If something is possible, I'll find a way to do it."

He took a county government job which involved using his newly acquired drafting skills and his established ability to read construction plans. "I had the ability to lead," he explains, "and I always liked working with people. So I found a job where all those things could be put together."

Four years after his accident, John bought a waterfront lot. He hoped to build a house there with specifications for a person confined to a wheelchair. A thrifty person, John carefully squirreled away most of his salary and later, with the help of his father and brothers, proceeded to build a home for himself.

He shopped around for the lowest bid from four electrical companies, got the lumber at near cost, and took out a bank loan using his parents' house as collateral after they sold it to him for five dollars. Once the loan came through and the house was completely built, John sold his parents' house back to them for the same price he had paid for it.

It is a beautiful home on the water with two fireplaces, three thousand square feet of space, and three bedrooms. With his youngest brother's help John built an expansive deck on the back and sides of the house that provides a view of the water from three perspectives. He is proud, too, of the handsome wood kitchen cabinets that he installed with the help of his father and brothers.

"I look outside," says John fondly. "I look at the trees. I look at the ducks that swim on the water outside my place—and there's beauty. But the average person just doesn't look anymore."

John tends both a vegetable and a flower garden. He mows his own small lawn in his electric wheelchair. He likes to tan himself on the deck and enjoys cookouts, motor boating, and sailing. "A lot of my friends just see me as a regular person," he says. "They don't see the wheelchair, they see the man. It does mean a lot to have people feel that way about me."

With small business loans from the federal government,

John has purchased in recent years a liquor store, a delicatessen, and a property which he rents out as a barber shop. His small businesses are in the community where he lives, a community to which he contributes by donating time to various service activities, including the sponsoring of two local summer softball teams. He continues his full-time government job, which helps him meet the loan payments that come due every quarter, and he tries to hire conscientious, community-minded employees to treat his delicatessen and liquor store customers with respect and courtesy.

"You have to work at it all day long if you want to succeed in life," John says. "There is also a certain amount of risk involved. I put my home up for collateral to purchase the businesses."

John says he sleeps only about five hours a night because "I'm thankful I'm alive and I don't want to spend my life in bed. Besides," he continues, "how can you help somebody else if you're sitting at home all the time or sleeping? I don't mind getting out of bed and shaving and going to work. I feel happy that I'm working, that I've made my way to be able to work and to enjoy living on the water."

Speaking of his father's recent death, John says, "My father and I were very, very close. I think we had a mutual admiration. I think my father was proud that I succeeded beyond what most men do with two good legs."

"NOBODY'S PERFECT"

Three times unsuccessful in marriage, John's longest romantic relationship lasted six years. A contributing factor, he says, may be a tendency to attract people "who need a stronger individual than what they are." One of his wives, for example, had a severe drinking problem which John mistakenly believed she had overcome before their marriage.

He is an engaging, energetic, interesting, and sensual man.

Women are drawn to him. His strength and vitality make one oblivious of the wheelchair. However, John demands a great deal of himself, I surmised, and can be excessively demanding of others, especially women. A generous and giving man, he expects generosity and passionate involvement in return. He is a "tough act to follow," and perhaps those who love him feel that his expectations of them are unrealistic, even burdensome, at times.

John is engaged to be married for the fourth time. "I love satisfying a woman," he says. "Discovering a variety of ways to please and be pleased sexually and having an active love life has probably been an important factor in my healing."

His father used to say, "Son, you're really good at solving problems but figuring out how to stay with the same woman is not something you're good at." His father's accurate assessment notwithstanding, John has found tenderness and intimacy over the years through numerous relationships. He sufficiently meets his personal needs as he sees them, and he is free to devote the majority of his energy to work, business investments, retirement plans, community service, and troubleshooting activities on behalf of handicapped people and their agencies.

Every weekday John gets ready for work in the electric wheelchair he uses only at home, ambulates to the garage, and gets himself into the driver's seat. As he has done for more than a decade, he picks up two riders, also government employees, and drives across the city to the office building where the three men work. One of the riders gets the wheelchair out of the trunk, and John unfolds it, gets himself in, locks the car, and pushes himself to work. The procedure is reversed in the late afternoon.

"I really enjoy life," said John, "because I almost had my life taken from me." These words were spoken twenty-one years after the accident that paralyzed him.

John Liller's mental approach and the actions that followed were built on the sturdy foundation characteristic of triumphant survivors: He helped himself by offering hope and encouragement to others and by seizing the available opportunities for meaningful human contact and self-improvement. He also identified satisfying activities he could still pursue despite his loss and accepted the fact that being human inevitably means having problems of one kind or another to contend with.

MARGARET: "THERE IS STILL TIME FOR ME"

"When I learned I was pregnant," explains Margaret, "I was thirty-four years old, unmarried, only fifteen months from finishing law school, and a few days from beginning a highly sought-after clerkship with the Court of Appeals. I loved Jonathan, the man by whom I was pregnant," she continues, "but I also knew I could never marry him."

Margaret was certain that Jonathan wouldn't *want* to get married. Twice divorced at the age of thirty, he was already struggling on a policeman's salary to make child support payments to two women, each of whom had borne him a son. "I loved him," Margaret explained, "but I knew he wasn't the kind of stable guy who could make a marriage work. I was also certain that if I had this baby, Jonathan would never be a real father to the child because he never visited his other children, never did anything for them except send money."

The pregnancy also presented a problem because Jonathan had been Margaret's student at the college where she taught paralegal and prelaw students. It would be embarrassing if word got out that she was dating and pregnant by one of her students, a policeman. The news might even threaten her job security.

Margaret wept in her doctor's office while she and the gynecologist discussed the pregnancy. "No woman in my family has ever even finished college," she said, tearfully. "I just can't give up this clerkship and negate all my hard work to go through law school. I would always resent the child if I gave up this career opportunity in order to carry out the pregnancy."

"Your tears say that you have mixed feelings about having an abortion," responded Dr. Eleanor Scott. A caring, soft-spoken doctor, she leaned back in her chair, resting one arm on the desk as if to communicate that she was prepared to talk awhile.

"I'm afraid I'll be too old to have children later," Margaret said, sobbing. "I feel that I've got to choose my career over having a baby right now, but what if this is my only chance?"

"If you're going to continue the pregnancy," said Dr. Scott, "we have to take out the IUD today so it won't injure the fetus."

"No, I know I have to have an abortion," Margaret replied. "And I want the people in the operating room to see you remove that IUD just before the abortion. I want people to know that I didn't want to have to do this. I've *always* used contraceptives. I've never had sex without being responsible about it."

Dr. Scott shifted her body a bit and folded her hands on the desk, facing Margaret squarely. As Margaret was to learn many years later, the doctor had been a medical resident in New York in the late 1930s and remembered that virtually every day someone who was bleeding or suffering a pelvic infection would be admitted to the hospital—the victim of self-induced or phony doctor's coat-hanger, catheter, or "slippery elm stick" abortion. Since no blood bank existed in those days and there were no antibiotics, many women died. Even after World War II, when penicillin was available, many women became sterile or died from the gross infections that often resulted from illegal abortions. Now, decades later, desperate women like Margaret could sit in a doctor's office and discuss a safe and legal option to continuing a profoundly troublesome pregnancy.

The doctor pushed her chair on rollers toward a shelf on

the wall three feet away. "This is my oldest child," she said, holding out a framed photograph and offering it to Margaret. "She's active in politics now. I was thirty-six when I had her."

Margaret reached for a tissue, blew her nose, and smiled. "And this is my baby," continued Dr. Scott, offering Margaret a second silver-lined photograph. "He was born when I was forty-one and is finishing law school now. So you see," the doctor continued tenderly, "there's still time for you."

A few days later Margaret wept again at the hospital and said a prayer before she was taken to the operating room. "Dear God, I'm sorry I have to do this," she prayed. "Somehow I know that You forgive me, but I still hope that You'll help me make it up to You."

Margaret never forgot the compassion Dr. Scott expressed nor her nonjudgmental response to the abortion decision. The doctor's empathic and encouraging words, spoken in a time of crisis, are remembered sixteen years later. Margaret is now a successful lawyer who has moved into public service law to realize her goal of helping others. She has married and is the mother by adoption of two young sons from Vietnam.

"Somehow I feel that things finally and fully have been made right again," explains Margaret. "I wanted very much to be a mother, and I also wanted to give a good life to two children from the Third World. Each of our sons was born into wartime and poverty and orphaned before the age of two. It gives us a tremendous sense of joy and meaningfulness to love our boys and to give them a quality of life they wouldn't otherwise have had.

"I still feel sorry that the abortion had to be, and I still try to live a useful, contributing life," she explains. "I believe that God's forgiveness and loving presence are with me," Margaret concludes, "and I feel at peace about the past."

DR. STARK: "THERE MUST BE SOME MEANING TO BE FOUND OR SEEN IN THESE EVENTS"

Dr. Meritt Stark, a pediatrician and father of six, was one of twelve hundred nonmilitary American physicians who volunteered to go to Vietnam. Since most of the Vietnamese doctors were involved in the war effort and away from their provinces, the Vietnamese civilians were left without adequate medical care. The children, who were victims of the war or were suffering from the diseases of poverty, especially needed doctors. Dr. Stark's son was in Southeast Asia with the marines when the doctor signed up for the two-month volunteer stint in 1967. "I had the feeling," he said, "that I should support the war effort, and that's why I went. I accepted the information that we got from our government that South Vietnam was being invaded from the north and that we were helping the people there regarding the choice of their government."

In 1969 Dr. Stark returned to Vietnam as a public health physician with the State Department. He took his wife and two youngest daughters to the safety of nearby Taiwan until Mrs. Stark was allowed to join him in Bien Hoa in 1972. Later a second son went to Taiwan to study Chinese.

Back home the Starks' two eldest daughters were in college and were serious protesters against the war. As they finished their education, one married and the other, Laurie, spent a year teaching in a community college. On her dad's suggestion, Laurie came to Vietnam to see the conditions there. "I invited her to come," said Dr. Stark, "because I thought that it might change her outlook on the war and that she might cease being a protester."

At the age of twenty-five, Dr. Stark remembers, Laurie started working with the street boys—Vietnamese children who had no parents and who were "little ragamuffins on the street." She made a serious effort to become adept in the language, helped at a medical center specializing in plastic surgery, and worked with a Vietnamese friend to establish and operate a preschool. Laurie held fast to high ideals. "She never felt the war was a good thing," explained her father.

In March and early April of 1975, at the very end of the war, hundreds of thousands of refugees poured into the south as the northern provinces of Da Nang, Hue, and Ban Me Thuot fell. Dr. Stark worked hard to set up relocation areas in Nha Trang, but that city, too, fell before it was possible for the refugees to settle. "On April 4, at 11 A.M.," recalls Dr. Stark, "I was told that there was a presidential authorization to use the C5-A, the biggest plane in the world, to evacuate the orphans, and that I had been delegated to accompany the orphans as medical advisor. They would begin loading at 2:00 P.M., and I was to be there then, accompany the orphans to the United States, and return to Vietnam." There were few escorts, and they were going to be taking out several hundred orphans, so Stark asked his wife if she could come. She felt she couldn't leave her work with the schoolchildren so he asked his daughter to go. Laurie had been scheduled to leave on a plane the next day to escort another group of orphans and would be leaving permanently, so she had packed all her things. "When I said we were going on the fourth and needed her more than on the fifth, she changed her plans and came with me," Stark recalls.

There were 253 war orphans and abandoned children on the plane and approximately fifty support people. Dr. Stark went with the babies and other very young children up to the troop compartment above the cargo hatch. Laurie stayed downstairs on the plane with the older children—some of them handicapped, some fathered by American servicemen. "If a woman had a baby fathered by an American and he left," explained Dr. Stark, "there was no way she could get a job in the country except to be a prostitute, because of the stigma. She would have to give the baby up." For several years certain agencies had worked to arrange for mixed-blood orphans to go to Europe, America, and Australia for adoption.

There was a great deal of confusion at the airport. Many Vietnamese guards didn't want the plane to leave. President Ford and Congress had granted permission to admit these orphans to the United States for adoption because they would be exceedingly vulnerable after the Americans left the country, and it was obvious that the United States would soon withdraw. There were no exit visas for the orphans, although Dr. Stark had a letter from the minister of welfare to expedite the plane's leaving.

Fifteen minutes after the giant airship took off, just as the plane was heading out over the South China Sea, there was a noise that sounded like an explosion. The cargo doors had blown off, and the stabilizing mechanism had been struck by a door and damaged. The pilot did not have full control but was able to get the plane turned around and headed back to Saigon.

In the crash landing, 138 babies, children, and escorts died, most of them in the cargo hatch, which took the bulk of the blow. Dr. Stark knew as soon as the plane crashed that it was virtually certain that Laurie had died. After he got the survivors out of the troop compartment that had been sheared off and took them away from the fire, he started walking around the burning ruins to see if anyone had been thrown free, looking for his daughter. She was twenty-seven years old when she died.

The day after the crash, on Saturday, there was a memorial service at the airport for all of the people who died. Laurie was mourned by French and Vietnamese friends as well as her parents' friends. A service was also held for her on Sunday at an international Christian church.

The Starks had little time to grieve. There was a great deal of preparation for leaving the country permanently. Dr. Stark was busy with the orphans for four days. Mrs. Stark threw all of her energy into trying to get an exit visa for the twelve-year-old son of Vietnamese friends who wanted the Starks to take the boy out and adopt him in the United States. The war was closing in on Saigon, and there was an atmosphere of impending doom. The presidential palace had been bombed and an immediate curfew decreed.

Dr. and Mrs. Stark left Vietnam six days after the plane crash as part of an urgent evacuation of Americans and orphans. The State Department sent Dr. Stark to Travis Air Force Base on the West Coast for a time to help receive the orphans who continued to come by planeloads from Southeast Asia.

Dr. Stark struggled with a profound feeling of disappointment and disillusionment. "So many South Vietnamese had put their lives and children's lives on the line," said Dr. Stark. "Four or five American presidents had said we would never abandon Vietnam, and yet we did." It was painful to know that many of his Asian friends would be sent to work camps to be reindoctrinated with a new philosophy, and it was disillusioning that "our efforts weren't appreciated by the people in this country."

Over the months and years that followed, Meritt Stark drew comfort from certain ways of thinking about his daughter and her death. Instead of blaming himself for inviting Laurie to come to Vietnam with the hope that she would change her antiwar views, Dr. Stark decided that "my daughter died doing what a Peace Corps volunteer might do." He realized that she also knew the importance of getting these young children out of the country. "My daughter's death had some meaning," Dr. Stark told me, "as opposed to the needless, mistaken shooting of a fifteen-year-old girl who rustled the bushes and was mistaken for a Vietcong soldier. I had the feeling that Laurie would herself have chosen to go on the flight even if she knew she was risking damage to herself or even the loss of her life."

Dr. Stark firmly believed that there was also meaning to be found in his daughter's death as a result of the fact that "Laurie seemed to live very fully, although she died very young." She had studied a year in France when she was in college and later helped young underprivileged Hispanics improve their English. As part of the year spent teaching in a community college, she represented them in court when they got in trouble. She had also lived and traveled in Mexico for several months, pursued an interest in ballet, collected many books and artworks, and taken postgraduate courses at the University of Colorado. She had founded a preschool in Vietnam and, Dr. Stark told me, by speaking the language as she did and by teaching, Laurie's selflessness and "her actions probably won more support from the Vietnamese people than the war effort did. Most of what the Vietnamese saw on which they formed their opinion of America," he explained, "was the American serviceman, who sometimes left not a very favorable impression." He was proud of what his daughter gave in sacrificing her life, and he labored unsuccessfully to have Laurie's name included among the more than fifty-eight thousand names of American war dead engraved in granite at the Vietnam Memorial in Washington, D.C.

There was another attitude that comforted Laurie's parents. "We knew," explained Dr. Stark, "that there were a lot of families like us in this country" who had suffered a precious loss in Vietnam, "and among the South Vietnamese *every* family had some tragedy like ours." Experiencing others' suffering firsthand seemed to alter the Starks' perspective. "There were hundreds of thousands of refugees, and every family over there had someone killed or injured in the conflict," he noted.

Finding meaning in suffering or loss, a concept to be discussed more fully in the last chapter of this book, is an essential element of the healing process for most people. Some come to believe in an ultimate or inherent meaning, feeling that God's purpose has been served somehow. Others reject the notion of a wider purpose and believe that a tragic event is inherently meaningless until the mourner himself or herself makes some sense of the event and imposes meaning on the situation or creates a purpose to be served. At any rate, meaninglessness is not something people can live with well. Those who resolve to find or create a sense of purpose or who can identify something to be gained from a tragic loss fare much better than do people who leave the meaning and purpose issue unresolved.

"I WILL NOT ASSUME THE VICTIM POSTURE"

Like Robbie Risner, a majority of the POWs in Vietnam were airmen, career servicemen dedicated to the war effort. Compared with the typical enlisted personnel on the ground, as a group they were older and better educated. They believed that the cause for which they were fighting was just and worthwhile.

"The guys I flew with," explained Risner in our interview, "were doing what they did best and what they thought they did better than anyone else in the world. We were America's fighting men, and we loved to fly. We often said we ought to be paying Uncle Sam to let us fly."

As they met with adversity and the severe hardships of prison life, Robbie and most of the other POWs did not struggle with the "Why me?" feelings common in a time of crisis. They were professionals doing what they wanted to do with their lives and what they believed in. It was neither in their character nor befitting of their situation to assume the victim posture.

From the air the enemy often seemed distant, the war bloodless. Air warfare is a clean, impersonal type of thing. When people die you don't see the pain.[3] It was different for the men in jungle combat, where they pulled leeches off their eyelids in the morning and never knew when the enemy might strike. Most of these servicemen were young men who found themselves drafted into service in Southeast Asia. Particularly in the later years of the war, many doubted the war's legitimacy and value or knew about the doubts in the minds of many Americans back home. It is extremely difficult to bear up under the stresses of a vividly personal and bloody war, experiencing an almost constant danger of death or injury, without the assurance that one's sacrifice is serving a meaningful purpose.

At the end of the war in Vietnam "it was commonly felt among the returning POWs (a majority of them airmen) that we didn't need to get well, because we weren't ill," explains Robbie Risner. "Many combat veterans who fought on the ground, on the other hand, feel they haven't healed yet."

Perhaps those veterans still unable to feel at peace with the scars they carry feel that society has not yet properly thanked them for the price they paid, or they see themselves as unwitting participants in a cause not of their own choosing or conviction. In order to find freedom from their discontent, it may be necessary for these soldiers to lay down the mantle of having been an unfortunate victim. What happened is finished. How one chooses to view the costly contributions that were made is what matters now.

Through tragic events, life often makes victims out of us. A child dies or is killed, a major illness or accident occurs, a sexual assault, war, fire, or natural disaster takes place, or some injustice is done to us, and we suffer. However dear, the price has been paid, and the events of the past cannot be changed. For healing to continue, a transformation in one's thinking is required. A disillusioned war veteran or the survivors of a soldier who died must begin to interpret events so that some purpose can be seen in the sacrifice that was made.

It is necessary for many of us to cease seeing ourselves as helpless victims. A ship cannot be launched on a new voyage until its enormous ropes are untied at the dock.

MY COUSIN CHARLES: "I CAN DO IT IF I SET MY MIND"

Charles was a college professor in upstate New York. His wife fell in love with one of his students and said that she wanted to live with the other man. Their daughter, Kristin, was thirty months old, and Charles requested sole custody. This was 1971, and neither the judge nor Charles's lawyer had ever had such a request from a father before. Kristin's mother wanted Kristin to live with her, but Charles was determined that his daughter would remain under his influence and care, firmly believing that he could better provide his daughter with emotional and financial security. "There was never any doubt in my mind," said Charles, "that she would always be with me."

"The very first night we were alone after the judge granted me custody," remembered Charles, "I suddenly wondered if I was capable of such an enormous responsibility. After Kristin went to sleep, I had one of the worst nights of my life. I felt a fear and panic that were almost out of control—I experienced heart palpitations, shallow breathing, cold sweat, trembling, and the fear of going crazy. I felt terribly alone, and it was the closest I've ever come to feeling near a nervous breakdown."

He stayed awake all night, pacing the floors and staring at the walls. "By the time the sun came up," Charles continued, "I knew that I was determined and that I had made the biggest commitment of my life. The pledge to raise a child makes the marriage vow pale by comparison. One makes a covenant with a child for at least eighteen years."

Charles came from the same German, rural Oklahoma background in which I was reared. Our grandfathers were brothers, and our parents' farms were less than a mile apart. "There was a dogged determination in those people we come from," remembered Charles. "When you've committed yourself to something, you just bull your way through it; the die is cast. It's a kind of commitment that sometimes can manifest itself as narrowmindedness," continued Charles. "Yet in crisis, in critical moments, setting your mind is a survival mechanism."

"I HAVE TO BE WILLING TO EXPAND"

Once Charles committed himself to the rearing of Kristin, he did not plan to get married again. "I wanted to be dad and mom myself," he explained, "and the more I took on the job of two parents, the more I liked it, because I learned new roles which broadened me to be a better human being."

Charles worked at trying to incorporate more of the so-called "feminine" traits into his personality. He wanted his daughter to receive from him the understanding, tenderness, and warmth of a mother at the same time that he planned for her future, loved, protected, and provided for her in a way normally associated with a father. "I was quite conscious of a need to become more open to the showing of affection," Charles remembered. "I saw the importance of touching, holding, and cuddling Kristin. I also developed that unconditional love that mothers often give which fathers who are strict disciplinarians are not allowed to provide. I tried to learn patience."

Brought up in an environment where male and female roles had been strongly delineated, Charles's attributes had been firmly and traditionally masculine. "It used to be that you could be an all-male, half a person, and hook up with another half person who was all female. As long as you stayed married for the rest of your lives, that kind of complementary relationship worked rather well," Charles explained. In a rural setting without the complications of city life, and in the days when women didn't work outside the home, the traditional roles and division of labor made sense, he said.

As Charles reflected on his life, he spoke with the understanding of a man who had studied society, social relationships, and social change. A sociologist by training, he was already intellectually aware of the sex role revolution taking place in the culture at the time. Now Charles found himself being changed by the literature of the women's movement and by the realization that what Kristin needed for her growth was to be parented by a whole person and to receive from one parent the best of what both men and women, mothers and fathers, have to offer their children.

Charles arranged his work schedule so that his college courses were lumped into a relatively short space of time, maximizing the time he would have at home with Kristin. As his initial hurt and anger subsided and Kristin's mother resigned herself to Charles's sole custody, Charles arranged for his former wife to spend time with Kristin while he was at work. Some months later he carefully selected a college-educated day care mother who was knowledgeable about the growth and development of children. She was a loving person who watched only a few children at a time and who planned activities for Kristin and the other children which encouraged thinking, learning, and peer interaction. Kristin spent the early morning with her father, then participated in the preschool activities from late morning through midafternoon, when Charles came to take her home again.

"We lived in the country then," Charles remembered, "and I liked to show Kristin the things that were outdoors. Taking our dog along, we went for walks in the woods and swampland, picked cattails, visited a nearby country store. I'd get Kristin out in the garden and we'd watch the seedlings grow." Charles also remembered that watching Mother Earth at work "was a real metaphor for the ways I needed to grow." He "tried to become more conscious of providing anything for Kristin that would produce growth," he said, including being willing to broaden himself as a person.

"I AM CONSCIOUSLY DECIDING TO BE IN THE COMPANY OF GOOD PEOPLE"

From his graduate work in sociology Charles was aware of statistics showing that the children of divorced parents can have many problems. He had also read that children raised by a single parent can exceed their peers in the development of academic and social skills. "I had learned," said Charles, "that some of the highest achievers are raised by single parents in situations where these kids have multiple role models."

Determined that his daughter would find the role models she needed, said Charles, "I placed myself in the company of good people who could teach her things, especially women who had those traits I was lacking or only beginning to develop. In becoming my friends, such persons became Kristin's friends."

Olga was someone whom Charles came to know as a friend, colleague, and close companion. From the time that Charles's daughter was four years old until she was nine, Olga taught Kristin how to be creative in various forms of artwork. "I would have tried to teach Kristin to be more concrete," said Charles, "instead of letting her just let loose and have fun and be abstract as Olga taught her to do."

From Olga both Kristin and Charles learned how to mend, sew on buttons, and cook. By the age of six or seven Kristin had become very good at crocheting and doing fine needlework. "She learned to pay attention to detail, something she wouldn't have learned from me," said Charles, "and *I* learned many of these things I wanted Kristin to learn. In fact, cooking became for me a new passion."

Another friend and colleague, Jane, offered Charles's daughter love and nurturing by taking Kristin shopping. Kristin began to learn quite young "how to shop for nice things instead of junk," said Charles.

Kristin's mother had visitation rights and saw her daughter on a regular basis. Her many personal problems, however, including an unhappy second marriage, the birth of a severely handicapped child, and a bitter divorce prevented her from providing full-time nurturance to Kristin. Years later, after Charles and Kristin moved from New York to New Mexico, Kristin visited her mother for two or three weeks every summer.

In New Mexico a woman named Mary Ann became a "surrogate mother," explained Charles, "an intimate part of Kristin's and my life, one of those friends you can really count on if you need help." From Mary Ann's professionalism and perfectionism, Kristin learned goal setting and logical thinking and got help with her math struggles. Mary Ann hired Kristin for odd jobs and babysitting and helped the youngster learn how to save money for a special dress and, eventually, how to save to buy a car. Mary Ann also coordinated the celebration of Kristin's high school graduation—according to Charles, "the largest family gathering that has taken place in years. If Kristin marries someday, Mary Ann will probably coordinate the wedding celebration, too."

We sat together, my cousin Charles and I, in the midst of a large and crowded auditorium in Sante Fe, New Mexico. Present were hundreds of Native Americans, Hispanics, and Anglos—friends and relatives on hand for the high school graduation of two hundred special persons. On my right were Kristin's maternal grandparents, salt-of-the-earth Oklahomans. Charles had seen to it, over the years, that his ex-wife's parents had had the opportunity to contribute their loving influence. Kristin had especially enjoyed learning quilting and canning from her grandmother on extended summer visits to Oklahoma.

On my left was my cousin Charles. I sat admiring his tall black cowboy boots, white pearl-buttoned shirt, black vest, large rectangular silver and turquoise belt buckle, and the black velvet jeans that looked so handsome on his tall, slender, bow-legged body. His plentiful gray-blond, curly hair added youthfulness to a man built and bearded like Abraham Lincoln.

My cousin's lovely blond daughter, almost eighteen years old, proudly marched down the aisle in her white, flowing gown, her dark, handsome boyfriend a few graduating seniors behind her in the procession. Kristin looked proud and pretty. Her dad's eyes glistened when he first spotted her. When the rest of us stood, Charles stood taller. The officiating priest at the graduation mass, an archbishop fully attired in red clericals, began the bilingual (Spanish and English) ceremony. Speaking words chosen perfectly for the lean, tall man standing next to me, the priest's firm voice proclaimed that "this celebrative moment would not be possible without the nurturance, devotion, and sacrifice of the parents of these young men and women."

"I felt proud of myself," Charles told me later, remembering his feelings during the ceremony. "Dammit, I did it. As one parent, I brought up this kid who has grown up to be such a lovely person. She did it. She made it. I'm just really grateful for that.

"While this isn't the end of our relationship or of her needing me," Charles continued, "it is the end of an era. I've gotten her to the place where she can build her own support system now, and if you can't do that as a parent you should raise dogs or cats, not kids.

"Being a single parent brings out one's potential, both male and female qualities and capabilities, that would otherwise never develop. It's the best thing that ever happened to me," Charles went on, "the most character-building, wonderful experience I could ever have had."

After the final procession, little family clusters formed at the back of the auditorium and in the hallways. The scent of pride from other triumphs was in the air as parents, grandparents, siblings, and friends snapped the lens shutters of their cameras. One graduating senior, said to be fighting cancer, wore a white scarf under her commencement cap and wrapped above her ears. This young woman and her family and friends were celebrating life itself.

Charles and Kristin posed for a photograph, Dad's proud arm around her shoulder. The beaming gray-blond curly-headed cowboy and his grown-up little girl surely looked happy. When I saw who the smiling and cheerful photographer was, I couldn't help but choke up a little. "Congratulations, you two!" exclaimed the woman from New York. "I'm proud of you both," continued Kristin's mother.

My cousin Charles's singlemindedness, willingness to grow, and conscious affiliation with kind, caring, loving, and giving people made it possible for him to succeed as a single parent. Like-minded persons are able to triumph over a host of difficult situations and experiences of personal loss.

THE SANBORNS: "WE WILL FIND A WAY TO GET WHAT WE WANT"

Dave and Mary Sanborn wanted children. They were among the one in every six American couples that struggle with infertility. The couple had been married four years and had been keeping temperature charts for two years. Their cousins were already having second children. Mary's gynecologist said, "Relax. You're just uptight."

"We wasted another year with this doctor," Mary says, "and finally we went to an infertility specialist." When the specialist made out a list of the available tests, Mary was astonished that so much could be done to study the problem.

Dave and Mary endured the exasperating ordeal of one inconclusive infertility test after another. They rode an emotional roller coaster—every month hoping that Mary was pregnant and having their hopes dashed to the ground, time after time. Dave was tested and checked out fine. Then Mary had minor surgery twice, was injected with gases and dyes according to various testing procedures, and had numerous blood tests. The testing took place in and out of the hospital, lasted six months, and included many instances of "having to make love on cue" during the four-day period around ovulation. Within twenty-four hours after intercourse Mary had to go early in the morning to the infertility specialist's office. Her cervical mucus would be checked to see how many sperm were still alive.

"The whole thing was very stressful for both of us," Mary

explains. "We cried together and I told Dave that I felt I was letting him down by not providing him with children."

Dave replied, "I married you for you." He was upset with the mental and physical exhaustion the tests were causing Mary and said he didn't want her to go through the ordeal any longer.

Finally, after six months with the infertility specialist, the Sanborns were thrilled to learn that Mary was pregnant. With joy and excitement they shared the news with everyone—their parents, friends, and work associates. Their infertility specialist seemed to be as happy about the pregnancy as they were.

The first five months of Mary's pregnancy were uneventful. Then one day she started spotting. On the advice of the specialist, she immediately went to bed. The following day, after a sonogram, Mary saw the tears in her physician's eyes and knew that the baby was dead. The doctor and patient held each other and cried. The specialist told Mary to call her husband because she was running a fever, meaning that an infection in the uterus was setting in and he would have to take the baby out right away. "I was actually wailing, just hysterical," Mary said.

Dave rushed to the hospital directly from work. He had hurried away from his masonry business because he felt he had to see his wife before the doctor induced labor. He arrived with wet concrete smeared over his trousers. He was so dirty that the medical support personnel draped him and his dripping shoes in layers of hospital gowns and wraps before they would allow him in the hospital hallways.

"Later I was in the recovery room with women who had had live births," Mary remembers. "Although the others weren't with their babies either, the nurses thought they were doing me a favor by wheeling me away from the mothers into the hallway every time they came to check my vital signs. The whole thing was handled very clumsily by the nursing staff. I swore that once I got back to work (as a lay Catholic chaplain) I would do something to help women who had lost babies."

When Mary got home from the hospital, she didn't want to see or talk with anyone, including her mother, who lived across the street. "The burden was on Dave to tell everybody we had lost the baby," explains Mary, "because I couldn't stand to talk with people." She took a month off from work, where her job was counseling the sick and the elderly.

Only a few days after the baby died, Mary received still more devastating news. Her respected and beloved doctor, only thirty-four years old, said he was stopping his practice. He had been diagnosed as having cancer and didn't have long to live. Mary understood another dimension now of the pain he must have felt when he couldn't help her continue and protect her pregnancy.

Referred by her dying doctor to another specialist, Mary went to the Johns Hopkins Medical Center. "The new physician there was very nice," she says, "but he wanted me to go through the same testing all over again. We had been married six years by then, and I felt that enough was enough."

Dave and Mary sat down together and agreed that they did not want to spend the rest of their lives without children. They decided to examine their options. Mary contacted several adoption agencies and learned that the child of their dreams and fantasies, a healthy white infant, would require a five- to ten-year wait. "I was already thirty-three years old by this time and Dave was thirty," explains Mary. "We felt terribly discouraged."

When Mary announced to Dave her discovery that they could avoid the long waiting lists in America by adopting a healthy baby from Korea, Dave said, "No way. I want a Caucasian child." Undaunted, Mary made a secret appointment with a social worker and, without telling her husband, got the couple on a waiting list for prospective adoptive parents. She began saying novenas, nine days of prayers, to Saint Gerard, the patron saint of mothers.

"After the nine days of prayers had passed, I asked Dave if he would go with me to a group called FACE, Families Adopting Children Everywhere, and reluctantly he agreed to go. I didn't have to light any more candles," she continues, laughing now, "or even light a fire under him!"

The course, taught by adoptive parents, featured various presentations made by couples and individuals, who brought along their children. "Who should walk in," says Mary, "but the cutest Korean twin girls, age three or four. I watched and saw his whole facial expression change. He just lit up with energy. Those little girls came right to him and sat on his knees and talked about Big Bird on the *Sesame Street* television program. Dave just melted."

"Remember what our priest friend Father Larry told you about our being able to have a baby through foreign adoption?" Dave asked Mary, a few days later. "I didn't want to go through with it but I do now if it's okay with you," he said.

"Good," replied Mary, "because I put us on the waiting list and we have an appointment with a social worker in just two days." She then told her much-surprised husband of the plans she had made, hoping and praying that he would change his mind. They had already been on the home study waiting list for one month, she revealed, in the first step toward being approved by the agency as prospective adoptive parents.

"On August 19, a year to the day that I lost the baby," says Mary, "we met an airplane from Korea. Our daughter Elizabeth, just two months old, was placed in my arms. To have a baby arrive that same day was like being reborn."

Throughout her life, says Mary, she has been like her grandmother, who had a habit of saying, "If one route doesn't get me there, I'll find another." Her grandmother, widowed young and having a six-year-old to care for, had married a widower with seven children under the age of fifteen. The grandmother worked hard, says Mary, but both she and all eight children had a happy life. The stepchildren soon loved her as their mother.

"I'm just the kind of person who finds options," says Mary. She had once held a job as a physician's assistant, she explains, but decided that what she really wanted to do was to combine medicine with church work in some way. She decided she wanted to become a Health Care Ministry chaplain, despite the fact that at the time there were no laywomen in such a role, only nuns. "I had to be certified by the U.S. Catholic Conference, and there was doubt that I would be approved as a Catholic laywoman," Mary says. She took theology courses, went through a chaplaincy training program, and passed the board exam. "To be able to walk into a hospital and minister to people as a chaplain, as a Catholic woman," she continues, "was really important to me."

Mary's long-standing philosophy of life, and her recommendation to others, is to "find a way to get what you want." Her husband's attitude, it turns out, is similar. Dave had imagined having a blond-haired, blue-eyed son or daughter whose appearance was reminiscent of photographs from his own childhood album. However, when he saw two adorable little Korean girls and observed that their parents clearly accepted and loved these children as their own, Dave realized that he could feel the same parental love. His doubts about being fully able to love a child from a different race and culture quickly evaporated while little twin girls were sitting on his knees.

Dave and Mary have their own two little daughters now. Elizabeth's sister, Julia, also from Korea, came by the jet-powered stork approximately two years after the couple's first daughter arrived. The family of four now lives on a beautiful farm surrounded by open countryside, in the company of three rabbits, two Holstein steers, two baby calves, two ducks (one rescued by Dave from a frozen pond, with a single foot), three California speckled quail named Winkin, Blinkin, and Nod, four goats, three cats, and two peacocks.

"When I was a teenager," says Mary, "I wanted to be a missionary and go to the Far East. In college I went out of my way to study Oriental philosophy, religion, calligraphy, and art. I was just fascinated and drawn to the Asian culture. To this day I enjoy doing reading on Taoism and Zen. We'll definitely go to Korea as a family someday," she says. "It just seems like everything has fallen into place. I'm glad I didn't miss this. I'm so lucky to have two Asian daughters."

Their spacious house, built by Dave, creates a warm and comfortable feeling. Earth tones and various soft shades of blue flow from one room to the next in the country wallpaper and colorful woven rugs. An elegant textured fabric in a royal blue Oriental print covers the living room sofa and dining room chairs. A splendid multihued peacock and other Oriental wall hangings perch proudly on both sides of the fireplace. Mary keeps the books for Dave's business and is a full-time homemaker who loves to arrange things indoors and enjoys caring for the animals outdoors with the little girls at her side.

A full moon is shining on the swing set in the back yard and illuminates the distant barnyard. I climb into my car in the Sanborns' driveway, my own international toddler belted into her car seat. We drive away and it is clear that my daughter thinks she has just seen the promised land. Amanda chirps about how wonderful it was to drink goat's milk for the first time and hopes aloud that we can return soon to pet the white-faced baby calves.

"Our family," I smilingly remember Mary's saying, "consists of two Korean children with Caucasian parents, a Jewish doctor for a godmother (the widow of the fertility specialist they regarded so highly), a Catholic priest for a godfather, and twenty-one animals. Pretty nice family, huh?"

"I WILL ACCEPT LIFE'S CHALLENGE"

According to an article in *The Washington Post*, in the 1980s the popular impression has been that "stress makes [people] sick" and "runs like a truck over its helpless victims." Fortunately, a more optimistic view has evolved from the studies of psychologist Suzanne Kobasa at the City University of New York. "It's not just what happens to [a person] that's important," Kobasa's studies suggest, but how one handles change, crisis or stress. "If you try to master stresses instead of feeling overwhelmed by them, they don't have to be bad for your health."[4]

Carefully examining the lives of hundreds of people, Kobasa and her associates found that certain ways of approaching life "buffer the negative effects of stress." The three inner resources that were seen as most crucial to psychological hardiness were the three C's: commitment, control, and challenge: "(1) Commitment to self, work, family and other important values. (2) A sense of personal control over one's life. (3) The ability to see change in one's life as a challenge to master."[5]

"When a man loses his job, for example," writes Maya Pines, a prolific freelance writer, "he can see it either as a catastrophe—an irreplaceable loss that shows he is unworthy and predicts his downfall—or as an experience that falls within the range of risks he accepted when he took the job. In some cases, he may even view it as an opportunity to find a new career that is better suited to his abilities."[6] Similarly, following a normal mourning period, a woman who finds herself on her own after the end of a relationship that she greatly relied upon for a sense of usefulness, security, and belonging can view her changed circumstances as a tragedy or as an event that has forced her to grow. She may discover for herself new opportunities in education, friendship, job training, travel, recreation, or hobbies. Doing certain things independently (the mere idea of which once was frightening) can yield a self-esteem and pride in her own accomplishments perhaps greater than any she has ever previously experienced.

People who are able to approach life's changes as a challenge "are willing to take some risks, but not excessive risks," according to Kobasa's studies. They also "are much more likely to transform events to their advantage and thus reduce their

SURVIVOR ATTITUDES | 255

level of stress." Less hardy people, on the other hand, are more likely to try to deny their stressful situations "by watching more TV, drinking too much, taking tranquilizers or other drugs, or sleeping more. These are self-defeating tactics, since the real source of stress does not go away."[7]

Particularly when one's loss is a traumatic one, a full-blown grief reaction taking months or even a few years may be needed before a person is able to transform the impact of a tragic event so that it is no longer destructive or crippling. Getting involved in work, family, self-improvement activities, and relationships with others instead of holding back from life, believing that you *can* make a difference in your own life circumstances, and accepting change as a challenge—all of these behaviors and attitudes contribute to good health and a positive outcome in times of personal crisis or stress.

No matter what problem life has given you to deal with, you may find it helpful to review the following attitudes which are typical of survivors:

- ☐ I will vividly examine the future.
- ☐ I will not be defeated.
- ☐ My God, I'm lucky.
- ☐ I will take advantage of the available opportunities.
- ☐ Nobody's perfect.
- ☐ There is still time for me.
- ☐ There must be some meaning to be found or seen in these events.
- ☐ I will not assume the victim posture.
- ☐ I can do it if I set my mind.
- ☐ I have to be willing to expand.
- ☐ I am consciously deciding to be in the company of good people.
- ☐ We will find a way to get what we want.
- ☐ I will accept life's challenge.

*There is, for all of us, a point at which
not growing means diminishing. A
point at which we can only choose
between despair or change.*

ELLEN GOODMAN,
TURNING POINTS

For most people the recovery process seems to take forever. Nevertheless, it is a process with identifiable components and phases. Milestones mark the way when people are growing, changing, and healing.

CARLOS LOPEZ: FINDING THE BEST HELP AVAILABLE

For most people, "fluency" in a language refers to the person's command of the language—how well the person deals with grammar, vocabulary, and pronunciation. For Carlos Lopez, a third-generation American, "fluency" in English was a problem of a different nature.

Carlos began stuttering when he was six years old and starting the first grade. Like most stutterers, throughout school Carlos was afraid of ridicule. He had a particular fear of words that started with hard sounds like "d" and "p." He hid his stutter by developing an elaborate list of synonyms for the words that would lead to stuttering. He also learned to avoid talking on the telephone and stayed away from other situations in which he would be called on to answer someone immediately. Carlos got along well with others and was popular in school, and in that way he felt good about himself. His parents never sought professional help for him, probably because he seemed happy as a boy and young man.

In college Carlos's life changed. After his first year on campus he married Maria, his high school sweetheart. They soon were expecting a baby and facing serious questions about having a family and career. Carlos's speech seemed to become more inept, or at least it worried him more. Feeling worse and worse about the stuttering, he also became more self-conscious. He realized that he couldn't continue avoiding so many situations. He wondered if something inside him was causing this problem, and he wanted to understand it. Deathly afraid of telephones, he went in person to a speech pathology center to inquire about getting treatment.

"The treatment was useful," says Carlos, "because it was the first time I really was able to talk about my stuttering and my feelings about it and to meet other people like me. You tend to feel there isn't anybody else like you." At two different speech treatment centers at major universities Carlos sought help for several years. From meeting other stutterers he learned to be more open so that he could discuss his stuttering with almost anybody. Another healthy benefit was that he no longer felt "weird and isolated in the world."

Many people believe nobody else feels what they're feeling and no one struggles as they do. In some cases social stigmas make it difficult to confide in others, but often healing strength can be found in the company of others who have had similar experiences. Even when there is no stigma attached to the personal crisis, talking with like-minded people contributes to healing.

Although treatment in college provided a useful support

system to Carlos, it also added to his problems. At that time he learned that a stutterer may cause his or her own problem by trying not to stutter. "It is you who are doing it, so stop trying not to stutter and the stuttering will cease," was the message Carlos heard. There was also an emphasis on looking for psychological problems presumed to be underlying the condition.

The treatment didn't work. Carlos ended up feeling worse about himself because this approach intensified a sense of hopelessness. "I blamed myself a lot of the time," Carlos explains. "I thought it probably was related to something about me that was screwed up, some hidden thing about my psyche, and here it was being expressed."

RECOGNIZING AND RECEIVING ENCOURAGEMENT

After finishing his bachelor's and master's degrees, Carlos decided to go on for a doctorate in political science. What attracted him most was the idea of teaching college students, but then he thought about lecturing daily to rooms full of people. What would it be like to have to make a living speaking in public? He was frightened when he thought about becoming a college professor, but he knew it was what he wanted to do.

In the year before he completed his Ph.D. at the University of Chicago, Carlos gave a seminar that most graduate students are required to present. One of his fellow graduate students said, "Carlos, you're going to be a really good teacher."

"I can still see him in that room. It's very vivid to me," says Carlos. "Here was a person who thought I could be a good teacher even though I stuttered. He was someone I liked a lot. It was important to hear it from him."

In graduate school Carlos took a number of political science courses with Dr. Harmon, "the best teacher I've ever had, a real model as far as teaching is concerned." This enthusiastic professor was a genuine human being, worked well with students, and could explain things in clear and understandable ways. "He was a character," Carlos says. "He liked to make jokes and said some very funny things. He made it fun to go to class. At the same time you felt like you learned easily and well, you felt comfortable there." Carlos decided that Dr. Harmon was the kind of political science professor *he* wanted to be.

It is interesting that what encouraged Carlos, a person who had been stuttering for almost two decades, was watching a professor whose strength was explaining ideas in clear and understandable ways. "This is how it can be to be a good teacher," Carlos thought to himself. Although he didn't express his doubts out loud, Carlos did wonder at times if he could do it.

The admired professor noticed Carlos's determination to do well in his studies and recognized his considerable promise. "He was one of the few adults I encountered in college and grad school who made me feel good about myself," says Carlos. "He made me feel that even though I stuttered, I was a capable person. He treated me in a normal, natural way. Other adults were patronizing. He treated me as an equal."

Being treated like a normal human being is a common thread among people who tell me their healing stories. When loved ones and others continue to behave toward the hurting person in the usual ways, healing takes place more readily. Virtually none of us wants other people to feel sorry for us. When those close to us clearly do not see us as broken and fragile, we are able sooner to see wholeness in ourselves.

It works both ways. Healing takes place more readily when we present ourselves to others as persons consisting of more than our emotional wounds or physical limitations. Continuing to meet our usual responsibilities and living normally as best we can helps others to treat us in nonpatronizing ways.

TAKING COURAGE FROM AFFIRMATIONS
PAST AND PRESENT

When Dr. Harmon left the University of Chicago to chair a department of political science at a new branch of the University of North Carolina, he asked Carlos to be the first full-time member of that department. It was a new university, where good teaching instead of academic research would be emphasized. Carlos jumped at the opportunity to go to such a creative institution. He remembers how good he felt that Dr. Harmon had the confidence in him to ask for his help in starting a new venture.

Carlos's life as a college professor was up and down. Unbearable days would be followed by several days of being reasonably fluent. During fluency periods Carlos's commitment to good teaching was sharply in focus, and he felt hopeful about his new career.

His struggle took place not merely in the classroom. Some situations were more difficult than others: talking on the telephone, meeting new people who were authority figures, having strangers ask him for some specific information. A stranger could stop her car and ask, "Where is Oak Street?" and ruin Carlos's day. Many stuttering situations embarrassed him.

"There were times when I could hardly get through my lectures, and I was exhausted. When you're stuttering and working not to stutter, you feel wiped out. On the tough days it would seem to me that every word was a struggle. I didn't want to be there. I didn't want to be with anybody, because every time I said a word I felt lousier about myself." There were many days when Carlos wanted to slam his book shut, walk out of the classroom, and never teach again.

At the beginning of a semester Carlos was fluent. "I would enter the classroom pretty hyped up. I would tell the students right off the bat that I stuttered, and it would make them more at ease. Having laid things on the table, we didn't have to hide things."

One student, a recovering heroin addict who had recently gone "cold turkey," sought Carlos's counsel one day after class. A Vietnam combat veteran, he told his professor of the struggle he was having staying away from heroin. He described the crimes he had once committed in his desperation for money to buy the drug. "I came to you for help," the student said, "because I figured if you can teach with that stutter maybe I can solve my problems, too!"

They became friends. Carlos saw the young man through the worst of his ordeal in the early months without heroin and also helped him find a professional counselor. "That experience was as important for me as it was for my student," Carlos says. "Here was someone with what seemed like an insurmountable problem, and I felt like I could help. I knew how important it was to have a person who could hold you up when you needed it."

In times of discouragement Carlos learned to invoke the memory of his fellow graduate student in Chicago, the friend who knew Carlos would become a good teacher. He also remembered his high school years. People had liked him then for his personality, his ability to accept different types of people, his way of treating others with respect and consideration. He remembered Dr. Harmon's faith in his abilities and promise. "Carlos, you're really a very capable person," he would hear Dr. Harmon say. "Don't put yourself down. You can do it!" He realized that voices of encouragement from the past could strengthen his determination to succeed in the present.

Carlos spoke slowly, was very well organized, and wrote a lot of things on the board. Students applaud such teaching techniques because they enable the students to comprehend easily. Like his mentor, he brought a sense of humor into the classroom and could even tell jokes about stutterers. He was an easygoing type of personality, yet a political scientist who was knowledgeable and well prepared. His students enjoyed learning. When a student would tell him that his classroom had a comfortable feeling, Carlos smiled. He remembered that feeling from Dr. Harmon's classes.

Several years after Carlos became a college professor in North Carolina, his students presented him with an award for outstanding teaching. "TO CARLOS LOPEZ, PH.D.," the plaque reads, "AN EXCELLENT PROFESSOR AND A FINE HUMANITARIAN." He had come a long way even without being fluent.

DELIBERATE SEARCHING

In the meantime Carlos read avidly and studied everything he could get his hands on that would help him learn more about his problem. He learned that a series of complex physiological conditions could cause stuttering. Four times as many males as females have the problem. There was also a theory that there is an inherited predisposition or biological basis for stuttering. Many new therapies were emerging with a focus on the mechanical aspects of speech production, and Carlos felt encouraged.

Years of deliberate investigation and a dogged determination to search out an improvement to his situation produced results. One Sunday, sitting at home in front of the fireplace with his wife, Carlos boldly declared, "I *don't want* to stutter. I want to find someone who can help me *not* do it." For so many years he had dared not speak aloud this yearning.

Carlos read about the Hollins Communications Research Institute in Roanoke, Virginia, where a new stuttering treatment program was underway. It was what he wanted. Instead of taking a psychological approach, the clinicians at Hollins emphasized physiology. Annie Glenn, former astronaut John Glenn's wife, had once been a severe stutterer, and she was said to give public speeches quite well since being treated in Roanoke. In an intensive speech retraining program, Carlos would learn to voice and articulate his sounds and words in a new way.

"It changed the world for me," Carlos says. "It's not as if I'm cured, as there probably isn't a cure for stuttering. Yet I learned that I can have some power over this thing. I'm not one hundred percent fluent, but I'm much more fluent than I ever was. I know that if I keep practicing the speech retraining techniques, I can be fluent. I feel much better about myself, have more confidence. Every stutterer can strive to be more fluent. I can't tell you how good that feels."

CONTINUING TO GET NEEDED HELP

Carlos was helped by the right marriage partner and the couple's determination to weather their periods of difficulty. "Maria has always been the kind of person who would not feel sorry for me, even when that's what I thought I wanted and needed," explains Carlos. "In past years the little boy inside would want Maria to not expect so much of me, but she wouldn't treat me like that. In the long run her attitude was beneficial. It helped me to grow, to confront things myself."

In having a wife who was warm and loving but would not foster a sense of dependency, Carlos was called on to account for things. Maria loved her husband but made him responsible for himself.

There were some problems in the marriage, and Carlos went for professional help. "The counselor helped me see a lot of the ways in which I was trying to depend on Maria. I was acting like a teddy bear, trying to get her to take care of me. My mother had died recently, and I was feeling dissatisfied with how my relationship with Maria was going."

"Carlos, your mother is dead," the counselor told him. "She is gone, and you can't make your wife be like her."

Carlos knew that he needed to hear what the counselor was saying. He continued in counseling for about six months and realized that he wasn't allowing Maria to be herself. He learned a lot about himself and made many changes in a relatively short period. The results have been lasting.

Carlos Lopez was a triumphant survivor long before he went to Virginia and gained a new level of fluency in his speech. The plaque that he received from his students in North Carolina was presented to him eight years before he entered the Hollins Communications Research Institute.

Dr. Carlos Lopez has been a successful college professor for many years. Sometimes he thinks his teaching was probably better when he had so much trouble with the stuttering. It was necessary at that time to prepare more thoroughly and speak more slowly. Then and now, though, his students consider him one of the best.

MAKING STRIDES TOWARD INDEPENDENCE

The story of how people grow and change is often the story of gradually widening strides toward independence that take place over many years. People rarely learn a new way of life quickly. Old patterns of thinking and behaving usually require a significant passing of time before they can be broken down and replaced.

Betty, described in an earlier chapter, relinquished a newborn baby for adoption, a decision that she later regretted. She simply obeyed her father. After her husband abandoned her and their toddler son, Betty also looked to her older sister and brother-in-law to take care of her and tell her what to do. Later her second husband, Dennis, took over the caretaking role. "It seemed I always had to have somebody look out for me," Betty remembers. "And Dennis did a good job. When our youngest child went to kindergarten, my husband found a part-time job for me—I didn't even have to go out and look for work."

After the first three years of therapy, in which Betty struggled to deal with the mental illness of one of her sons and the grief she felt over relinquishing her daughter nearly twenty years earlier, Dennis urged her to quit therapy. She continued without telling him, managing to pay for the monthly sessions by selling some of her artwork and by carefully budgeting household expenses. She opened her own bank account and grew in independence and self-confidence.

Betty's therapist encouraged her to "stand on her own two feet" and speak up for what she wanted. She had considered quitting school because her husband didn't like the idea of her going to college. Both the college courses and seeing the supportive therapist were critical elements in Betty's continuing personal development and eventual ability to make peace with events in the distant past.

In recent years Betty has begun to assert herself at home, contributing her opinions to family decisions. "I used to be passive and obedient," she explains. "Whatever Dennis wanted, that's what we did. I was brought up to believe that this is the way a woman should be, and that's how I had been with my father, too."

Their marriage was turbulent until Dennis accepted Betty's college activities and her assertiveness at home. Betty says, "He is trying to understand me now."

THERESA: SURVIVING A BROTHER'S SUICIDE

When Theresa was eighteen years old, her brother committed suicide by taking a drug overdose. The story of Theresa's shock, anguish, and anger in the months immediately following her brother's death is told in *Living Through Personal Crisis*. Theresa struggled with her own suicidal yearnings while mourning bitterly the tragic loss of her twenty-five-year-old brother. Most suicide survivors have a long and difficult bereavement journey. Theresa's pilgrimage toward a new life spanned an even longer period of time than usual because she came from a family of negative-thinking, frightened, self-destructive people.

Her mother was a virtual recluse who stayed in the house most of the time as Theresa grew up. The mother was afraid of social situations, was dependent on her children to accompany her in those rare instances when she did go out, and was described by Theresa as someone who always seemed "helpless and without self-confidence." Theresa remembers her as always wearing the same housedress and spending much time in front of the television set. She seemed to have a difficult time coping with routine household chores, and Theresa has memories of dishes not put away, empty boxes and jars not disposed of, and old newspapers and magazines accumulated in great stacks throughout the house. Even as a young girl, Theresa saw the cluttered house and accumulated junk as a symbol of her mother's life in disarray. The giant stacks of messy newspapers everywhere were also, she remembered, a tremendous fire hazard in a family where both parents were chain-smokers.

The father in this family with five children had a "back-breaking factory job," as Theresa remembers it, "and kept the same job for thirty years without making any effort to improve his lot." She remembers him as a self-defeating person without goals. Theresa felt her father showed his fear of hoping for any improvements in the quality of his own life by making negative comments whenever Theresa expressed high expectations such as announcing her desire to be the first in the family to attend college. He was a man with a fatalistic attitude about life, neglectful in self-care and health habits, who always said he didn't need a retirement plan because "I'm just going to die anyway before I live that long."

Her parents' options were narrowed by negative thinking, by fear, and by reason of having married and had children at an early age, she concluded. Theresa made a decision in early adolescence, which she expressed in the journal she kept almost daily in her teens: She would not marry as young as her parents had done and she wanted to make something of herself.

There would be numerous "relapses and dark times," as she puts it, "tragedies and setbacks," even repeated periods of depression over the years when she contemplated suicide. Nevertheless, while still quite young, Theresa determined that she would have a better life than her parents'.

My good friend Rick Lamplugh once used the analogy of a champion thoroughbred racehorse to talk about triumphant survivors. "Something in the horse makes it want to run for the roses," said Rick, "but you can't just put the horse out on the track. You have to have a good trainer and a plan to go with it."

Theresa's early training and the plan she fashioned came from reading books. She developed the reading habit at an early age. In her early teens she got a part-time job in a neighborhood drugstore, where there was a lending library, and she got into the habit of bringing books home. She read books by and about women, fiction and nonfiction, including every feminist book out at the time. "I read about people trying to make a life for themselves," she told me, "books by women who had had husbands and children and decided that wasn't enough, and books by women daring to develop their full potential."

While a teenager she also spent a great deal of time talking to other girls' mothers in search of advice, companionship, and role models. "I got to see," Theresa remembers, "that there were other kinds of females, other kinds of families. I began to realize that once I got on my own, I could create my environment and have life be the way I wanted it: I could *be somebody* and make a good life for myself."

Her journal writing, her short stories, and her poems were a way of helping Theresa to release troubled feelings and hopeful yearnings. During some family tragedies she would temporarily be unable to write but would eventually get a handle on the crisis by describing her reactions on paper. In keeping with the self-destructive family theme, the tragedies she observed included an elder brother who was an alcoholic and had several run-ins with the law, an elder sister who was the victim of repeated wife beating, and a younger sister who had some disfiguring scars on her face, an unfortunate reminder of the days when she would recklessly "play" with dangerous cleaning supplies, until, at the age of nine, she had an accident with some of the chemicals. Clearly Theresa was endeavoring to cope with and escape from the impact of severe family problems even before her brother's suicide dealt another massive blow.

Another sister, just two years older than Theresa, managed to escape her negative environment. Her stability was due in part to a teacher who had become interested in her during her freshman year in high school and who had helped her to gain some self-esteem and motivate her desire for a better life. Marrying young and moving out of her parents' home at the age of nineteen after high school graduation, she found a decent and hard-working young man who treated her with respect. They were able to share a good, if not luxurious, life.

Theresa, an eighteen-year-old college student living at home, began to see me for professional counseling for a nine-month period beginning shortly after her brother's suicide. I had been her psychology teacher and had taken a special interest in this bright young girl who had seemed depressed even before her brother's death.

Earning money for her tuition and books by taking placebos and experimental drugs for a government-funded research project, Theresa lacked financial resources. I arranged for her to receive counseling at a greatly reduced fee and to work it off by doing such odd jobs as painting my garage. I also encourged her to apply for an educational loan and quit that awful job of putting unknown drugs into her body for money!

Laboring through sorrow over the loss of her brother and battling the anger she felt at the self-destructiveness rampant in her family, Theresa moved through the early stages of a grieving process. As her suicidal depression gradually began to lift, it became possible for her to make decisions for the future.

"I've got a tooth that's really bothering me," Theresa announced one day at her therapy session. "The dentist says I need a root canal and I wish I could do that, but it costs an awful lot of money. My dad said to just have it pulled."

"That's typical of him," I remember muttering to myself, feeling protective of Theresa like a mother or older sister. "Eighteen is really too young to start pulling out your teeth," I said aloud, restraining myself. People who are planning to kill themselves don't go to the pain, trouble, and expense of getting a root canal, I reasoned silently. I wanted to support Theresa in building her life, and this dental problem was an important symbol of her future. "Let's try to find someplace affordable so you can have the root canal and save that tooth," I continued. "There's a dental school downtown where perhaps you can get the work done for a lot less money."

Years later Theresa told me that those practical things I did, such as offering odd jobs and advice about self-care were helpful. She also recalled, however, that at times she resented my not helping her more by offering therapy free or even by having her move into my house in order to get her away from the influence of her self-destructive family. She looked up to me and relied on me for strength and support as a surrogate family member, she said, and at that time she didn't see why I couldn't just help take care of her. Now, of course, Theresa understands that she had had to learn to be independent and that I was helping her to grow by gradually separating her not only from her parents but also from me.

SURROUNDING ONESELF WITH BENEFICIAL PEOPLE

Theresa had always chosen her male companions well, perhaps as a result of reading so many books by and about women from early adolescence and also as a consequence of having determined in her youth to have egalitarian relationships with men who would support her need to be an independent person. Her boyfriend from the age of eleven was Raymond, a fun-loving and good-hearted person with whom she enjoyed a pleasurable, nurturing relationship and the ability to communicate honestly about innermost feelings.

When Raymond went away to college, Theresa began dating Jay, always being honest with him about the fact that she continued to love Raymond. She was dating Jay at the time of her brother's suicide and for several years thereafter. The fact that this was a loving relationship was helpful to her during this difficult time. Jay was a kind, sensitive, and caring young man who drove her or loaned her his car so that she could come for our weekly counseling sessions. She was so deeply depressed that I was afraid that she, too, would commit suicide, and having her come at least weekly for counseling was very important.

Once Theresa had gained a small measure of independence, she and Jay, armed with scholarships and student loans, decided to go away to a college hundreds of miles from home, where they would each live in a dormitory and have a first taste of life totally away from family. It was hard for Theresa to leave therapy and her relationship with me, since she didn't feel ready to function without my active and present support, yet she felt a great need to get some distance from her family and to grow independent. After a year of dormitory life, Theresa and Jay moved into an apartment, which they shared while continuing their studies. Once or twice she tried to establish a new counseling relationship for herself but was not successful. Instead she drew strength from the healthy relationship with Jay, benefited from several important new friendships, and kept in contact with Raymond throughout. She also contacted me from time to time through letters or an occasional session when the couple came home for holiday visits. I remained for Theresa a symbol unlike the self-destructive people in her family. Even after moving away she relied on me as a role model and got energy from our relationship. A sense of competency gradually emerged from her college teachers' positive response to her academic work, as well as from such personal victories as overcoming her fear of speaking in public by giving speeches in class, learning to drive a standard transmission automobile, and getting herself through college with scholarships and loans.

Jay was "a deep-down optimist," Theresa remembers. Over the following years they enjoyed "a playful relationship," prompting others to remark on how much fun they had together. They enjoyed a stuffed animal family and joked that the animals were their children, shared "inside jokes," wrote humorous notes, and enjoyed tickling each other and having playful wrestling sessions. The young couple also shared their innermost feelings, ideas, and aspirations. Her choice of a good man like Jay to be her lover and almost constant companion over the critical years between eighteen and twenty-one made a tremendous difference in Theresa's having the ability to grow and change.

Eventually, however, Jay and Theresa amicably went their separate ways. Theresa and Raymond married, and Theresa went to graduate school for a master's degree in journalism. Shortly after she married Raymond, Jay met a woman, married, and happily had three children.

HAVING A POSITIVE ATTITUDE

While working on her master's degree, Theresa found a good counselor, another woman who became in her mind what I had been earlier: a combination teacher, role model, friend, and the positive-thinking healthy big sister she had lacked at home. From the therapist's important influence and Theresa's continued reading of psychology books, she learned at least four important new ways of thinking: (1) It is not a disaster when things don't go my way, (2) I have control over most of the circumstances in life that cause me to feel unhappy, (3) I can depend on myself and don't always have to have somebody nearby who is stronger than I, and (4) it is not the past that shapes who and what I am or will be but my own attitudes, values, and actions.

From her good work in graduate school, Theresa learned that she really could succeed even while fearing failure. From her therapist and from doing well on her own and achieving her educational and career goals without family support, she learned that she could be proud of herself and be encouraged. "And I learned," she says, "that when I do things competently or work hard to excel, I make life better for myself and make my future more hopeful."

Theresa says that she feels like "the composite of all the women I ever met who seem assured and who seem to be achieving something they enjoy in jobs or through motherhood." She has advanced in her journalism career to an important editorial position for a nationally known company, continues to enjoy her marriage to Raymond and their friendship with several other couples who have become extended family to them, and is considering having children.

CHOOSING A LIFE OF HOPE

"It was a long way from there to here," I said to Theresa, remembering that she had had serious thoughts of suicide throughout her teenage years. I was now interviewing her for *Coming Back*.

"I see I've come a long way," Theresa replied, rather quietly. "I never thought when I was eighteen years old, with a brother dead from suicide, that I'd ever get well enough to be an example to someone else. I still have cycles of depression. Some months are better, some are worse. Yet I've managed to recognize my bad times for what they are and cope with them. Seeing that you come out on the other side every time and that usually things will look much better later on has taught me a patience with life that helps a lot."

Often where there is a family history of depression, alcoholism, or suicide, a depressed family member may need antidepressant medication in order to get better. A chemical imbalance can cause depression, as can destructive family patterns and learned perspectives on life. Medication prescribed by a physician knowledgeable about the treatment of depression may be necessary in addition to receiving help from a professional counselor and other "beneficial people."

"There's still a lot to work on, ways I can grow, yet even when I feel really, really down, I don't want to die anymore. No matter how bad it gets, I'd rather think of a way to get through it instead of giving up. I just feel a lot less passive now. I can't stand to see this fatalistic thing that you can't change your life."

Theresa did manage to break the family pattern. She learned how to take care of herself, how to dream, live hopefully, and choose healthy relationships and good people to share her life with.

Theresa, at the impressionable age of eighteen, saw in me someone who was a symbol of hope. I was in my early thirties, divorced, a college professor and counselor, was studying for my doctorate, writing a book, and had recently purchased a home on my own. Other than the fact that I was at the time a heavy smoker like her parents, it must have appeared to Theresa that I was living a life very different from the members of her family who always seemed so unhappy, lacking in goals and the ability to take care of themselves adequately. My friend and one of my own most important mentors, the late Dr. Richard Goodling, said, "If you push people" who are triumphant survivors to account for their ability to prevail over adversities of various kinds, "they will always be able to identify a role model."

Theresa also grew from reading books, talking with her

friends' mothers, choosing her male companions wisely and well, and keeping a journal that enabled her to reflect on and examine life in a careful and intensive way rarely typical of a person so young. Another important aspect of Theresa's growth was her determination to go to college. There she met many role models and new friends, was affirmed in her intellectual and creative abilities, and grew in independence and self-knowledge. Her decision to get an education was a key factor in her continuing growth and ability to forge a life for herself far removed from the alcoholism, suicide, domestic violence, victimization, tragic and careless accidents, and other self-destructiveness in her family.

I was once asked what was the most important decision I had ever made in my life. I was then in my thirties, but I'll give the same answer now and would expect to always reply similarly. College. The decision to attend college changed and shaped the course of my life more dramatically than any other decision. While the decision to have a child has made me happier than anything ever pondered, virtually every opportunity and most satisfactions in my life have come because of the doors that were opened by my educational pursuits. Not everyone is as dependent on education to open up life's treasure chest as I was.

One can see other examples of fortuitous, positive decisions. A friend tells me it was moving to New York after graduation from college that changed her life in the direction of permanent improvement in the quality of her relationships, family life, and career opportunities. Although it was thirty-six years ago, my friend still looks on her life as being in two parts—*before* moving to New York and *after* moving to New York. For many women a decision made to get a job outside the home divides their lives, or the decision made by any individual to leave a job or marriage that has ceased to satisfy or be growth-producing. One of the most significant ways that people grow and change is by having the courage to move in completely new directions, sizing up the available opportunities and taking the plunge.

I sat across from Theresa and couldn't avoid smiling. Here she was sitting in the same soft chocolate brown corduroy chair in my study where she had sat in sorrowful days, ten years earlier. The corduroy chairs had been new then. That was before they had become decorated with baby formula and other assorted food spots, miscellaneous crumbs, and Cheerios under the seat cushions—signs of my own life changes. Theresa, who as a much younger person had once fought so hard to find strength and a reason to live, is now well educated as a result of her own efforts, is thriving in a good marriage and rewarding job, and is functioning well and independently.

At some point Theresa may still suffer episodes of depression severe enough to require professional help. Antidepressant medication under medical supervision may be needed, although it has been unnecessary up to now. Severe depression often runs in families and is clearly a major theme in Theresa's family. Just as people with diabetes must take insulin, people with a biological predisposition to bouts of depression often require medication for a period of time in order to find relief.

"I used to think things would all be solved to the point of doing away with relapses and dark times," Theresa told me. She is aware now that life does not work that way for any of us and perhaps especially not for suicide survivors.

The journal that Theresa kept over the years has contributed toward her progress. Journal or letter writing can be an important source of strength and a way to record one's journey. On reading back over journal or diary entries one can see progress and growth that were not evident at the time of the writing.

Paula D'Arcy, pregnant when her young daughter and husband were killed in a car accident in which she was injured, found that writing was meaningful and extremely helpful in preparation for the new baby. In her book *Song for Sarah*, she writes many lovely letters and poems to the daughter who was lost, sharing the struggle and her hope for recovery. On one occasion she turned to a priest for counseling. She then tells the lost child of a new revelation, beseeching her daughter for permission to go on with her life:

> You may not believe it, but Father Jim said that the way I am is normal! All of it. All this craziness, normal. NORMAL! I may not be a madwoman. In fact, one day I could be me again. I know that right now that's just an idea. But it's such a strong, positive one. Do you understand? I could keep having these awful moments of remembering you both, and even think that I won't live past the pain. And still one day I could find that it is better. That I'm all right. It's the strongest hope I've had. I might be me again! Please don't resent it if I do recover. Don't resent it if I want this new baby. I think I do. I think I dare to love again.[1]

STARTING OVER

"My first impulse," Ed said, talking about his feelings following the death of his young son, "was to put my wife Jan and my surviving son in the car, set fire to the house, and drive away. I knew soon after we lost Mark, there was no question about it, that the family would leave the house, the city, the state, and try to start over in a new environment."

Not everyone finds it necessary to make a clean break when a loss occurs. In my counseling experience with grieving people, those suffering an especially traumatic or violent loss seemed to have the greatest need for a major environmental change. Rape, incest, murder, suicide, and violent accidents, for example, which occur at home, at work, or close to one of these places often has an abiding psychological impact that can be tied to the setting where the event took place. In certain situations creating a permanent physical distance can be an important element in the chemistry that produces healing.

Ed's little boy had been struck by a speeding driver in front of their house while Ed's wife watched from the family car. Although it would be painful to leave their friends in the neighborhood and community, Ed and Jan knew that they would need to move when Ed completed two years of advanced medical training there. This couple decided it would be just too difficult to go on with their lives unless they moved far away, to another state.

People who escape the powerful hold of tragedy over their lives are often those who have made early decisions about how a new beginning is possible. In addition to the important decision to move, Ed and Jan benefited from a decision that each made separately, based on each one's individual reason not to be broken by their loss. "I thought that I owed it to Mark not to lose my life, too," Ed explained, wanting to honor his lost son's memory by going forward. "I have to be alive for John," Jan concluded, referring to her younger, surviving son. "John needs us, and he isn't going to stop needing us because Mark died."

Starting over becomes possible after one clearly and specifically weighs the advantages and disadvantages of any changes that would support growth and becomes clear about why life is still worth living.

SEEING HOW HAPPINESS IS POSSIBLE AGAIN

For a long time Ed wondered whether he "could ever be happy again." He thought that "being happy meant not being sad," but that would be impossible, he realized, since he would *always* be sad to have lost his son. Finally Ed's understanding changed. "I realized it has to be possible to be happy and incredibly sad at the same time. Otherwise I was just doomed."

Four months after Mark's death, Ed and Jan attended an

outdoor music festival and saw cloggers dancing on stage. Jan "burst out laughing" when she saw the folk dancers "looking like marionettes with none of their body parts connected." She realized she hadn't laughed like that since Mark died. The couple started clogging lessons about a year after their bereavement began and have continued the lessons in the years since. It is interesting that Jan and Ed have kept up with the activity that first made laughter possible in those horribly difficult, early months of mourning.

JIM: A VIOLENT CRIMINAL WHOSE BEHAVIOR AND LIFESTYLE DRAMATICALLY CHANGED

Jim Townsend grew up in the Great Depression of the 1930s, when life was difficult, especially for a family with five kids spaced over twelve years and an alcoholic father. Jim's mother was always sick with asthma. Jim remembers only once or twice when she was out of bed and able to do anything.

From a very young age Jim was always "busting into someplace, stealing something." He was only eight years old when he was classified as an incorrigible delinquent and sent to reform school. "I had a reputation for having more guts than common sense," Jim says.

He was in and out of reform school until the age of twelve. Then his mother died, and his father placed him in a Christian Brothers' orphanage. He kept running away and eventually was returned to reform school. When he was fourteen years old and at his father's urging, Jim lied about his age and joined the marines. He couldn't take the discipline, and he lasted only six or seven months. Because he was underage, he was given a dishonorable discharge instead of time in the brig.

The first time Jim went to prison, for assault and battery and attempted rape, he was sixteen years old. He came out at twenty. He got a painting job, continued to commit various crimes, drank a lot, and joined a gang. Once, during an argument, a girl named Judy slapped him. He broke her jaw. The female gang leader came to Judy's defense. She gave Jim a fierce beating, put her foot on his jaw, and then literally picked him up and carried him to her place. That humiliating experience stayed with him for years.

"If I was an animal before," says Jim, "I was really an animal then. I hated women. I learned everything ugly about women and sex."

Jim decided he wanted a particular girl, Alice. According to a rule in the gang, a girl had to get inside a circle and the guy had to bid money for her. "When she went into that circle I wanted her so bad that I threw nine hundred dollars out there. But no matter what I bid, Judy put in twenty-five cents more. Judy said, get her legal, meaning get married. I took Alice to dinner, to the movies, bought her flowers and candy, and the con worked. She said she'd marry me.

"The idea of connecting with one person was galling me. I thought I'd marry her and then I'd go my way and she'd go hers. I'd go back and laugh at Judy, is how I saw it. But I had never had, from anybody, the warmth and understanding Alice was giving me, so I didn't leave as I thought I would. I stayed with her.

"I still kept going with the gang and other girls, and that got back to Alice. I told her it was all a lie, and she believed me. I learned about forgiveness then, funny as it seems."

Then Jim lost his painting job, and he and Alice went to a farm, where he worked as a caretaker. "Alice fell in love with the place," says Jim, "loved the baby chicks and other animals. I did my job but I didn't like it there even though it was a pretty place."

"One day I hitchhiked in to Johnstown, Pennsylvania, and found my kind of people. I drank and played cards with them, but when I realized they were cheating me, I got mad and started to fight. All five guys beat me up. I was drunk and went home after a rifle to shoot those guys who beat me. When Alice tried to stop me, I pushed her back. The second time she pushed me I shot her. She was pregnant at the time.

"I became cold sober. I had never taken a life before. But I was so mad I kicked Alice's dead body, blaming it all on her."

Jim tried to make it appear as if he and his wife had been attacked and robbed, but the police saw through his story. He was sentenced to life in prison.

"For the first time in my life," explained Jim thirty-nine years later, "I realized I had lost something that was lovely."

I interviewed Jim in a busy, noisy airport restaurant, riveted to my chair for nearly five hours. I stared at his clerical collar. "How does a guy," I wondered, "kill his pregnant wife in a drunken rage, spend a lifetime in prison, and end up a brother in a religious order?" I was utterly amazed by Jim's story and absorbed in trying to figure him out.

Could someone really be severely damaged emotionally and morally incorrigible at the age of eight and become rehabilitated? Was it even safe for me to be sitting there talking with him? I suddenly realized that I had arranged to meet Jim in a place with a lot of people and activity because I was afraid.

Embarrassed by my private thoughts, I looked down at the plastic cafeteria tray and soiled dishes from our lunch together. When my eyes lifted, I fixed them on Jim's wrinkled black shirt and suit. This stockily built, balding, almost-sixty man in clerical clothing might have been a lumberjack or an oysterman in younger days. There was a rugged outdoor look about him. He had the appearance of a hard-working, honest-living type, not someone capable of robbery, rape, assault, and murder.

HAVING A CONSCIENCE

Nightmares tormented Jim after his first few months in the penitentiary. Again and again his pregnant wife appeared in the nightmares, staring at Jim with a sad expression. She held a little boy who asked, "Why, daddy?"

The tormenting sleep continued for many years. When he became violent after nightmares, beating on walls, yelling, and banging on a chair, he was put in a padded cell. He couldn't get the thoughts of Alice and the baby out of his mind. "The whole thing was like a glue, really sticking to me, and I couldn't get rid of it."

In his waking life Jim was furious at Alice. "Get away from me! It wasn't my fault—it was *your* fault! You don't understand," he argued in silent conversations. He shared his struggle with no one, presenting to others only toughness.

At times Jim couldn't help remembering the good moments with Alice. He tried not to let his thoughts get him down, yet he often despaired, at times realizing there was no hope that he would ever get out of prison. He was not eligible for parole.

That he still had a working conscience that could agonize over destroying Alice and their unborn child was the first indication that some hope existed for this violent, destructive, and immature man. Even though Jim was self-centered when he suffered for having robbed himself of "the only lovely thing I ever had," he recognized the difference between warm, lovely, trusting Alice and hostile, animalistic, cheating Jim.

ENCOUNTERING FORTUNATE FATE

"One day I woke up and realized I had done six years in prison and I was still looking at a life sentence in the place. About the same time there was a guy named Jack who wanted to have sex with me and was really persistent about it. I decided to kill myself and take him with me.

"We lived on the fifth range, meaning five stories high. I was going to throw him the hell off the range and go with him. I made arrangements to get together with him, but the day we were to meet, a big truck of goods came in and he had to work overtime unloading it.

"I went to my house [cell] and figured I'd just lie down a while until it was time for dinner. I had one of the best sleeps I'd ever had in my life. I woke up feeling good and rested. It just hit me that committing suicide was being a coward.

"I wasn't going to let these people beat me. The tougher they get, I decided, the tougher I'll get. So I went to Jack and told him, 'Leave me alone or I'll fix you and take the punishment.' He didn't bother me anymore, which is good because I would have killed him."

Jim was fortunate that fate kept him from committing another murder and then suicide. He was still alive. Waking up feeling well rested and good about the reprieve perhaps indicated a partially functioning conscience. Even a man who didn't deserve it, he decided, was going to have another chance.

ALLOWING ONE'S HEART GRADUALLY TO SOFTEN

As years went by, Jim schemed and planned for his escape. From another convict he learned about a nearby honor farm. Jim decided to get transferred there, build a good record, go to church, ask if he could learn how to drive in order to haul farm produce in the prison truck, eventually work outside the gates, then one day just keep driving and escape.

He managed to maneuver himself into the honor farm after nearly fifteen years in the penitentiary. "In my mind I had decided I'm going to 'Yes, sir' everybody, keep clean and neat, and have the best house you've ever seen."

As a way to get out of his cell at the penitentiary, Jim had gone to church in earlier years. He would sit in the back and walk out after the service got started. He didn't believe in God at the time. At the honor farm Jim also went to church. One day the prison chaplain asked him to join a religious group he had organized, the Third Order of St. Francis, an order for laypeople.

"I almost told him where he could shove it," Jim recalled, "but I figured this would go on my record."

The chaplain, Father Walsh, was shrewd. He set up a schedule in which they would all meet to study the scriptures, go to confession, and receive Holy Communion. Jim said to himself, "What the hell is this?" but he decided to go along with it and "make up some champion sins."

"I hated the chaplain's guts, anyway, so in confession I told him I had had sex with men and played with myself ninety-six times. It was all bullshit."

The chaplain would answer, "I know what you're going through; I'm a human being. It took me a long time to live with being celibate, too."

BEING INFLUENCED BY A STRONG AND DECENT HUMAN BEING

Jim went regularly to the religious meetings and reluctantly read the scriptures. One day he likened the Stations of the Cross to a baseball game and gave an interpretation that seemed to impress the chaplain. "I just wanted to please the priest and get that smile," he explains. "Some part of me wanted his approval as a father, even though I didn't see it that way at the time. At the time I saw it as conning him.

"Meeting good people can change things," observed Jim. "The priest was gentle and kind. I'd look at him as that 'little man,' but I began to wonder about him. 'I wonder, does he live his life the way he says?' I'd ask myself."

Jim found himself watching how the chaplain dealt with the other prisoners. He overheard a conversation between the priest and someone in the punishment cell where there are no visitors, no privileges, and no leaving the cell for a week or ten days. "How are you?" the priest asked the inmate. "What the fuck is it to you?" the man replied.

"Doesn't mean a fucking thing to me," answered the priest. "I just wanted to know if you're all right."

In some strange ways, Jim's respect for the chaplain grew as he observed this religious man who could be called a motherfucker and reply, "Well, so are you!"

Then the inmate who was head of the Third Order was transferred to another prison. Father Walsh wanted to put Jim in charge and give him various leadership jobs. Realizing that his being a leader would also look good on his record, Jim accepted.

Only inmates who seemed genuinely interested were allowed to join the Third Order of St. Francis. There were various stages of membership. Each participant had to be a postulate for three months and a novice for one year. After that he became "fully professed," which meant he would promise to live his life in a Christian manner. The inmates continued to have their regular prison job assignments, and there were no vows of poverty or celibacy because this was a religious group for laypeople.

It began to mean more and more to Jim that the priest thought well of him. Here was the attentive parent, the caring father Jim had never had. He would never have admitted it, even to himself, yet little by little his heart was opening. He was becoming less argumentative, less violent, and less negative in his attitudes and behaviors. He smiled more often, did his work well, even stopped smoking. He started to notice beauty—staring at a deer while on a work detail and noticing nature's colors as the seasons changed. The nightmares about Alice and the baby were abating.

The inmate janitor for the building where church services were held was going home in six months and asked Jim to leave his job as a painter and take his place. This was to become a major event in Jim's unfolding transformation. From his new job inside the church building, Jim was in a position to observe Father Walsh closely and to watch the men who came to him or were sent for counseling. "I saw guys come in crying and leave happy, come in tough and leave downcast, looking thoughtful."

CARING FOR ANOTHER PERSON AND BECOMING VULNERABLE

"I saw Bill, a new guy, coming in," related Jim. "He was real young, had blond hair, blue eyes, and rosy cheeks. I thought, 'Boy, is this kid going to be a sex object.' " Bill offered Jim his six-dollar-a-month commissary allowance to "be his pal" and protect him.

"All of a sudden," Jim explains, "I started looking at Bill as the son I never had. My wife had blond hair and blue eyes. I told Bill, 'I don't want your commissary, but I'll tell you how to take care of yourself.' "

Several weeks later Jim heard that Bill had had a nervous breakdown and had to go to a hospital outside. He was upset that the boy had had a problem and didn't share it with Jim.

Bill came back, six weeks later. Jim pushed him up against the wall and said, "You've got something on your mind, and you should have told me." Bill said he couldn't.

"I grabbed him by his shirt, took him to the first pew, and we sat down. I said the first prayer in my life and made Bill tell me what was wrong." Bill told Jim he had a twin sister. He had fallen in love with her, and they were living like man and wife. He had wanted to buy her a gift and had stolen for it.

"I saw all the hell he went through feeling so guilty about his sister," Jim told me. "I just loved him." Jim took Bill immediately to Father Walsh. Later he saw Bill come walking out alone, his shirt all sweaty. He looked relieved.

FACING AND TELLING THE TRUTH AND RECEIVING ACCEPTANCE

Later that afternoon Jim went into the confession box and kneeled down. When Father Walsh threw open the little door, Jim knew he "couldn't continue lying like a creep," but he was speechless. The priest said, "Do you need some help?"

"Father, I didn't do anything," he answered.

"Jim, it's about time," said Father Walsh.

Jim wondered how the priest knew it was he in the confessional and asked him. "I'm like a mechanic; I know my cars," he replied. "I know my people. Let's go into my office and talk turkey."

Father Walsh put a stole around his neck, signifying his priestly role and authority to receive confessions, and said, "This is just between you and me and the Lord."

Jim cried. He started from the beginning and released the whole story. "I'm no good," he said. "I did all these crazy things. I lied to you. I'm a con man. I hurt my parents. I stole from them. I robbed people. I committed rape. I drank too much. I only married Alice in the first place to prove something. I cheated on her. I killed her and blamed her like it was her fault. I killed our baby."

The priest listened and asked questions from time to time. He told Jim that these things had to follow each other, that Jim had had to hit rock bottom before there could be any hope for him.

After Jim's first genuine confession, which lasted about an hour and a half, Father Walsh prayed for Jim to be relieved of guilt and filled with love and peace. He asked God to let Jim "be an inspiration to others" and to help Jim understand that he was not a lost soul even though he was in prison.

"As a priest of God," he continued, "I forgive you your sins."

Jim never had another violent dream after that first honest communication. He returned to confession faithfully after that.

For three and a half years he poured out his heart in dozens of face-to-face sessions with Father Walsh.

LEARNING SELF-FORGIVENESS

"With peace coming into my heart," Jim explained, "I was able to bring things forth that I had hidden from myself. I talked about the women I had assaulted, my wrongs with Alice, my lies, everything that there was."

"One day I went in there and I just cried and cried. Father Walsh touched my hand and said, 'Hey, it takes a big man to cry.' Then he said, 'Always remember, Jim, yesterday is gone. You always get up today. Today is what matters.' "

"Father Walsh was my priest, my brother, my mother, my father, my friend. He would ask God to give me grace to live my life in quiet, to do my work well, to be at peace with myself, and to be able to help others when opportunities came. He would pray for the total healing of memories, even those I did not consciously remember."

At one point the priest actually had Jim say, "I forgive myself as well as others." They also prayed for Jim's victims, that wherever they were now they would be at peace, and that any scars left would go away.

"I knew that the crime of rape is very traumatic, that the women I raped would feel dirty and feel that no decent man would want them now. I prayed for them to know that's not true and be released from such thoughts."

Father Walsh would say, "Lord, you know the needs of these people," and he would help Jim find the words to pray for those he had hurt.

A dramatic and almost unbelievable transformation took place in the life of Jim Townsend, a violent and destructive individual, a seasoned criminal, a con man with a hardened heart. Jim changed over time because a decent human being entered the picture. Little by little, Jim's heart opened to observe and experience genuine caring and goodness in life. Through this straight-talking priest, Jim gradually saw a different way of looking at life.

When he allowed himself to approach Bill as the son he had never had, the child he had destroyed, Jim's transformation went into third gear. He made a decision to care about Bill, to look after him, to become vulnerable, perhaps for the first time in his life. Their kinship offered an open, understanding love. They could talk honestly and receive no judgment.

Jim learned to forgive himself with the help of Father Walsh, who offered him unconditional acceptance and positive regard. It was not easy to learn to trust this priest and to unravel his own twisted life in the sunlight. Father Walsh had the wisdom to teach Jim how to pray for his victims, and these prayers became an important part of his healing.

Some years passed. One night Jim had a dream in which Alice and the boy came to him again. This time she was smiling and the boy gave a message of love instead of torment. Jim never again dreamed of either of them.

HELPING OTHERS

Five times turned down for commutation of his sentence, Jim finally was freed from prison after serving twenty years for killing his wife. Counting the years in reform school, he had spent twenty-seven of his forty years in prison by the time he was released.

The last fifteen years of the nineteen that Jim has been free have been lived as a member of the Capuchin Brothers religious order. He made his final religious vows about ten years ago.

Jim is not harming society, and he is not unhappy. His lifelong problems no longer plague him. He has devoted himself to a life of prayer, serving his community as a building- and groundskeeper, and helping others by telling his story.

He speaks from time to time at church assemblies, at youth conferences, and in retreats held inside the prison walls he knows so well.

"I still pray for my past victims," says Jim. "I ask God to heal them and bring them peace."

His memories of his earlier life won't ever be easy for him. Jim strongly believes and feels, however, that he is forgiven. He lives his life out of the mainstream of society, away from the stresses of modern daily living, doing well in an atmosphere where he can function easily. Jim lives in celebration of the reality that new beginnings are almost always possible. So can we all.

ACCEPTING THE NORMALCY OF DIFFICULTIES, DOUBTS, AND UNCERTAINTY

When I had major surgery in my forties, it was the first time I had been so physically ill that I was unable to take care of myself. A single parent, I looked at my child and saw her vulnerability in a new way as well.

I had been contemplating the adoption of another child, but now I was feeling doubtful. Locating capable, responsible child care people was difficult, sometimes overwhelming. I had my share of horror stories to tell—of being abandoned when I was most in need of help.

My situation could have been worse. My illness was wholly curable, and many wonderful friends had come to my aid. I know that most of you who are reading this book have had far greater troubles to cope with. As Viktor Frankl wrote in his book on concentration camp survivors, suffering is like a gaseous substance: It completely fills the room no matter what is the source of the suffering.[2] At the time, I felt miserable and hopeless.

How am I going to look at this issue of single parenting? I asked myself. I can decide it's too much for me to think of adopting another baby, mourn, and then resign myself to having only one child. Or I can figure out ways to make it work even in times of sickness and vulnerability. There must be a means by which it is possible to screen out those child care people, I decided, who can't be counted upon to do the job for whatever reason. And surely, I told myself, I can build a support system for myself, as a single parent. Talking out loud in the dark helped me to feel not afraid. It worked. I began to get my courage back.

Numerous periods of doubt, worry, and concern followed. I went ahead with the parenting of my toddler, continued my work, let a few months go by, and started the elaborate paperwork to adopt a second child. I still wasn't sure if I was completely ready or how I would handle parenting two small children.

"What if my next child is a really difficult, disruptive new person in the family?" I asked one of my agency social workers. "Things are going really well now. Amanda is an easy child to raise, and we have a good life. What if there are big unexpected medical or psychological problems and our comfortable family life gets turned topsy-turvy?"

"Then you'll get help and you'll find solutions," the social worker answered.

Her reply made a lot of sense and began to bring a feeling of relief. "Oh, right," I said to myself. "Instead of catastrophizing all the things that could go wrong, I need to remember," I decided, and said aloud, "that most problems have solutions and are best solved one at a time as they arise. Even if the worst scenario of events took place and my happy little family was suddenly beset with problems, there would be trained people from whom to get advice and there would be findable solutions for coping with most of the problems."

There would occasionally be other times of doubting, but I was growing even though I couldn't recognize it at the time.

For the longest time it had been hard for me to believe that fate would allow me to have my own family, a place where clearly I belonged and where others felt they belonged as well. I had wrestled for years with the irrational feeling that since I often wasn't content it must be because I somehow didn't deserve to be. I wondered if a satisfying family life or marriage would ever happen for me. My way of thinking was a big part of the problem.

"The deep wish to be taken care of by others is the chief force holding women down," writes Colette Dowling. "I call this the Cinderella Complex. Like Cinderella, women today are still waiting for something external to transform their lives."[3] What needed to happen in my life was for me to take action and set about to make a good life for myself.

"CHANCING IT"

"Life needs mystery or else everything else flattens into a routine so familiar you wonder if you will ever get out of the rut," wrote sportswriter Dave Kindred. "We need the sweet pain of anticipation" to "tell us we are really alive." He was explaining why multimillionaire Sugar Ray Leonard would try to make a boxing comeback at the age of thirty, his boxer's prime behind him, having fought only one fight in the previous five years, and take on Marvin Hagler, a more aggressive and heavier fighter. "Leonard fights because life without it was a knockout" read Kindred's lead.[4]

In *Chancing It* by Ralph Keyes, the tale is told of the fascinating feat of wire walker Philippe Petit, who in 1974 seven times crossed a wire stretched between the two towering pillars of the World Trade Center in New York. Surviving crosswinds and a natural sway in the towers which some conjectured would render the twenty-one-ply, $7/8$-inch cable "likely to snap . . . like cheap cotton thread," Petit strolled and danced across a "138-foot cable strung 1,350 feet above lower Manhattan." During most of the forty-minute walk, he carried a fifty-five-pound balancing pole and at one point hushed the crowd below by lying down in the middle of the cable.[5]

Keyes wrote that several years after the famous feat he asked Petit how the wire walker came to be such a risk taker, and he was surprised by the Frenchman's reply. "In no way, shape, or form did he consider himself to be a taker of risks," said Keyes.[6]

"I have no room in my life for risk," Petit continued, as recorded in *Chancing It*. "You can't be both a risk taker and a wire walker. I take absolutely no risks. . . . I plan everything the most that I can. I put together with the utmost care that part of my life."[7]

Petit had been preparing since the age of six for his accomplishment at the World Trade Center and for other wire walks performed in Australia, France, the Astrodome in Houston, and elsewhere. At six he asked his parents for a book about learning mountain climbing. As a young man he apprenticed himself to a master wire walker, whom he later consulted about the Trade Center walk. He had first begun to ponder the walk in 1968, when he saw a sketch of the proposed 110-story structure. He and his associates visited and studied the building possibly a hundred times as it was being built.

He was twenty-four years old at the time of the World Trade Center wire walk, a man who knew how to build and study models to rehearse for his performances in gymnasiums where an "inch-by-inch, second-by-second plan" for a walk could be executed.

Petit is afraid of deep water, snakes, spiders, numerous animals, and marriage, and he walks up the stairs instead of risking a ride on an old elevator with creaky cables. Writes Keyes, "Philippe Petit is one of the most *prepared* people I've ever met. . . . He prefers to leave nothing up to chance." Definitely not a daredevil, Petit is a man with a "passion for preparation." Keyes explains that "according to insurance company actuaries, the average citizen is more likely to die in an accident than is Philippe Petit."[8]

Having assessed in advance all of the things that could go wrong is a healthy and productive way to prepare for a risk, Keyes concluded in researching *Chancing It*. Rehearsing events related to the risk in a safe setting such as a support group of some kind also prepares us well.[9]

"When we think of what it means to 'take a big risk,' we usually think first of something like a retiring civil servant leaving his family and going off to climb the Himalayas," wrote Keyes. "For such a person, that probably would be a big risk. But equally risky, if not more so, would be the climber of the Himalayas committing him or herself to something or someone ongoing: having a family, say, and becoming a civil servant."[10]

Americans, continues Keyes, associate taking a risk with doing something dramatic. What may be a far more courageous act for many people, he states, would be quietly to attune ourselves to our own needs and fears and bring to the surface "fears of commitment, responsibility, and rootedness." Staying put, for example, committing oneself to a marriage partner, career, or family, or making some commitment to something that is important to us may be far riskier than a more sensational action.[11] In the final analysis, Keyes feels, it is the "spirit of being adventuresome" that provides excitement, and it is the ability to make and keep commitments that brings happiness.[12]

AN INTERNATIONAL FAMILY: SEIZING AN OPPORTUNITY FOR A NEW LIFE

The mother of an almost-three-year-old, I listen in the car to a tape of Christmas music over and over again. It's April. Our tulips and Japanese cherry tree are in bloom, and my daughter is in her car seat singing "Winter Wonderland" at the top of her lungs. I look up at her pretty little face in the rearview mirror, smile, and find myself thinking about the life we have together and hope to have.

"Mommy, are you from India?" my daughter asks. She was born in Calcutta and was two months old and weighed five pounds when I became a mother at JFK International Airport in New York.

"No, Amanda, I'm from Oklahoma," I answer. Her question moves my thinking to a place ten thousand miles away.

Somewhere in Calcutta at this moment, I realize, a young adolescent girl walks along crowded streets or bathes in a river where hundreds bathe with her. The young girl is dressed in a colorful sari and has beautiful, silklike hair. She is poor, probably hungry, unmarried, and carrying my second child.

Unable to provide for herself, let alone a child, within a few months the young girl will grow desperate. Presenting a fictitious married name, she will enter a clinic, give birth, and slip out unnoticed, leaving the baby behind. A social worker from the International Mission of Hope will come to receive the baby into immediate, loving care.

How I wish that desperate young woman, herself still a child, running away from the clinic, could hear what I have to say: "Your baby will have the best education I can provide. She'll have an Indian sister, learn music, ride horses, have good nutrition, be exposed to Indian food and culture, take swimming lessons, wear pretty clothes, play on the beach, swing in the park, bring joy to her family, and always, always be loved. Please be at peace."

Following my usual eighteen-month pregnancy, eventually the waiting list will get to me. I'll receive a cable saying, "Baby girl, Ann Kaiser Stearns." Perhaps I'll shed some happy tears or give Amanda all the vanilla ice cream with chocolate sprinkles she wants, and I'll spend a hundred dollars making happy long distance telephone calls. "Before *Coming Back* goes into print," I'll explain, proclaiming it to everyone, "my new little baby will come to America!"

When the cable announcing Amanda came, I did the completely unorthodox thing of pouring glasses of wine for myself and the woman I was counseling in my office at the time. My action must have had therapeutic value, however. My client was a childless career woman who decided to get pregnant a few months later. Now she and her husband have a little daughter with a pink bedroom and rainbows everywhere.

It's risky, I remember thinking as I looked into the rearview mirror to see Amanda's face. We are very happy as we are now. My daughter is healthy, affectionate, bright, full of happiness and fun, talkative, a child easy to love.

A single parent with two children under the age of four? Can I still handle writing books and teaching college students? We'll have the chicken pox to look forward to, and fifteen cities in three weeks on a book tour with my daughters along. What if we lose our reliable and loving child care person after having finally found someone long-term? The old questions returned: What if I get really sick? What if the new baby develops serious health problems?

I'll be forty-four years old when my new baby arrives. Can I keep myself young enough to be full of fun through all the years my girls will need an energetic and lively mom? Will I get to live a long life and watch over my children as they finish their educations and establish their own families?

Amanda is singing along with the Christmas music even louder now. She is practically shouting, "to face unafraid the plans that we've made, walkin' in a winter wonderland."

The tears filling my eyes tell me that the meaning of the words is sinking in. There isn't any other way to go forward, I remember.

You have to take chances. How frightened I was at the prospect of becoming a single parent the first time. Well-meaning friends, assuming that biology is destiny, kept asking what I would know about my child's background, implying that problems were ahead. "Your life will drastically change," they cautioned, as if getting a baby at forty is like going to jail for a few years.

What resulted is best summarized in my social worker's report. "Dr. Stearns," she wrote, "has found motherhood and the parenting of Amanda fulfilling beyond her greatest expectations."

What an unspeakable improvement in my life Amanda has made. As a single parent in midlife, taking on a malnourished baby girl who had weighed 3½ pounds at birth was the biggest risk of my life. But look at what she's brought me: I have such a happy life being Amanda's mother that I want another brown-eyed baby girl from the same country so I can enjoy the parenting experience all over again.

Psychiatrist David Viscott has written, "Taking a risk is central to everything worthwhile in life."[13] You have to go for it.

If you find that you can't work for
the best possible result, then work for
the best result possible.

In our imperfect world, our family structures and other institutions inevitably lead us to deal with the frailties, disappointments, and excesses of human life. We begin to discover that it is necessary to let go of certain unrealistic expectations of life, to release some of our favorite dreams.

Most people who marry look initially to the institution of marriage for a sense of belonging and a feeling of connectedness to another human being. On their wedding day, men and women look ahead to a life of mutual and enduring love, the sharing of pleasures with spouse, children, other relatives and friends, and a lifelong feeling of being valued by the other person. Often marriage doesn't provide us with what was expected.

In all marriages and other relationships there are periods of discouragement—times when feelings of loneliness, frustration, resentment, hurt, and anger prevail. Often there is enduring disappointment and disillusionment. One must decide if or how to remain in the relationship and whether or not it is worth the effort and struggle required.

FATHER BILL: DEALING WITH A TROUBLED RELATIONSHIP

Bill had wanted to be a priest as long as he could remember. The nun in the first grade asked, "How many of you boys would like to be priests?" Bill's hand went up, along with several others. As the years progressed fewer and fewer hands were raised.

"It's hard to understand why I was so intent on the priesthood from such a young age," says Father Bill, a tall, athletic man with a handsome gray moustache. He looks much younger than his fifty years. "As a boy I admired the parish priest," he continued, "and, as I look back, I can see that the priests were the primary role models I experienced in growing up." It seemed to Bill that all the other men he knew well, including his father, had a problem with drinking. None of the men in Bill's family were well educated. They all worked hard and drank hard. As he grew into adulthood, the son of an alcoholic, Bill was intent on being "responsible, good, and holy. I was also determined to do something with my life to help people," he remembers.

When Bill entered a seminary high school, he was ecstatic at the opportunity for a good education. Although a high school seminary would be considered obsolete today, for him it was a "good time in almost every way." There was a routine of class, study, prayer, manual work, and sports which appealed to Bill. "One area that was not addressed," he remembers, "was the area of relationships with girls. Since we were preparing to be priests, the expectation was that our friendships should be with others who were also preparing for the same vocation. Those who got into dating seemed to leave the seminary and not come back, so the recommendation not to date seemed to make sense in keeping with my vocational direction."

Bill found college equally fulfilling. His love of study and sports, the routine of daily mass, meditation, prayer, and his sense of mission in preparing to serve others in the priesthood was sustaining. "The atmosphere," Bill recalls, "was very much asexual. I was not aware of any homosexual inclinations or activity in the seminary during my college years, but the emergence of sexual drives was a cause of concern. There was an ongoing struggle," he says, "to control sexual impulses."

Bill's study of theology excited him. He was getting close to his goal of being able to help others, and it was meaningful to him to learn the theology which he would be teaching and preaching. "I felt close to God," says Bill, "and called by God to serve and to make the sacrifices that the priesthood required. Ordination as a priest and offering my first mass were 'peak experiences.' " After ordination Father Bill earned a master's degree in counseling and was assigned to teach in a boys' high school. He quickly got a reputation for being a good teacher and preacher as well as a good confessor, someone who was kind and understanding.

He found his confessor role deeply meaningful. To bring some comfort or peace to a person struggling with anxiety and guilt was very rewarding. He found himself listening carefully to people and found that their human struggles were different from what he had learned about sin in the moral theology manuals. "I came to be convinced that most people do the best they can under the circumstances and that so many of the ideals that are set forth we can only achieve over a period of time and perhaps only partially."

The first seven years of Father Bill's ministry were filled with giving. "I had never learned to say 'no' or to regulate a schedule," he remembers, "since in seminary everything was properly regulated and after so many years of preparation, I was eager to serve." He consistently overextended himself as a teacher, counselor, and helper. The strain of long, long days with very little time off began to take its toll, but he did not recognize this. "One thing I did discover at about thirty-five years of age," said Father Bill, "was that having a drink at night was very relaxing. I did this occasionally at first, and then it became a regular event. The drink also seemed to release creativity. I remember many a Saturday evening sipping a Scotch and getting some of my best sermon ideas."

During the next few years, the "honeymoon" of the priesthood seemed to be over, he now recalls. "Externally everything was going well, but I was finding the teaching had become routine and was feeling the lack of something in my life." He took time off to attend courses in counseling at a secular university in what became a pivotal summer of his life. One class was an experiential course in which participants learned to do therapy by having group therapy sessions among themselves. There were ten in his group: five men and five women, including a male and a female leader. The group met for four hours each day. "It's hard to express what happened," says Father Bill, "but for the first time in my life I got in touch with the affective or feeling dimension of my life. I had always kept a stiff upper lip and had never shared problems or frustrations. That was not what men did. But after several days in the group, I cried in front of others for the first time. It was like a dam bursting. For the first time in my life I allowed others to take care of me: to hold me, to comfort me, to draw me out, to listen to me, to care for me. In the past I had always been the helper, always in control."

Father Bill also had the new experience that summer of falling in love. "One of the women in the group, Marjorie, touched me deeply with the beauty of her personhood, and I found myself fascinated by her. Two weeks into the therapy course I woke up at night during a wet dream in which I had the fantasy of making love with Marjorie. New desires and ways of thinking about myself were awakened."

What was even more surprising to Father Bill was to discover that Marjorie was also deeply attracted to him. They openly discussed their feelings in the group and had "several beautiful sharing afternoons at the beach," he remembers. "We were able to accept our attraction to one another," Father Bill went on, "and at the same time accept her commitment to her husband and my commitment to my vows. It was a beautiful experience and led me to celebrate the fact that my vow of celibacy was indeed a sacrifice that I willingly offered to the Lord as part of my commitment to a life of service."

The affective or feeling dimension of Father Bill's life had been awakened, however, and with it the awareness of himself as a man with sexual drives. He successfully served in several new ministries yet felt a growing restlessness. After a long day of working with people, Father Bill came home to an empty rectory. There were often other people around, but there was no closeness or intimacy. "The deepest needs of my being," he recalls, "were not being satisfied. Prayer, the liturgy, work—I was beginning to wonder if it made any sense. After all, early in the Old Testament, God said that it is not good for man to be alone." Recognizing that many men were leaving the priesthood because of the loneliness they felt made Father Bill question his own ability to sustain a life of celibate ministry. Another study period of about six months gave him new energy to plug away for a few more years. Meanwhile, Father Bill's evenings were still lonely, and he continued "having a few drinks" before retiring. "As I look back on this," he acknowledges, "I'm sure the drinking was a substitute for the intimacy that I was yearning for but continuing to deny."

Then while involved in the work of his ministry, Father Bill met Eileen, another "very special person." In meetings that took place several times a week at the church, they planned and carried out many projects and injected new life into the parish. There was also "the opportunity to attend meetings together and to have some outings," Father Bill remembers. "I felt alive again," he says. "Gradually our attraction for one another became obvious to both of us. We exchanged cards on all the appropriate occasions, went out of our way to support one another, and began to share affection with restraint." The progress of Father Bill and Eileen's relationship was clear, yet he had not given any thought to leaving the priesthood and knew that he needed to be honest with Eileen about this. Their joint ministry project was completed, and, although they lived in the same town for two years thereafter, their contact was relatively minimal. "An occasional lunch or dinner," explained Father Bill, "was all that I needed to make me realize that pursuing this relationship would lead to an inevitable choice between a commitment to Eileen and my ordination to the priesthood. By now I had been ordained twenty years."

Father Bill found his work satisfying in many ways, but there were other needs which cried out for fulfillment. He took some time away for travel with a priest friend but all the while wished that the trip were with Eileen. For months he prayed and struggled with the decision of whether to continue in ministry or move into another helping profession which would free him to marry Eileen. By this time Father Bill had earned certification as a counselor and would have had an immediate means of making a living if he chose to leave. "The priesthood had been my lifelong dream," he says, "and it was a life that was working well for the most part, even though it was taking its toll." The drinking continued, almost always when Father Bill was alone or when he was traveling with a trusted friend. "By this time," he recalls, "I was being careful publicly, somehow sensing but yet denying that alcohol was becoming a problem. Public drinking was always very controlled; but in the evening drinks became heavier and more frequent. As a counselor I realized, from working with others, that I needed to address the issue of alcoholism in my life."

He confided in a psychiatrist friend and called the friend weekly to give him a report on his drinking. He stopped for six months but then began again—always alone and at home at the end of the day. Drinking was no longer serving the function it once did; it did not lead to comfort or creativity but more and more to remorse and guilt the next morning. Father Bill knew he had to resolve the alcohol issue in his life before making any kind of decision about remaining a priest. At this time he grieved the loss of his parents, who died within three years of each other. Father Bill had been especially close to his mother and was deeply affected by her slow decline and great suffering.

A breakthrough came when the troubled priest, now in his late forties, started attending Alcoholics Anonymous meetings twice a week and stopped drinking for another six-month period. There was a major problem, however. Father Bill had just been appointed to a significant administrative position with high visibility and did not want to jeopardize his reputation. "To me," he explained, "alcoholism connoted moral weakness, lack of self-control, and lack of trust in God. I didn't really commit myself to AA. I thought all I needed was some confidence that people could quit drinking; then I got the complacent and overconfident feeling that I could now do it on my own."

He stopped attending AA meetings for another two years and engaged in "relatively controlled drinking," Father Bill goes on. "I worked very hard and continued to enjoy success, but when the day was over, my solace was an increasing amount of Scotch. I was becoming less and less comfortable with the dual life: one of service and ministry, and the private life of addiction.

"Finally I surrendered," he recalls. "It was a most unlikely experience. I was watching a Sunday-morning evangelist—I don't even remember the man's name—but the message of healing and hope and surrender sank in. It was a highly emotional experience, and I begged to be healed from my addiction. I begged to be free again: free to live and to love and to serve. I felt unburdened and freed up for days, but knew that this kind of spiritual high would not last. I committed myself to becoming a 'full member' of AA."

"It is ironic," Father Bill continues, eloquently, "the son of an alcoholic, who despised everything associated with alcohol for some thirty years, now began to find God once again through the disease. I came to understand that alcoholism was not a moral problem but an illness. I had gradually become addicted, and in the process of spending myself in helping others, I was losing my own personhood. I was a stranger in my own home."

It seemed to Father Bill that he had never achieved balance in his life. "The drive to achieve, perhaps to make up for my dad's limitations, to be the very best, to be superhuman and selfless left me with many unmet needs. I longed for love and intimacy and yet could not reconcile that longing with my commitment to the priesthood. Alcohol helped to delay the resolution of my ambivalence." With the twenty-fifth anniversary of his ordination approaching, Father Bill knew that he had to come to a resolution and realized that a long period of sobriety would be necessary in order to gain perspective. "Becoming a 'full member' of AA meant that I had to acknowledge that drinking was no longer a viable option for me."

It took Father Bill several years in AA to reach his first anniversary of sobriety. "It was not just being 'dry' but now an enjoyment of sobriety and of life," he explains. "Now I was free to visit the person I loved. She had not yet married but was finding fulfillment in her career and enjoyed an active social life. I knew that my recommitment to the priesthood was coming into focus. Eileen and I were able to spend important days together, deeply sharing our personal goals and aspirations, acknowledging our deep love for one another and the fact that my vows excluded a commitment to an exclusive life together. Our relationship has been precious through the years and continues to be precious."

There are many days when Father Bill experiences a new excitement about life, wakes up praising God for life's goodness, relishes the beauty of the unaddicted life, and looks upon maintaining sobriety as his number one goal: "One day at a time." There are nights when yearnings stir, and Father Bill struggles with feelings of loneliness and isolation. The battle to stay sober then is fierce. He has come to see clearly that living each day creatively and in a balanced way will give him the health he yearns for and that sobriety is an important component. So much of his life, Father Bill realizes, has been consumed with doing, as opposed to taking quiet time for being and reflection. "I know that it is not a matter of either-or, but happiness for me must be one of achieving balance. Balance, I have come to believe, is the crucial factor in a life of celibate ministry."

Drinking, he now realizes, is an "attempted shortcut to bypass pain, frustration and weariness." He now better understands and accepts unhappiness and fatigue. "When I am tired, I'm learning to go to bed. The results of going to bed when weary rather than drinking into a false sense of well-being are so much more effective." He also cherishes the comradeship, acceptance, and understanding of other AA members. "At these meetings," he says, "I'm not the priest, I'm just Bill. AA has brought me a long way in learning how to receive from others. I also find myself doing a better job of receiving in my ministry now as well as giving. In my recovery I am also coming to value relationships more than achievement." Recently he has started a support group for colleagues who meet every other week to share their lives and ministries.

"Balance" in his life means that Father Bill is gradually learning to take the time not only to be quiet and meditate but also to share in warm and loving relationships with others and to replenish his spirit. "I seem to have less need to earn God's love and acceptance by overinvolvement in work," he explains.

As he thinks back, Father Bill sees that there were some very difficult years in which he could not face the intensity of his attraction to a noncelibate life. "I yearned for intimacy at the end of a day of giving." Alcohol, and his addiction to it, served to ease that pain. It bought him some time. His life is different now. Sober for a year, he is finding renewed meaning in his priesthood and largely accepts the sacrifice of intimacy as the price for enjoying the ministry of being with others in so many important and satisfying ways.

There are days when Father Bill would like to resign and go in another direction, yet as a counselor he knows that all people, irrespective of their commitments, have such days.

Feelings of isolation, ambivalence, and periods of doubt or disillusionment come and go in nearly every personal relationship, career, or other involvement. Father Bill has found ways to identify and appreciate the benefits in his chosen vocation. Others find their fulfillment outside of a marriage, job, or career. For example, an unsatisfactory marriage may be acceptable because one's work is fulfilling, or someone may stay in a well-paying but unrewarding job and find happiness through family, friends, sports, travel, and the like. In this case the individual doesn't like having to compromise but has come to terms with doing so. Some decide that seeking certain kinds of fulfillment elsewhere would jeopardize what *is* precious in an imperfect situation. Father Bill decided to limit the extent of his involvement with the woman he loved. Similarly, a married person might decide not to initiate or continue an extramarital affair.

Sometimes, of course, a decision is made to sever oneself completely from a relationship or institution that repeatedly has been demonstrated to be destructive to one's best interests, survival, or growth. The best life within reach may involve a choice of walking away and not staying when one makes an assessment that the rewarding moments are all too fleeting.

SUZANNE: LIVING WELL WITH LOST DREAMS

Suzanne, dressed in well-cut wool slacks and a cashmere cowl-neck sweater, settled back into a deep leather chair and related her story. She is the picture of success, a highly respected principal of a residential school for handicapped children and the mother of a son and daughter in high school.

"The first-born child in my family, I felt close to my father as a little girl, following him around in our small Midwestern town," she said. "Like him, I wanted to be a teacher when I grew up." On weekends she loved to go along with him when he drove to the hardware store to buy seed, or to the rented plot he gardened with Suzanne's mother to stretch his meager teacher's pay. A tomboy, Suzanne accompanied her father on summertime fishing expeditions at the river outside of town and routinely enjoyed working with him around the house, painting, wallpapering, and doing the never-ending chores necessary to keep their late-Victorian house livable. "He clearly enjoyed my company," recalled Suzanne, "delighted in my interest in what he did, and called me his 'pal.' From an early age I worked hard at the chores he gave me and always strived to please him. I was mostly successful."

There was a dark side to Suzanne's father which she sensed as a child and then saw more clearly as an adolescent and adult. It was hard to understand that a man who patiently taught teenagers math formulas and theorems for over forty years could be so difficult at home with those he supposedly loved most. The life of the family and the behavior of all family members had to center around him and his wishes. Whenever he did not have things completely to his liking or when his authority was challenged, he was capable of considerable meanness through teasing, name calling, putdowns, and other excessive discipline, usually verbal and mental rather than physical. He was a moody, short-tempered person who could reduce a child to three inches tall simply because he or she broke something, made a mistake, prematurely asked for a pair of new shoes, or wanted to play rather than work.

Suzanne and her father got along well when she was a small child because she thought of him as knowing everything and always being right. "I learned to do whatever Dad wanted me to do—everything from having the right table manners to thinning the carrots or painting the gingerbread trim on our front porch," she remembered. "I felt some sadness that I couldn't go swimming in the summertime because the garden needed tending and that we never took family vacations because the tomatoes would rot in the patch or we would miss the green beans. About the only thing that ever really got to me were the times, not infrequent, when my father belittled or viciously teased my mother, my brother and sister, and me and left us in tears or silently fuming."

It was also upsetting to Suzanne that her father would never attend functions which were important to her. "I've been in that place all week," he'd say, if it was a play at school. Yet his answer was the same no matter where the event was held. A choir performance at church, a Girl Scout father-daughter banquet, a band concert—"he just wouldn't go," Suzanne recalled. "He did attend my younger brother's high school basketball games but would criticize him later for such minor offenses as tying his shoelaces during time-outs in the game."

Suzanne's father was especially cruel and severe in his treatment of her younger sister. A man with many axes to grind against women, having been the only boy in a family with four sisters and a mother who frequently belittled him, her father seemed to be constantly ridiculing her sister and finding excuses to poke at her with words. She was a bright girl, but her interest in schoolwork floundered in elementary school when her father punished her for every mark below ninety by making her give up all her playmates until her marks improved.

Suzanne thinks of her mother as a "kind, patient, giving, and loving woman limited in the ability to rescue us from our father." Although she was devoted to her children, her mother was born before women in America were allowed to vote and was deeply schooled in the tradition that husbands and fathers make all the important decisions in a family. "Our mother found a host of secret ways to show caring, compassion, and generosity, including buying birthday and Christmas presents with money she saved from selling our garden vegetables," Suzanne said. "We would have to pretend these gifts had come from our maternal grandfather. The pretty dresses Mom bought for my sister and me were especially appreciated since Dad seemed so reluctant and resentful of buying clothes for a girl."

When Suzanne was in high school, she lost tolerance for the way her father used criticism, threats, and ridicule to impose his wishes on the family. She had had a close look at other families, and it was clear to her that fathers could be loving and gentle.

She urged her mother to stand up to her father when he criticized her appearance or found fault with the way she went about her work. "She almost never defended herself," Suzanne told me. "I would find Mom standing over the old wheelbarrow in the garden or on her knees in a sea of weeds crying. Sometimes I begged my mother to leave him. It was not within my understanding then that Dad was Mom's life. She had never held a paying job and couldn't imagine ever getting one. In my hometown women stayed married then. I don't remember ever knowing a child in school whose parents were divorced."

Sometimes Suzanne fantasized killing her father when he joked about her mother's taste in clothes or treated one of the children "like a dummy." In her imagination she would take a gun and stop his ridicule and meanness forever. Luckily she realized that violence would destroy not only her father but also her mother, whom she loved dearly. And violence would put an end to any happiness life had in store for her. "I had to find another solution," Suzanne explained, "another way of preventing my father's behavior and my parents' interactions from hurting and destroying me. What I did was simple. I left home to go to college, and I didn't go back."

Staying away from her parents for six months to a year and limiting the length of her visits to their home was Suzanne's way of curtailing the pain she felt in relation to her father. Sometimes she stayed away for two years at a time. While feelings of loneliness and homelessness plagued her, she tried to make up for it by writing and visiting her widowed grandfather and occasionally on weekends going to a college friend's home to visit another family. While she was still in college, Suzanne married Andrew, her first love, whom she had dated only a few months. The intensity of their love affair, she says, was probably built on a combination of physical attraction and a mutual lack of attachment to family.

As she and her husband made plans for having children, Suzanne resolved to learn from experience the importance of being present and available to her own family. "Even if one of my kids gets married in Alaska to some jerk I can't stand," she declared, referring to the fact that her father didn't want to drive three hundred miles to her wedding, "I promise to go to the wedding and to give them my support!"

She and Andrew had two babies in rapid succession, within eighteen months after they were wed. Their marriage, so good at first, suffered from the stresses associated with being busy young parents trying to hold down part-time jobs while taking a heavy load of courses in graduate school. Their physical attraction to each other wore thin in an atmosphere of almost constant mutual fatigue, and the couple separated about the time that both children were enrolled in preschool.

Once again Suzanne made an effort to attach herself to other families. She sought out and befriended surrogate parents of various sorts—an older couple her parents' age, several professors, a minister, a male therapist, and a female psychiatrist, as well as numerous friends in the half generation between her parents and herself. By attaching herself to various role models and to various families, she found that her feelings of loneliness greatly diminished. Many of these relationships grew into enjoyable, satisfying, and enduring friendships.

It has been twenty-four years since Suzanne left her parents' house to live on her own. "The times when I have felt sorriest for myself for not having visits from Mom," she explained, "were when I received my master's degree in special education, when my children were born, when I got my divorce, and when I was recovering from a bad automobile accident."

Her mother does, however, write to her every week. "Every letter," says Suzanne, "is a precious reminder of her love, pride in my accomplishments, and interest in my life, home, work, and children." Suzanne is trying to accept the fact that her parents do not have a terrible life together; they are actually good companions. "Mom says she loves him, that she does not have an unhappy life, and that she knew that my father was a domineering man before she married him." Suzanne knows that in recent years her father has done a great deal less belittling of her mother and treats his wife somewhat more gently now that she has crippling arthritis. "It's certainly not the way I would want to live, but I am not my mother," comments Suzanne.

Suzanne has tried to build a close relationship with her sister and brother and their families. However, she says, "My brother grew up to be undemonstrative and hard to get close to. He is also quick to criticize, like my father. This combination has more than once left me feeling bruised when I've flown down the East Coast to visit my brother and his family in Florida, only to leave earlier than planned because I felt so uncomfortable in their home."

Before she had a family of her own, she shared some close times with her sister, who escaped home by marrying before she even finished high school. Suzanne traveled to be with her sister during special holidays or various family emergencies. "When she was first married, she asked me to visit her because their budget was tight," recalls Suzanne. "Now that many years have gone by, her commitments to her husband and children—even her bridge club or her prize-winning show dogs—keep her at home. In the past two decades she has traveled to visit me on only three occasions. My brother has about the same track record."

Politically, philosophically, psychologically, and religiously, Suzanne and her siblings are far apart. They all vote differently, think differently, behave differently. "We're just not close. We don't share feelings," says Suzanne. "Sometimes I wonder whether they haven't forgiven me for being the oldest and the first to leave home, even though they both left as soon as they could, too."

Suzanne's disappointment with her biological family is keenest around Christmas. Since her divorce, the holiday brings feelings of sadness. On Christmas she misses the family she never really had. But she has found that she sometimes feels lonelier with her biological family than when she and her children share the day with close friends.

Today Suzanne celebrates Christmas with her two teenagers, their friends who drop by in the afternoon, and her friends. The sadness at missing her parents and siblings is deep but short. "My friend Lucinda and I," she explained, "share Christmas and our family birthdays, for ourselves and our children. We attend church together on Christmas Eve, and then my children and I have a lovely dinner and gift-opening evening with Lucinda, her husband and daughter, and their dogs. Lucinda is the sister I have always needed, actively involved in my life in a way that my biological sister has not been able to be. She really makes Christmas a wonderful event."

For the past twenty years, Suzanne has had two other "sisters" as well. Charlene lives in Georgia and Louise in Wyoming, but their families visit back and forth across the miles several times a year, and their husbands and children are extended family for Suzanne. They have seen her through the grief of her separation and divorce. They shared her joy when she finished graduate school and years later when she bought a new home. "They were with me through all my highs and lows," says Suzanne.

When Suzanne delivered her first baby, she was frightened at being responsible for a tiny infant. Her husband was supportive and helpful, but Suzanne felt she needed what a mother or sister could offer. "My friends took their places. Charlene was there for the first week, and Louise and her husband and little boy came for the second. Leaving their own homes in distant states to be with me, they bonded early to my daughter and shared my joy along with the worry and sleepless nights."

Later, when she had her second child by Caesarean section, her husband was away on a fishing trip because labor had come earlier than was expected. Lucinda took a day off from work to be with Suzanne and slept in a chair beside her hospital bed the first night. Charlene arrived by plane the day after the surgery and took over for Lucinda, staying with her in the hospital until she felt Suzanne could be safely on her own.

"They have been such wonderful friends," reflects Suzanne. "They and their families are my family now. I'm godmother to their five children. We manage to all come together for Thanksgiving or Easter every couple of years, and we share family celebrations, such as school graduations. Those are wonderful and joyous occasions—real family get-togethers."

The love of such friends has made Suzanne free to enjoy what her parents *are* able to give. Suzanne remembers some very pleasurable times. Now, as long as she is the one who takes the initiative to phone or travel to see them, they are happy to see her and her children. "They try to make us feel welcome in their own way," says Suzanne. "I have accepted that my parents are the way they are and that they're not going to change. Mom and Dad are old, I realize."

For the most part, her father no longer has the power to hurt her. "He seems to have mellowed a bit with age," she says, "and quite simply, I'm no longer so vulnerable. His caustic remarks don't destroy me." Getting along with him lets Suzanne have access to her mother, and her children have an especially loving relationship with their grandmother.

Suzanne feels uncomfortable when she has to explain to somebody why her parents never come to visit her and probably never will. Usually she makes excuses for them, saying that they aren't comfortable traveling now that they're getting older. In reality, she knows it's still her father who is holding back and her mother who stays to please him. "At times I feel a sadness that this is the way things are," Suzanne comments, "but then I remember my joy in my new family of friends. It isn't the life I would have chosen, and it isn't the one I will give my children, but I am content. I'm happy."

That Suzanne has found "the best life within reach" is illustrated by the fact that most people who know her would be astonished to hear the story that she has told here. Her co-workers, neighbors, friends, and acquaintances see her as a happy, talented, fulfilled person who is capable of enjoying life.

Suzanne admits she once held regular "pity parties" for herself. She does so only occasionally now. Like a lot of people who have painful family situations to deal with, she found the professional help and the support of friends she needed to make a good life for herself.

"You get what warmth, caring, and meaning you can and fulfill the dreams that are within reach," Suzanne says. Like Father Bill's consideration of leaving the Church, Suzanne had to make a decision whether to walk entirely away from her parents and siblings or whether to meet what needs could be met realistically in those relationships while connecting elsewhere with more nourishing individuals and groups. "You make up for what is missing by making a life for yourself that is the next best thing to the dream you had in mind," says Suzanne.

She is not alone. Millions of families know the sorrow of unfulfilled hopes and hurtful relationships. Many have had to deal with a violent, incestuous, alcoholic, drug-addicted, or mentally disturbed person who inflicts psychological or physical damage on his or her innocent victims. We *all* must deal with an imperfect world, with our own humanity and that of others, and still find the best life within reach.

ESCAPING SELF-PITY

At the Feast of Tabernacles it is the Jewish custom to build a *sukkah*, a temporary structure in the garden or yard. For eight days the structure stands as a reminder of the temporary booths in which the ancient people of Israel dwelt during forty years of wandering in the wilderness. The *sukkah* must be insubstantially built to convey the idea that human beings should never be haughty and that things of luxury are not lasting and do not bring lasting happiness. The roof must be partially open so that one can see the stars as a reminder of God's protection and blessings.

A structure that preferably has four walls but sometimes has three walls with one side open, the *sukkah* may represent the fragility of life. "Life would be preferable with four walls, but most people have to learn how to live with three walls because few of us have escaped tragedy, disappointment, or misfortune," said Rabbi Simon Glustrom of the Jewish Center in Fair Lawn, New Jersey. In a recent conversation, Rabbi Glustrom was using the three-walled *sukkah* as a symbol for describing how to cope with human brokenness. The insubstantial structure symbolizes God's protection under which frail human beings are able to stand erect and manage to survive.

From the vantage point of a three-walled structure from which one can look to one's neighbor's *sukkah*, continued Rabbi Glustrom, "we are clearly reminded that we are all united together in pain and sorrow. Because a wall of our own is missing, we see that our neighbor, too, is missing a wall. While another person's pain doesn't necessarily lessen our own," he continued, "by looking past our predicament to the other person's *sukkah*, we move from self-pity to the healing that comes when we try to bind up other people's wounds."

Suzanne managed to escape self-pity by looking at the parents of handicapped children at the school where she was a principal and by realizing that virtually everyone experiences some form of pain or brokenness. Seeing others struggle with their own families, marriages, love relationships, financial or work situations, or health problems led her to experience personally the wisdom of Rabbi Glustrom's words.

Suzanne has devoted her energies to loving her children and to providing for her son and daughter a role model of strength, sensitivity, and self-determination. She lives independently of any permanent love relationship with a man at this time and knows that if she should marry again, she will not be doing so from a position of loneliness and a desperate need for familial connections, as when she was young. She would like to be married, but she would prefer to stay single rather than to be in a marriage where she might be diminished or otherwise mistreated as her mother was. Dedicated to her work in special education, devoted to helping handicapped children, Suzanne feels useful and worthy as a person. By helping others she has saved herself from self-absorption.

Father Bill made a decision to stay. The priesthood was a lifelong dream which he began to find rewarding when his needs as a whole person were addressed. He still struggles with the issue of finding "balance" in his life but has made significant progress in that direction. Like many priests, Father Bill's primary issues or problems to be resolved are living with celibacy and loneliness, overcoming his vulnerability to addiction, learning how to receive from others, sharing his humanity, and weathering some midlife years to emerge with a sense of peace and fulfillment. With the exception of the celibacy factor, these are the primary issues of many men and women who must decide whether to stay where they are or to take their leave.

Suzanne had to learn to live with the limitations of her biological family members and their circumstances, to protect herself from her father's destructive influence and ability to hurt her emotionally in her younger years, and to build a family life apart from her parents and siblings. Like Father Bill, she needed a "balanced life" consisting of a feeling of usefulness, meaningful work, caring, support, sharing, warmth, and a feeling of connectedness to others. Her children and work filled many of her needs as the priest was fulfilled in part by his parishioners and ministry, yet more was needed in order for each of them to feel happy and largely at peace.

QUESTIONS TO ASK WHEN DECIDING WHETHER TO LEAVE OR STAY

In deciding whether or how to remain in a relationship, a long-held occupation, or other way of life, many of the triumphant survivors I have observed have asked themselves a series of questions. Perhaps some of the items below will help you to search out the best answer for yourself regarding where you want to be and why:

- ☐ How much satisfaction can I find in this relationship?
- ☐ Can I see myself living the rest of my life in this situation?
- ☐ What can I do to make my present situation more fulfilling?
- ☐ If I stay, what will be missing and where else can I find it?
- ☐ Are any of the "benefits" of my remaining destructive ones—i.e., do I seem to have a need to be unhappy or to be abused?
- ☐ Will the situation be like this forever or is there a realistic chance it will change?
- ☐ What are the advantages of staying? Leaving? What are the disadvantages on each side?
- ☐ How will others be affected by my decision to leave or stay?
- ☐ Is a clean break necessary, or would a major change be too costly?
- ☐ Do I lose anything by leaving? Would it be a permanent

> loss or one I could eventually replace or learn to live without?
> □ In what settings and with which persons can I best meet my needs?
> □ What dreams and expectations are within my reach?
> □ Will I have to get outside help to find the strength to choose what is best for me?

CAROL: LEARNING TO LIVE WITH A CHRONIC ILLNESS

Sometimes we are in a position of deciding to leave or stay in a situation, and sometimes we are not given a choice. When a loved one dies or becomes profoundly debilitated or when we fall seriously ill, for example, there is no choice but to learn to live with the unchangeable. It can still be possible to fashion a good life.

For five years Carol, a management consultant, a tall, slender, bright, and personable woman in her early thirties, lived with a serious but undiagnosed illness. She suffered abdominal cramps so severe that she would cry. She was sent to various specialists and evaluated for gynecological problems and gallbladder and other diseases. She experienced joint stiffness, swelling, and pain, muscle weakness, and extreme fatigue. Her glands were swollen, she often ran a high fever, was troubled by sores in her mouth and nose, and suffered diminished dexterity, grasp, and sensitivity in her hands. She came down with pleurisy, an inflammation of the lining of the lung. Carol's symptoms would mysteriously come, leave, and then return. Her joints ached even in the mild San Francisco winters. During much of the summer she would feel well again, except on the weekends, when she would be out in the sun and feel ill.

"Lupus is a very difficult illness to diagnose," Carol explained, "because the symptoms vary from person to person and because one is better or worse at different times. My symptoms seen together formed the classic picture of lupus erythematosus, a systemic illness in which the body builds up immunities to itself. But my doctors looked at each complaint in isolation; they ruled things out—said what diseases I didn't have—but never ruled anything in. There were days," she continued, "when I thought maybe I was dying of something and nobody would know why."

At lunch with college friends one Saturday, Carol dropped her coffee cup. Coleen, a nurse since graduation, asked Carol a few questions and listened to her replies. "I'm not supposed to say this because I'm not a doctor," Coleen said cautiously, "but I think you have lupus. You should see a specialist in connective tissue conditions."

Carol saw a specialist, and her history, a physical exam, and diagnostic laboratory work confirmed what the nurse had suspected. Carol's symptoms were due to systemic lupus erythematosus, a chronic disorder of connective tissues which affects many bodily organs.

"After five years of being sick and hearing medical people tell me that I didn't have this or that illness, I was very glad that the doctors now knew that I had something," said Carol. "I was glad I had a disease that had a name and that people knew I wasn't crazy."

In the first few weeks, Carol refused to let her physician put her on corticosteroids, powerful antiinflammatory drugs which Carol had heard sometimes caused bone damage and other serious side effects. Her pain worsened. Finally Carol became extremely ill and decided she had no choice but to begin taking the steroids along with the five or six other prescribed medications she was already taking.

STAGES OF "SURVIVORSHIP"

Like many people who learn that they have a serious illness, Carol denied the full reality and severity of her illness for some time. About a month before she received the lupus diagnosis she had discovered that her husband of thirteen years (whom she had long suspected of being unfaithful) not only was seeing someone else but had gotten the other woman pregnant. There were too many crises in her life all at once for Carol to cope with the full reality of lupus. Denial is often a healthy and very necessary defense mechanism.

"I spent three years," she said, "in the phase of 'well, I'll take these drugs even if they kill me.' I did very unhealthy things—worked all day, stayed at my desk until three or four A.M. working on my doctoral dissertation, slept awhile, got up the next morning and got myself and my daughter off to work and school, stayed out later on the weekends, drank too much alcohol, and went to political meetings after work two or three nights a week."

It was "a crazy way to live when you know you are sick," Carol acknowledged. She went for professional counseling, complaining that her life was "out of control." She told her social worker therapist that she was "doing whatever people wanted" her to do, being out late at night, chauffeuring her daughter and all the daughter's friends, having big dinner parties, and *resenting* it. People thought she wasn't ill, she confessed, because she worked hard to convey healthiness while taking increasingly higher dosages of steroids to control the disease.

"The therapist was very helpful," said Carol. "She was nuts-and-bolts oriented—practical—and didn't talk to me about my mother and father or try to raise any deep psychological issues from childhood. She talked to me about what I wanted to talk about and agreed that my life was out of control."

The social worker helped Carol to practice handling various situations in order to get back in charge of her life. "I'm sorry,

I can't do that. I'm terribly sorry, I can't do that right now," Carol learned to say. "On Tuesday? Gee, sorry, no way I could do that on Tuesday," she said, practicing. The therapist told her she should lie if she had to in order to protect her health.

Discovering that there were specific behaviors that would give her more control in her life, Carol began to look for other ways in which she could play a role in shaping the course of her illness. "I began reading more about steroids. It seemed you could control your diet with proper nutrition and possibly offset some of the effects of the steroids. Another side effect of the drug can be great hunger and weight gain," Carol continued, "especially gaining weight around the middle. I decided that I was going to lose the twenty-five pounds I had gained; that I was getting a divorce and wanted to look nice and wanted to date."

Carol saw that there were things she could do to help herself and that she was not simply at the mercy of a disease which was stalking her. Neither, she decided, was she going to be the passive victim of the medications she was taking. "I saw a study that looked at an increased risk of heart attacks and strokes because of the effects of steroids, and the disease itself affecting cholesterol and lipid levels. I saw another study related to the fact that exercise can impact positively on cholesterol. So I decided that doing something was better than doing nothing. I began an aerobic and weight-bearing exercise program—walking and running."

She discovered that she could say no to people who placed demands on her time, such as telling her lonely and emotionally needy next-door neighbor, "I have to go now." Carol learned to give certain people ten or twenty minutes instead of wasting several hours. She learned to go to bed earlier and to budget her hospitality as a hostess and her generosity as a community servant. She asked her teenage daughter for more help at home and began expecting other parents to do their share of the taxi service for the youngsters. She limited her intake of alcoholic beverages, took vacations and an occasional long weekend for rest and recreation, and built into her usual daily routine moments of serenity as a way of reducing the stressfulness of her position as management consultant. "I know I can't will away my illness," Carol said, "but I still have a lot of control over the disease, a lot more than if I didn't actively do anything to help myself."

Carol took an active role alongside her doctor in overseeing her illness, and she accepted the responsibility for self-care in some small ways that gave her an important role to play. She learned to listen to her own inner voices. For instance, the steroids caused an infection in her mouth and an upset stomach. Her doctor prescribed a specific mouthwash and recommended an antacid. Over time she was sure she felt better if she used an over-the-counter brand of mouthwash instead of what the doctor prescribed, and she noticed she felt better when she forgot to take the antacid or ran out of it. She would report these findings to her doctor, who told her to use her own judgment. Sometimes she made a mistake, but it added to her store of knowledge of the workable.

People with a chronic illness, many who are bereaved, and those with ongoing family problems find that there is not a specific point in time when they can feel that they have dealt with the crisis. They keep dealing with the problem or loss event on an ongoing basis. One advances in the stages of survivorship by "trial and error," summarized Carol. "You keep learning and assuming responsibility for your own healing. It is not the doctor, fortune-teller, therapist, priest or minister or rabbi, or anyone else who is responsible and whom you can then blame and say it's their fault that you're not coping better. You have to listen to the knowledge within yourself."

Carol had decided to finish her doctoral dissertation after learning that she was seriously ill. Even though the combination of such highly stressful activities as graduate school and a full-time job can exacerbate illnesses of various kinds, including lupus, she pressed on. "I heard other lupus patients say they had dropped out of school," she remembered. "I'd feel like saying, 'You're not really dropping out because of your illness. It's just an excuse.' " The time came, however, when it was necessary for Carol to reevaluate the high expectations she maintained for herself and others.

Carol one night had a dream that served to clarify her situation. She dreamed that she was trying to get on a boat that was sailing away but that she had packages strapped to her body, was wearing winter boots, and had children ahead of her to put on the boat. "I had all these encumbrances," Carol said, recalling the dream. "And just as I was getting on the boat, I saw a woman there and I said to her, 'Can't you help me? Can't you give me your hand? Can't you take my packages?' Finally I got on the boat," Carol continued, "and I said to the woman, 'Couldn't you have given me a hand? How hard would it have been? Can't you see that I'm sick and have a lot of burdens?' "

"You are sick and have a lot of burdens, but you didn't get on the boat because you're lazy and not strong," harshly replied the woman.

After she awakened, Carol sat somberly trying to interpret the dream. "Who *is* this woman, this mean and evil woman who wouldn't give me a hand?" she wondered. The woman's cold and tough-looking face was still vivid in her mind.

Later that day she told a friend about the dream. "Well, who do you know who's like that?" he asked. "If it's so important for you to figure it out, who would be that mean to you?" he asked.

"I don't know anybody who's like that woman," Carol replied, just before the answer dawned on her. "Except me— *I'm* like that!" she exclaimed. Carol recognized that it was she—she was the one pushing herself, showing no mercy, showing no kindness, offering herself no help with the encumbrances!

Carol decided that it was time to stop being self-judgmental.

She realized that the illness may require some of one's most cherished goals or self-expectations to be released. "People can miss the boat if they want to," Carol concluded, and so could she. "After all," she continued, reflecting on the lesson of her dream, "once I got on the boat I realized that it wasn't all it was cracked up to be."

She knew there would still be times when she might labor with many encumbrances. In the future, however, Carol planned to ask herself in advance of a laborious effort, "Is all this struggling worth it?" and "What will I achieve if I pursue this goal?"

Designing and executing a self-care plan was no small task. After completing her Ph.D. in management, Carol was promoted to senior partner in an important consulting firm. The promotion increased her responsibilities but cut down significantly on the travel required of her. Even when she had worked a ten- or twelve-hour day, it was difficult to decline when her boss suggested that she and the two other senior partners go out for a drink after work and talk over a particular problem. "The president and the other partners are all men," she explains, "and for a long time I wasn't included in those informal sessions after working hours, when many of the important decisions are made. Saying no is just unacceptable. It's not just a matter of closing myself out of a social situation: Such informal meetings significantly improve the quality of my work and influence." Some days "go on forever" but Carol continues to participate in those after-work meetings.

When she has deadlines to meet, she is sometimes forced to work several consecutive twelve-hour days, and for these Carol pays a much dearer price than most people. The extreme, debilitating fatigue associated with lupus can be compared to having major surgery and feeling completely spent after walking twelve steps to the bathroom and back for the first time. "I have to sleep fifteen hours a day for several days to recuperate from periods of overwork," she said.

Carol learned to go to bed early whenever possible. She

devotes her weekends to rest and to spending time with her daughter, who will soon be starting college. Knowing the dangerous side effects of her medications and the importance of taking as low a dosage as possible, Carol repeatedly has had to learn that taking care of herself is essential. By trying to avoid having more than two consecutive work days that are long and stressful, and by protecting her personal time, Carol finds that she can sometimes cut back on her medications. She returns to the higher doses, under her doctor's direction, when she has a business trip back East or another highly demanding, stressful obligation.

Looking back over the ten years since her illness was diagnosed, Carol sees periods of denial, followed by periods of self-care, followed by more episodes of hard work and stressful living, more pain, and higher doses of the medication. "You can see my stages of survivorship," she explains. "People keep growing. You don't just say at one point in time, 'Okay, I understand this illness, or my divorce, and I've come to terms with it.' You keep seeing crises differently, and you keep coming to terms with them over and over again."

COMING TO TERMS WITH ONE'S LIMITATIONS

One of Carol's favorite ways of relaxing is to sleep late and then to while away a lazy Saturday. She and her daughter like to lounge around the house in their nightclothes, catch up on each other's activities from the past week, and literally share their dreams. Remembering aloud their respective nighttime escapades, they enjoy interpreting their dreams together and cherish the moments of closeness that follow.

Mother and daughter each have a house about which they recurrently dream, and each especially delights in sharing the nocturnal tales involving her house. "My house," said Carol, "is a twenty-room mansion, a wonderful house with renovated ceilings and doors that open into whole other houses with more rooms. There is always plenty to see or do in the house. The place is so huge that I've always thought of it as representing my life."

For many years Carol dreamed of an attic in her mansion where handsomely etched, expensive glassware was stored and where elegant Oriental rugs had been rolled into colorful cylinders and were gathering dust. "Oh, I love these beautiful rugs!" Carol would exclaim in the dream. "I should bring these rugs and the pretty glassware downstairs where I can enjoy them."

She has interpreted the attic and its treasures as all the things she had loved in the past but was not now bringing into her life, in part because of the lupus. "I used to sew, draw, consider myself an artist, go to gallery openings and the opera, and belong to a weekly reading and discussion group," she remembered. "I especially found great satisfaction in being politically active—getting signatures on petitions, driving people to the polls, distributing literature, and selling tickets to fundraisers." It was sad to think that she could no longer be active in these things.

Carol struggled in therapy in an effort to figure out which treasures in life had been relegated to the dusty attic because of her illness and which treasures were left behind for other reasons. On important decisions, Carol found that she needed to examine the possible effect of the illness on her life. "Have I given up sewing because it's hard for my hands to accomplish those fine motor tasks and hard to grip the scissors?" she wondered. "Am I staying home from work simply because I have caught the flu from my co-workers, or am I sick because of the lupus? Did my marriage end because I have a serious, major illness, or would it have ended anyway? Did it take me two additional years to finish my doctoral dissertation because of the lupus, or would I have taken that long to finish my degree under normal circumstances?"

Carol's therapist listened patiently for a time, then grew

somewhat exasperated. "Why is it so important to sort out whether all or *any* of these things are due to your illness?" the social worker asked. She wisely saw (and helped Carol to see) that while people have a tremendous need to understand how major life events are related to each other, at some point such thinking becomes a meaningless exercise. "Who can really say what the precise relationship is between your illness and these other events?" the social worker asked. "What matters is how well you live with things as they are."

Carol began to have a new perspective on the treasures in her attic. She saw that she was attributing all of the changes in her life to her illness. "My daughter said, 'Mom, I don't think you're the sewing type anymore,' " Carol remembered. "And it struck me that maybe I'd have given up sewing anyway, whether I had joint swelling and a problem with my hands or not!"

Carol acknowledged, "I have a serious illness. I can't live my life just any way I want to." At the same time, she realized that anyone's life involves making choices. It just isn't possible to do everything. "Life is constantly putting some limitations on every human being," Carol continued, "and some people have severe limits. But if my hands got so crippled that I couldn't write letters, I could talk into a Dictaphone if it was really important to me. If I really *wanted* to sew, I suppose I could get a special sewing machine and find ways to do that too."

When a loss becomes the central focus, one no longer has a sense of proportion about all of the other things going on in one's life. Paraphrasing the philosopher Socrates, Carol said, "While it's true that 'the unconsidered life is not worth living,' once one has thought about life to a reasonable degree, it's time to get on with life. To say that I've lost an attic full of treasures for a particular reason (lupus) puts the illness at the center of my life. There's nothing wrong with closing a door and just saying, 'That's something I used to do; I don't do that anymore.' "

In her management consulting work, Carol helps people in institutions plan years in advance. "I am by nature somebody who looks way down the road into the future," she says as she learns how to live well with a life-disrupting, unpredictable illness. "Some people with lupus go into remission for months or years," she explained. "There is one famous case still in remission after twenty years. Maybe I'll get a whole lot better. Maybe I'll get a lot worse or die of a stroke. I am carefully saving my money as if I will live to have a long retirement."

All things considered, Carol wouldn't change places with anyone else. "Even if it meant not having the disease, I wouldn't want to live somebody else's life," she said. "I really wouldn't."

ACCEPTING WHAT IS POSSIBLE

"There are a lot of unhappy people who have an unrealistic image of themselves or who have unrealistic goals," said Sam, a physician friend. "Such persons aren't happy because they're not willing to relinquish this image of themselves. There's a great deal of our whole culture and moral philosophy opposed to this idea of accepting what is possible." He is gay and wishes that he could have had children yet accepts that "in this lifetime" it probably won't be workable for him.

Most of us must compromise. It is only realistic, for example, for millions of women who are widowed or divorced (and outnumber men the older they become) to plan on finding happiness without a fine new potential husband. In this way, a woman can put herself in situations where she has opportunities to meet men, and if an available good fellow shows up along the way, fine, but she has decided to make for herself a satisfying life *in any event*.

We all have to find a balance between living for the future and not banking on it. Serendipitous events occur more frequently to some people than others because some people are more open than others. Still, instead of striving to live "happily ever after," it makes more sense to do what you can do, to be reasonably happy, accepting the reality that almost no one, to use a common expression, "has it all."

Many people reflect on a major loss with resentment and regret. "If only *this* hadn't happened, then *this* wouldn't have happened and my whole life would have been different." Triumphant survivors have learned not to view life in this way. Whatever would have been *one will never know.*

It is certain, however, that as long as life itself continues and one is not in a coma or mentally incompetent, a host of possibilities still remain for the brain to ponder. Once a decision is made to go forward with life as it is and realistically can become, we move toward the best life within reach.

In a recent play about author Lillian Hellman, Hellman is speaking to Dashiell Hammett in the last months of his life, summarizing their thirty-year love affair, a relationship with many good years but also plenty of pain. Cancer and a lingering coma would soon and permanently take him away from her. "It's been *fine!*" Hellman exclaims.

"Fine's too big a word," replies Hammett, a person she always admired for his precise truthfulness. "Let's just say, 'We've done better than most.' "[1]

*In the midst of winter
I find in myself at last
Invincible Summer.*

HAIKU BY SOEN NAKAGAWA
IN NINE-HEADED DRAGON RIVER,
BY PETER MATTHIESSEN

Survivors of crisis events can fall into one of three groups. Roughly one third of the trauma victims who were investigated by the International Committee for the Study of Victimization appeared to be broken by their experiences, showing a lasting psychological impairment, reduced ability to function well in work and in relationships, or medical problems. Another third passed through a period of emotional difficulty and adjustment but eventually returned to their pre-crisis level of adaptation. The final third underwent an adjustment and healing period that resulted in great personal growth. Those in this last group eventually emerged wiser, stronger, psychologically healthier, and more productive than they had been before their ordeal.[1]

The wife of a U.S. government official who was one of the fifty-two Americans held at the U.S. Embassy in Tehran for over a year is reported to have said that her husband is not the same person he was when he was taken captive and that she rather prefers the person he is now. This former hostage,

Moorehead Kennedy, is a survivor who seems to fit the general category of achieving an improved life as a result of his traumatic experience. Kennedy emerged from the hostage ordeal "a very different person," he explained, with strengths and sensitivities "I didn't know I had."[2] About one third of such survivors "will reassess their lives, set new priorities, find new values,"[3] according to Dr. C. Richard Spates, a member of the International Committee for the Study of Victimization.

All of the triumphant survivors I studied have done more than come back from crisis. While their circumstances have been extremely painful, distressful, difficult, or challenging, these men and women have managed—most with great effort and mental resolve—to go boldly forward.

FINDING NEW MEANING AND PURPOSE IN LIFE

There are many who believe that God has an active hand in tragic events—not only in helping people to survive and transcend their pain but in "causing" or "allowing" the tragedy to occur. Some believe such events happen for a reason known only to God. Whether you believe in a God but not a God who works in this way, don't believe in a God at all, or believe tragedy has an inherent ultimate meaning—finding or creating meaning in or from suffering is something virtually all triumphant survivors are prone to do.

My friend Marian has a saying I especially like. "Survivors make sense out of what happens to them," she says. Many of the people I interviewed or learned about while researching this book have done just that.

Francis and Alfred Newman, for example, lost their thirty-one-year-old son and Mrs. Newman's father to cancer. Their son had battled the disease for seventeen agonizing years. From their experience the Newmans, a black couple, became aware that educational programs and support services for cancer patients and their families were virtually unheard of in the black community. Two years after their son's death they established a foundation to help victims of terminal illnesses and their families. The Jackson-Newman Foundation, named for the son and his grandfather, develops and finances educational programs on terminal care, death and bereavement in Prince Georges County, Maryland. The Newmans are retired professional people whose "days are filled with designing education and volunteer programs, and with visiting the people who call them for help."[4]

On Thanksgiving Day four years ago, writes Norma Phillips, "a drunk driver killed my son. Dean's death was the worst tragedy of my life. At first I thought there was no place to turn for the comfort and support I needed. . . . But I found help in a nearby Mothers Against Drunk Driving (MADD) chapter." Soon Norma Phillips began a MADD chapter in her hometown of San Diego. In 1985 she was elected national president of MADD. "The day I took office," she says, "I recommitted myself to the goals of reducing the incidents of drunk driving and the pain and suffering it causes."[5]

Theresa Saldana, an actress, was nearly killed in a premeditated, violent stabbing attack that resulted in surgery, more than a thousand stitches in her body, and a long war with pain, rage, and terror. In her recent book, *Beyond Survival*, Saldana writes, "My rage gave me the drive to keep fighting death, pain, and the sick wishes of the person who harmed me."[6] Too, it was her rage at the treatment victims receive in society that led her to form a victim advocacy group called Victims for Victims. Miss Saldana feels that she needed to know that the anguish "that plagued her body and soul was not a total waste." Now offering inspiration and help to others who have been victimized by violence, she feels that her pain has "served some useful purpose."[7]

Seventy-one-year-old Ruby Mathieson nursed her gravely ill son and helped him plan his funeral before he died from AIDS. A widow, she left her comfortable life in Boston and moved into the San Francisco home where David Mathieson, a forty-year-old former minister, had lived the last part of his life. Mrs. Mathieson has stayed on in San Francisco, where she has embraced David's gay friends. She has found new meaning in life taking care of others who are mourning the loss of their loved ones from AIDS. " 'All my life, my way has been to do something. I'm not sure I can explain it, but I love these young men. I love them all, just like my own. They're my family now. I want to be here for them if they need someone, just as they were here for David,' Mrs. Mathieson said."[8]

United States Senator Bob Dole, in his youth a fine athlete, had his right shoulder destroyed and his neck broken as a young soldier in World War II. He was hospitalized for more than three years and almost entirely lost the use of his right arm and hand. Knowing what it means to be disabled, the senator established the Dole Foundation, which has provided training and jobs for physically or mentally disabled people to the tune of more than half a million dollars and has funded nearly two dozen projects around the country. "I don't think you're trying to prove yourself when you're disabled," Mr. Dole told Jonathan Fuerbringer in the writer's special report to *The New York Times*. "But I think, at least, you're trying to make certain that everybody understands that you can carry your load, your fair share."[9]

Ted Kennedy, Jr., son of Senator Edward Kennedy, lost a leg to cancer at the age of twelve and likes downhill skiing and sailboat racing as a way of demonstrating that he and people like him can still pursue excellence. At the age of twenty-five, "his full-time job now is to use his Boston-based foundation, Facing the Challenge, to push for the better enforcement of laws providing jobs and access for the handicapped." He fights against the all too prevalent perspective that "society should isolate, protect and care for" people with disabilities. "Anything that serves to exclude a person or foster dependency on others is an obstacle holding someone back," he says. "We want opportunity more than we do sympathy." Kennedy is a tireless advocate for thirty-six million Americans with some type of disability. "I prefer to talk about the 'physically and mentally challenged' or 'persons with a disability,' " says the young man with conviction, "to stress human beings first and limitations second."[10]

After the tragic suicide death of her seventeen-year-old son, Jody, Susan White-Bowden wrote a book called *Everything to Live For*. She is a Baltimore institution—a popular, talented, energetic, forty-six-year-old television newscaster who has survived the traumas of divorce and the suicide of her ex-husband in addition to the suicide of her son. Then, as if she hadn't borne trauma enough, six months after her remarriage, lightning destroyed most of her house. Susan attributes her survival to having meaningful and important work to do, to receiving a great deal of supportive mail from her viewers, and to telling her story through countless talks to young people in schools and through her writing and media appearances while promoting *Everything to Live For*.

Six months after her basketball star son, Len Bias, died tragically of cocaine intoxication, Lonise Bias found what she calls a mission for herself by traveling around the country to lecture in schools and churches. Her message to young people: "You don't need drugs." She usually travels alone and often without payment other than airfare. According to *Baltimore Sun* correspondent Amy Goldstein, "although [Mrs. Bias] has no prior experience as a public speaker, her style is gripping" and her message powerfully spoken.[11]

In order to heal, it isn't necessary to write a book, establish a foundation, lecture widely, or give a large amount of time and money to some cause related to your personal crisis. One woman whose adult son committed suicide remembered that he was a loner as a boy and that he liked libraries, and she makes it possible for an author of children's books to be "in residence" one day each year at a school that her son had once attended. Many others who mourn find meaning in giving a single book to a library in memory of their loved person and in countless other small meaningful acts of giving and gifts of time. Faithful participation in a self-help group with other persons who have suffered a loss similar to yours, visiting patients in the hospital or a nursing home or people who are housebound, stuffing envelopes, typing a newsletter, answering a telephone or hotline, writing letters or baking cakes for fundraisers, participating in a prayer group for persons ill or dying, making a decision to go back to school or work—any of these activities may be a part of an agenda for healing and recovery, a way of making sense out of your pain, a way of moving ahead.

In *Coming Back*, one person after another has found new meaning or a sense of purpose in the aftermath of adversity:

Georgia, whose two beloved horses were felled by lightning, has found new meaning and purpose in training and preparing the new horse, Sunshine, for showing. Recently she has acquired and begun to train another filly.

Molly and Ben, whose daughter once was lost to a destructive religious cult, remain active in a "cult awareness" group, a support group for families of those who had or still have a loved one under the spell of such a group as well as for former cult members themselves. This couple rejoice in their family and children, including their reunion with a daughter once so distant, detached, and psychologically damaged.

Former U.S. Senator Daniel Brewster, no longer owned by ambition and alcohol, contributed his time and talents for a number of years to various political, military, religious, and community groups as a spokesman on alcoholism treatment programs and education. His primary meaning in life for quite some time now has been found as a loving father and husband.

Hope and George Curfman, whose daughter Claudia was murdered, share a special closeness with each other and with their sons and daughters-in-law, and continue to wish happiness for their former son-in-law. Each continues to write to various bereaved parents whom they know or learn about, particularly to those who have lost a child to a violent death. Long before their daughter was tragically killed, both Mrs. Curfman (trained as a social worker) and Dr. Curfman (an oncologist) found great meaning in caring about and helping others. They continue to find purpose in their religious faith and their active concern for people who are hurting.

John Liller, from his wheelchair, finds meaning and purpose in his full-time job as a government employee and in his community service activities as a businessman. When he was called to jury duty last year, John concerned himself with helping to remove the physical barriers that often prevent other "handicapable" people from exercising their rights and performing their duties as citizens.

Lynn, who was rejected by her first husband while she was gravely ill with Crohn's disease, says that the most meaningful thing in her life continues to be her supportive family, including her present husband. Her work with special education students and curriculum design is also very important. Recently Lynn was called by the Ostomy Foundation and asked to visit a young high school student, said to be an athlete, who was having a very difficult time after his ostomy. Since one of her own students was in the same hospital at the time, she decided to visit both young men that day. On arriving at the hospital, Lynn was surprised to learn that the two patients were one and the same: The young athlete had been her special education student for four years. "It was wonderful for both of us," she said, referring to the encouragement and hope she was able to impart to the young man. She told the eighteen-year-old that his teacher also had had an ostomy and that she continues to keep athletically fit.

Steven and Naomi Shelton, whose son was stillborn, have participated as panelists and speakers for medical groups and childbirth education classes. Steven's job in social work often calls upon the knowledge and sensitivity he has gained from dealing with the loss of his stillborn son. They and their daughters, aged ten and three, have recently purchased a home they had been living in and wanting to buy for a long time.

Kathleen, who lost ninety-two pounds and has kept it off, is starting her eleventh year with Diet Workshop as a dedicated, personable staff member. She continues to help others learn new thinking, skills, and behaviors for weight loss and maintenance.

The Sanborns, having happily resolved the painful ordeal of infertility by adopting two beautiful daughters from Korea, have been adding to the number of animals on their farm. They also have appeared as guest speakers for Families Adopting Children Everywhere (FACE), a Baltimore group that offers courses to prospective adoptive parents.

Charles, the single parent who raised a toddler daughter and enabled her to go out on her own sixteen years later, has found purpose in a new job setting. He also delights in the fact that his coed daughter still seems to need her dad now and then, even though he is proud of her independence and self-sufficiency.

Carlos continues his life as a college professor in a southern university. While a lot of people seem to have forgotten that he ever had a severe stutter, so fluent is his speech most of the time now, Carlos remembers. He is proud of his accomplishments in a career that involves public speaking. He has been successful both as a person who stuttered and as a person who was determined to become fluent.

And a great many more persons, unnamed here, have made sense of their losses and pain. People who find new meaning as a result of their pain or a new sense of purpose despite having had to struggle rarely are permanently broken by the losses that happen to them. Over time, tragedy and transition, adversity and having to adjust to it can be transformed into something that is useful for human growth, even something widely beneficial and lovely.

ROBBIE RISNER: HAVING AN IRREFUTABLE, NONDISLODGEABLE ANCHOR

In 1973 Robbie Risner came home after seven and a half years as a POW. He sent a letter to Admiral Moore, Chief of the Joint Chiefs of Staff, saying, "After a good night's rest and three good meals, we're ready for duty." He asked for one of the most difficult jobs in the Air Force, a fighter wing. Robbie explains, "I didn't feel I had any healing to do. I had been down a dark trail and now I was walking in the sunshine."

Robbie realizes that it was an illusion to think that he had no adjustment to make and could pick up where he had left off with his contemporaries.

There were hard times ahead. The Air Force did not give Risner the orders he had requested. They understood that he needed an opportunity to get reacquainted with his loved ones.

The circumstances, however, were not conducive to family healing. After joyous and loving reunions, the family that had learned to live without a father and a husband struggled to absorb major changes. The four Risner sons who were still at home didn't like having to live on a military base when their dad was sent to a new assignment. Risner drew up a set of rules, trying to put regimentation back into the boys' lives, and gave them all duties to perform. Kathleen, Robbie's wife, resisted some of the rules, saying that her husband was giving the boys too much to do. The boys themselves disliked the new regime yet felt some need of it.

A further difficulty for Robbie was dealing with the fact that his mother and a much-beloved brother had died while he was in prison. The many transitions and adjustments were difficult for everyone in the family.

Robbie's life as a former POW was exceedingly busy. He was in the public eye and in demand as a speaker. Publishers tried to persuade him to write a book. Kathleen, who also needed healing time, didn't welcome the fast-paced life Robbie was forced to live. When her husband was promoted to brigadier general, the demands placed upon her increased, pushing forcefully against her natural inclination to retreat and to live in privacy.

"I had been engine idle for seven and a half years and Kathleen had been at full throttle," Robbie explains. "When I came back we wanted to go in opposite directions." The strain on their marital relationship probably was heightened by everyone's idealized fantasies concerning how wonderful the family reunion would be.

In 1974 Robbie's book, *The Passing of the Night*, telling the story of his captivity, was published. Robbie was on a radio and television tour promoting the book when tragedy struck. The Risners' oldest son, Rob, died suddenly of a massive heart hemorrhage. He was twenty-six years old. Doctors had predicted that a congenital heart defect would prevent Rob from living past infancy, then elementary school, then high school. Notwithstanding medical predictions, the young man had achieved a second-degree black belt in karate, had lived a normal life, and had recently married. His death was a shock and a devastating loss. The entire family had trusted that God would preserve Rob. Several months after Rob's death, Robbie and Kathleen divorced.

Grieving horribly, Robbie eventually found comfort in the knowledge that his son had done well and had led a good, rounded life. "I've always felt thankful," he said, "that God loaned him to me for those years."

"What I went through as a POW prepared me to lose Rob and then my marriage," Risner told me. "I was tough. I had been through so much, yet I had emerged holding the hand of God. I was so strengthened by my faith that death itself would not have been unbearable."

"But don't you feel bitter sometimes?" I asked. General Risner was driving me back to the airport after our long interview. I was vigorously taking notes, still trying to assemble the puzzle of this remarkable man's seeming lack of lingering regret.

Answering so characteristically, Robbie replied, "Why look on something with remorse that you can't change?" Having no control over what had happened to him, he explained, shaped his perspective. "When life has done something to you that you couldn't have changed, how can you be remorseful?

"God had already proven Himself to me," said Robbie. "I knew that God was with me, that Rob's death hadn't gone unnoticed."

On paper Robbie's life could read like the biblical story of Job, and yet it doesn't. He has lived triumphantly through isolation, hunger and malnutrition, physical torture, brain-washing, and darkness. Through more than seven years as a prisoner of war, he maintained his fighting spirit, his stature as a leader of men, his perpetual optimism, his faith in God, and even his physical fitness.

There was a time when Robbie looked at the losses that kept happening to him and wondered if he hadn't already suffered enough—the indignities and cruelties as a POW, coming home to the painful absence of his mother and brother, and returning home to lose his eldest son and his marriage.

For three months he sought refuge and time for reflection in a mountain cabin in the wilderness of Utah. Other than the park ranger and the ranger's wife, there were no human beings within thirty-five miles. He needed to be alone. "You might have thought," he says, "that in prison I had had time enough in isolation to last ten lifetimes." He learned in prison, however, the need for solitude.

Breaking in untrained horses, riding the game trails, searching his feelings and thoughts, and experiencing the beauties of nature helped. It was as if in taming the horses he tamed his own restless, troubled soul.

"I determined," Robbie remembers, "that all the trauma I'd suffered since I came home was just a part of my life and I was going to go on. I decided something good can come of everything if I retain God's influence in my life."

Robbie also needed to mourn the loss of his mother and

brother. He has now come to a place of comfort, remembering his mother's loving influence and her strong confidence that he would safely return. He is warmed by cherished memories of riding mountain trails with the brother he lost, memories of their "knees brushing" up against each other as their horses climbed the slopes.[12]

Robbie married a woman whose husband was for many years missing in action in Vietnam and was declared killed in action. He has remained in respectful and caring communication with his first wife and in contact with their grown sons while enjoying the companionship and love which he has found in his new marriage.

Twice in the last decade Robbie has battled a life-threatening cancer. Prior to his first surgery a physician told him his chances of beating the cancer were "fifty-fifty." Ever the positive man, Robbie answered his doctor, "Well, those chances are pretty good."

A few years ago, when surgery for cancer was again required, his chances were said to be "substantially less this time." Robbie's upbeat attitude, he felt, was easily explained: "I have already lived a richer life than most people in the world—I've known more excitement, been more wonderful places, met more wonderful people. I don't have any regrets."

Also, Robbie continues, "Along with one of the best doctors in the country, I have an irrefutable, nondislodgeable anchor—a belief in God so strong that it sticks with me despite the hardships."

Retired from military service now, Robbie has worked for some years as the executive director of an organization called Texans War on Drugs. He was also appointed by the president to serve as a public delegate to the United Nations. Robbie and his wife live in a beautiful rural setting outside Austin, Texas. There Robbie continues to train and sell horses, and he'll tell you how he loves to listen to the mockingbirds, which are capable of about seven hundred imitations of other birds.

"I missed nature so much while I was gone," he says

thoughtfully, as we walk together outside the sprawling, gray stone ranch house. "I wanted to have pets, so we have dogs, cats, and horses. Out here in the country we see fox, wolves, even cougar. Deer cross the yard fairly often. The mocking-birds stay with us. I'm at peace—contented and happy."

In a spacious, comfortable den with lounge chairs, large windows on two sides of the room bring the pastures and wildflowers inside. The horses seem to be grazing alongside of us while I scan the memorabilia decorating every surface. Plaques, military and community service awards, models of the many fighter airplanes he has flown, war ribbons, and photographs with distinguished government figures nearly cover the wall space. An inscription on one of the awards is a quote by American patriot Dean Alphange: "I do not choose to be a common man—it is my right to be uncommon if I can."

This is a humble man, somehow not quite the person I expected a brigadier general to be. We met first in a not-so-fine restaurant at what turned out to be the modest motel my travel agency had booked for my family and me. When our breakfast came, I was secretly harboring petty thoughts about the rotten service and mediocre food when General Risner said, "Isn't this nice looking fruit and bacon?"

He said aloud a little prayer of thanksgiving for our food and families. I remembered that in a rat-infested cell with a concrete bunk, Robbie had similarly thanked God for every meal and for his family. Even on a constant diet of bread, water, and sometimes a little soup, he was genuinely thankful.

There was one trait abundantly evident in General Risner which I found present among most of the triumphant survivors I studied. It is the absence of what I call an "attitude of entitlement." These men and women who have had to bear such pain and endure many changes might understandably feel that life now owes them something—and yet they don't.

After a terrible loss or difficult battle of some kind, it is human to think that we are entitled now to an easier life, special treatment from others, or even deserving of unusual prosperity and good fortune—at least for a while. Certainly many triumphant survivors I met have felt that there isn't any need to go looking for more suffering, that they've suffered aplenty, and that a period of respite is needed and perhaps even "due" them. Nowhere in evidence, however, was a demanding, haughty, self-righteous attitude as if others should now cater to these individuals because of the struggles or tragedies they have encountered. While General Risner is an especially gentle and humble man, I met many others who were genuinely modest and rather quiet about their accomplishments as survivors and who lacked almost entirely an attitude of entitlement.

GLORIA BACK: "LIKE BEING REBORN . . ."

It is a giant step from telling your gay son that he should see a psychiatrist if he wants to keep having a mother to getting a master's degree in social work with the new aim of helping other parents of gays to accept their sons and daughters. As a part of the study project she designed in graduate school, Gloria Gus Back interviewed scores of other parents with gay children and observed that many were shaken, as she once was, by "their perception of homosexuality as a calamity."[13] It had taken Gloria about six years to overcome her own reaction, which began as disgust and shame, gradually softened to uncomfortableness, and led eventually to an acceptance of her son and the man he loved. She wanted to help other parents through this difficult transition.

Investigating the resources available to help the families of gay people, Gloria was surprised to learn that even in the metropolis of Manhattan there was not a single professionally led class, workshop, or group where the parents of gays could find the kind of help needed. Self-help groups and private therapists were available, but nowhere could troubled parents reap the benefits of group sharing with other parents and also receive needed information and guidance from a qualified professional.

The families of gays often live in their own closets—afraid of others' finding out that their child or sibling is gay, ashamed, and uncomfortable when talking about their gay family member. Gloria had been there. She remembered being unable to tell her husband that his stepson was gay and feeling horrified at what her parents and friends might think of her. Even when her views began to change, she attended her first gay rights parade, in the streets of New York, disguised in dark sunglasses and a giant floppy hat. She wished she could help other parents of gays explore those closets and be comfortable enough to come out themselves and not be ashamed of their gay children. She wished she could help them feel the same pride in their gay child as they had in their other children.

"I thought more and more about the problems of families of gay people," Gloria remembers. "Finally, I decided to stop thinking and move on it."[14] She began to initiate, staff, and conduct workshops for these families at New York area YWCAs. During six weekly meetings the topics included a historical overview of homosexuality and the views of the individual parents who attended. Many siblings of gays also attended. Professionals in social work, psychiatry, and psychology served as speakers and workshop resource persons. The focus of the workshops, wrote Nadine Brozan of *The New York Times*, was "the preservation of family ties."[15]

Reviewing the literature and observing that little had been written about the families of gay people, Gloria decided to write a book based on her experience and the experiences that dozens of parents were bringing to her in the workshops. She wanted her book to offer the parents and siblings of gays the kind of help she once urgently needed.

"You do not have to be phony," Gloria advised her readers in *Are You Still My Mother?* which was subtitled *Are You Still My Family?* (The titles were a quote from Ken, her gay son.)

"You do not have to pretend to be comfortable . . . if you are not. . . . It gets easier with time," Gloria went on. She advised the parents of gays to "redefine the word family" and to give their gay child the sexual privacy that would be granted to a straight child or expected for oneself.[16]

In her book, Gloria was able to say, "I am proud now. At thirty-three, Kenny is a licensed psychologist with a doctor's degree. He has built his own home with the help and loving support of his lover of over six years. He has strong emotional bonds with his family, friends, professional associates and 'in-laws.' By most standards (mine included), his lifestyle would be considered 'successful' if not superior." She was also able to say that she felt that Ken and Sam were "lucky to have found each other" and that she hoped their relationship would continue to grow and endure.[17]

Gloria was delighted that her husband, Gene's, relationship with her son and Sam was blossoming into a relationship of mutual respect and fondness. As for her relationship with the young men, "we were more than accepted by my mother," Ken remembers, "we were cherished.

"My mother always had a feeling," Ken went on, "that time was running out and that she had to do whatever she had been put here on this earth to do." She finished looking over the book galleys, did several radio interviews around the country to promote *Are You Still My Mother?* and appeared with Ken on the nationally broadcast television program *Hour Magazine.* A promotional tour was scheduled by her publisher, and she sat for a series of professional photographs which portrayed her marvelous smile, her attractive personality, and her beauty.

In June 1985, while preparing to leave her home on the Upper East Side of Manhattan to have lunch with an old friend and then tape a television show related to her book, Gloria Gus Back suffered a sudden cerebral hemorrhage and lost consciousness. She was found by her husband some hours later in their home. For ten days Gloria was in intensive care, where it was discovered that the stroke had been caused by a dormant aneurysm. She died without regaining consciousness at the age of sixty-one.

"When she died, she wasn't the same person I married eleven years earlier; that's how much she had changed," Gene told me. "Possibly why I was as supportive as I was had to do with the fact that I was impressed by her potential for growth. As she learned and got involved, I learned."

We sat on the handsome gray wool woven rug on the floor of the modern country home Ken and Sam have built together. A large framed photograph of Gloria was prominently displayed on the table. Her striking attractiveness and vitality were evident, as was her continuing presence as a much-loved person.

"My mother talked constantly about her life, saying that it was like being reborn," Ken said.

Sam listened while cooking in the kitchen and reminded us all of a wonderful story Gloria loved to tell. A parent in one of her workshops had said that when she saw that her son and his lover were cooking on a hibachi, she wept. It had dawned on the woman that her son was a regular person like everybody else! As regular people, we agreed, was how Gloria came to see Sam and Ken and their friends.

"Sam is so thoroughly integrated into our family," Ken explained proudly, "that when my grandfather died—my mother's father—she asked Sam to be a pallbearer. That may be shocking to some people that a gay lover was so embraced by the family. That was two years ago, the year before Mom died."

JAN AND ED: MOVING FORWARD

Like his wife, Jan, Ed was infuriated when people suggested at times that it was by some interior design or act of God and not merely by accident that his young, innocent son had died.

"I don't think there is any meaning in the death of a child," Ed explains. "It is an utterly meaningless event.

"There is no meaning in certain events at any level, and we have to choose how we're going to live in the face of that truth," he continues. "That's probably the hardest thing for a human being to do. We try to use our minds to put order into our lives and to make sense of life. But some things come along that have no sense and can never be redeemed no matter what we do."

In the anguish of his battle with what he saw as the "irredeemably tragic and meaningless death" of his son Mark, Ed determined that he had two choices. One was to choose not to live at all, and the other was to choose to live with the tragedy in the best way that he could. Because he is grounded in something that he feels does have deep meaning, his life with Jan, his son John, his friends, and his work, Ed found the strength to choose growth, hope, and life over resignation, bitterness, and death. "How you live your life, relate to the people around you, and how you care about them is what life is about, what makes life worth living," he says.

Ed recognizes that he is a better doctor than he was before he lost his son. Since Ed is an oncologist, all of his patients have cancer, a disease frightening to most people. With his new insight and sensitivity, Ed finds that he can "be with people" in their crises because of what his own struggle has taught him. He has surprised himself by finding the emotional ability to take care of children dying of cancer, work he had not expected to be able to do.

"I feel much freer than I ever have felt in my whole life. There is now almost nothing that I experience as a threat to me. If all my property is destroyed, if I lose my job, even if I lose my health—I'm really not bothered by things that used to worry me, because they seem inconsequential."

He sets his own agenda and accomplishes his own goals. Describing himself as someone who used to worry about everything, especially performance, Ed explains, "I've been

an achiever all my life and I still want to achieve, but I don't
worry about it. I just do it. I simply do my best, and that has
to be enough. And I don't compromise on what I believe just
to achieve."

Ed greatly enjoys his work—"I still get a lot done"—yet he
spends considerably more time with people now, particularly
family and friends.

Losing Mark has prompted Ed to reorder his priorities and
readjust his values. He has been deepened and enriched emotionally, spiritually, socially, and professionally. "Whatever
personal growth has occurred as a result of losing Mark," says
Ed, "I would trade in a minute to have Mark back. But that's
not a choice." Nevertheless, he lives well with the new pleasures and meanings that have entered his life.

After Mark's death, Jan avoided buying clothes for her second son, John, seasons ahead of time, when things were on
sale. In the immediate years following a terrible loss, people
often feel almost superstitious about not taking the future for
granted. Recently, however, she bought some pants on sale
for the next school year, when John will be in the second
grade. That's the grade Mark would have been in next had he
lived. Jan feels proud of herself.

Their daughter Kate is now eleven months old, at the age
where life is a complete adventure for her, and Jan and Ed
don't take one second of her life for granted.

Jan says, "I wish that Kate and Mark could be in each other's
lives, too. It's very painful to think that this won't happen.
But I believe that Mark will be present in her life and be a
part of her identity because he is a part of ours. Mark's gift
to us now is to live with an awareness and appreciation of
what we have, what we have had, and what the moment brings
in a way that was, of course, impossible before we lost him.
The risk of having Kate is the risk of choosing to live. I hold
my little baby in my arms, and I am so happy to be alive. I
feel full and also so happy to have John. And I feel thankful
to have had Mark, to be the one who got to be his mom for

those seven years. It's not that I live without pain from losing him. It's just that I also live with great joy and blessings."

John is now almost eight, a red-haired, blue-eyed, and sprightly little guy who lives to play soccer. Like his elder brother, John is taking Suzuki violin lessons. When he first wanted to play the violin, it was hard for Jan and Ed because they associated it with Mark, but they felt John should choose whatever instrument he wanted. Now it seems appropriate that their second son plays the violin as Mark did.

"We enjoy being alive now in very many ways," Jan says. Ed plays the guitar and banjo and sings for the kids. The couple and John take clogging lessons together. Their family life is a far cry from the rugged days of gnawing, aching pain and grief.

They are now planning a trip to Japan, where Ed was invited to give a medical lecture. Before tragedy struck, Jan and Ed had a penchant for adventurous activities. As young marrieds with toddler Mark along, they had journeyed to a mountain village in Nepal where Ed had worked while a senior medical student. "We haven't risked an adventure since losing Mark," Jan explained. "The trip to Japan represents getting back some of the spirit we used to have."

Allowing that "anything can happen" when a family is far away from familiar territory, Jan says such concerns didn't hold them back when Mark was a baby and won't make them stay home now. "Time isn't guaranteed," Jan explains. Somehow Mark's dear little soul, alive in the universe, it occurs to me, seems to be urging them on.

ALEX: CHANGED THINKING

"Losing 150 pounds was a loss of strength to me both psychologically and physically," Alex told me. "Part of the reinforcement I got for being overweight was being able to run people down. While I was never the athlete I wanted to be,

I *was* strong, because I weighed so much. I played organization football in an open league. It was tackle football and was very competitive. After dieting, I lost all that strength and the ability to feel powerful physically."

Alex's feeling of physical power was transformed into a spiritual, inward power. That he had the ability to overcome his weight problem gave Alex a feeling of might mixed with peace and tranquility. This was the first major accomplishment that he felt he had achieved on his own.

Although Alex felt empowered, he didn't feel omnipotent. He often wondered how much was luck and how much was hard work, and guarded against his own feelings of smugness. Overweight people asked how he did it, and he didn't want to paint an easy picture for them. He has tremendous empathy for overeaters, chain-smokers, and alcoholics, he said. At the same time, Alex gained a feeling of mastery and competence, a belief that he could do things, a sense of power that he has never forgotten and never since been without.

"In my world," says Alex, "nothing parallels the achievement of losing weight and keeping it off these fourteen years. It's a bigger accomplishment to me than any of the three degrees I have, including my Ph.D." Racquetball, he explains, also provides a sense of mastery and competence. His athletic skill is an achievement that far outstrips his doctorate. It was always a difficult decision whether to work on his dissertation or play racquetball. While education was important and valuable, the priority in Alex's life is to remain at normal weight and to enjoy the accompanying and deeply satisfying sense of personal accomplishment and control.

Recovering, for Alex, involves a lifelong monitoring process. He had to learn that those with a history of obesity must live under a different set of rules. He had to stop feeling sorry for himself that he couldn't eat like other people. He realized that while it always felt good to eat, he was trading in that pleasure for all the satisfactions he wanted in life—sports, women, self-satisfaction, pride, and a sense of competence.

Alex also changed his thinking and consequently his be-havior in another way. He saw that whatever limitations peo-ple are born with, it is necessary to learn to compensate for them. "In reality," he said, "this constraint on eating was something I could learn to cope with. After all, all I had to do was limit my diet in order to live a normal, happy life," Alex explained, "whereas somebody with cystic fibrosis or a child born retarded has a different battle." At the same time, Alex acknowledged, "my emotional need for food did not wear off for years and years."

Alex's experiences have also given him "some intuitive in-sights into being human." He finds, in his work as a teacher and school vice principal, that he has a tremendous tolerance for diversity. He is able to relate well with a wide range of people. "I'm just very aware that every person has strong points and weaknesses," he says.

It is a trait of triumphant survivors to rise above both their limitations and the experience of life's unfairness. Mary Fore-man, a lifelong social worker in New England, shared with me an attitude which she had found helpful for many years. When burdens must be borne, Mary tries to say, to herself or to her clients, words to this effect: "That being the case, how can this situation be redeemed?"

"That being the case . . ." is familiar language to many of the triumphant survivors I interviewed. Persons who are bro-ken by life's tragedies seem to keep thinking, "If only that weren't the case." Survivors have a way of saying, "That being the case, how can I move forward?"

COPING POWER

"In my work with people," says psychiatrist Joy R. Joffe, "I try to get them to see that there is power in coping. So many people try to put their power into control," she says. "Coping is deciding, 'I will do the best I can.' You triumph in life when you learn to forgive yourself in the struggle to build your life as you want it."

Dr. Joffe feels it is important to accept that we can't always completely control our lives and to abandon the notion that one has to get control or all is lost. Luke, who is battling with multiple sclerosis, didn't say, "I can't lose the strength in my hands." He said, "If and when I do, this is how I will cope." Carlos didn't say, "I can't do anything until I conquer the stuttering." He said, "I'll do what I can with my life while having a stutter; I won't let it hold me back." According to Dr. Joffe, "That's the difference between coping and insisting on control."

Not everyone can achieve the long-term success of formerly obese persons such as Kathleen and Alex. In view of how difficult it is to maintain a significant weight loss, coping can even make good sense for many overweight people. June Bailey, in her book *Fat Is Where It's At*, emphasizes that the person with a weight problem has "the right to have good mental health and self-esteem."[18] Part of the victory in this case can be to reach self-acceptance and to live fully the life that one has.

Most individuals who lose an arm in childhood do not grow into the baseball captain of the college team, as Ray Bevans did, or take up golf at the age of forty and develop a handicap enviable to most amateurs of any age. Most people with a serious, debilitating, unpredictable, probably progressive illness like lupus aren't philosophical, optimistic, exceedingly resourceful, and full of humor and grace like Carol. Most hardened criminals capable of rape and murder will *never* change, as Jim did, into a nonviolent, trustworthy, or safe person. Most mastectomy patients haven't gone to the bedside of a hundred other women suffering such a loss as Rachel has done. And most colostomy patients who wear a plastic bag for waste products do not work out at Nautilus, have a drawerful of sexy swimsuits, and enjoy life as buoyantly as Lynn does.

The criteria for being a triumphant survivor do not include

being capable of miracles, exceptional in accomplishing athletic feats, or eligible for canonization. While I have presented a number of noteworthy individuals here, I have chosen them in the belief that we can *all* learn from each person something that is readily translatable into our own lives. Each person described in this book can show us identifiable, practical coping skills and attitudes that lead to triumph.

PEOPLE WHO TRIUMPH

In order to help you remember and synthesize some of what I have been saying about survivors and surviving, I wanted to pull together a handy summary statement. By itself, the list that follows will not do much for you and is certainly *not* meant as a checklist for "ten quick steps to triumphant surviving." What the guidelines that follow *can* provide is an aid to recalling some of the lessons the book has offered you. I hope that you find it helpful.

People who go beyond brokenness, overcoming tragedies and hurts, do some things differently in a grief and healing or transition process. Triumphant survivors think and behave in ways that lead to recovery. So can you.

- ☐ You can establish positive memories, loving moments shared with others.
- ☐ You can search relentlessly for answers and find whatever help is needed from friends, family, experts, helping professionals, your church or synagogue, books, healing activities, or support groups.
- ☐ You can develop survival strategies such as dealing with pain in small segments.
- ☐ You can make an early decision to go forward and actively reinvest in living.
- ☐ You can learn to live with the past by getting whatever

help is needed to face life squarely and to live in the truth.

☐ You can examine events fully and acknowledge the full range of your human emotions.

☐ You can decide to grow in self-acceptance and take active steps in that direction.

☐ You can remind yourself that prior to recovery it is necessary to deal first and fully with the pain and that your healing process may take longer than you and most others expect.

☐ You may experience a crisis of faith and encounter feelings of terror and a continuing struggle, yet you can become aware that forward movement is taking place.

☐ You can fight off and resist feelings of helplessness by deciding not to remain passive and powerless, engaging in active learning or decisive action when the time seems right.

☐ You can leave encumbrances behind—old resentments, grievances, axes to grind, remembered injustices—the harbored memories that grow increasingly heavy. You can decide not to waste your life by permanently losing yourself in sorrow, defeat, anger, fear, or guilt.

☐ You can listen to the rumblings of a need or desire within yourself to forgive and choose wisely the setting where a sense of peace can best be worked out within yourself or through an interaction with another person.

☐ You can work on getting a good mental picture of your loss or crisis event. Gradually you can form a clear sense of the emotional issues and make concrete plans for your future based on your changed circumstances and the "new person" you have become.

☐ You can plan ahead.

☐ You can solve problems one at a time and treat well those who help you.

☐ You can decide that you *want* to learn and grow.

☐ You can look for inspirational role models.

- ☐ You can associate with and learn from people who have the ability to laugh, enjoy, and see humor.
- ☐ You can become anchored in your religious faith, love of family, friends, or nation, your beliefs and values beyond the material realm.
- ☐ You can make a firm decision that you *want* things to work out well, *want* to recover, *want* to build a new life for yourself.
- ☐ You can take advantage of the available opportunities.
- ☐ You can become willing to expand yourself, willing to think and behave in new ways.
- ☐ You can consciously decide to be in the company of life-giving, positive-thinking, hopeful, nurturant, kind, and understanding people.
- ☐ You can vividly examine the future and plan how to realize your yearnings for a good life, remaining realistic yet daring to dream.
- ☐ You can decide that meaninglessness is intolerable and set out to make sense of things and construct a meaning for your life.
- ☐ You can strive toward independence and self-sufficiency at the same time that you learn how and when to rely on others.
- ☐ You can open yourself to finding and receiving encouragement from the available sources.
- ☐ You can recall individuals and events in your past that can provide strength, hope, and encouragement in difficult, discouraging times.
- ☐ You can allow yourself to care for other people, become attached to others, and be vulnerable with those who are trustworthy.
- ☐ You can open yourself to serendipitous events.
- ☐ You can know and use to your benefit the power of a symbolic achievement.
- ☐ You can use rituals and symbolic acts as an aid to healing.

- ☐ You can reach out to help others while you yourself are still hurting.
- ☐ You can find a variety of fitting ways to say goodbye— frequently and fully.
- ☐ You can find the people who will help—friends, family, peer support groups, role models, professional helpers, neighbors, authors, treatment programs, wig or prosthesis makers, carpenters, advice givers of varying and sundry sorts.
- ☐ You can accept the best life within reach.
- ☐ You can do the best that you can.
- ☐ You can go forward, knowing the sorrows and hardships you've had to come through—but looking ahead far more than looking back.

MOON WATCHING

The moon was full the night my husband left me. For several years after that I hated looking up in the sky at a round, radiant moon. I felt robbed of my long friendship with the bright night, a fondness that had begun in childhood when I watched with my mother for falling stars. Sitting on a blanket on tall grass near our farmhouse, we saw an Oklahoma sky that was brilliant and seemed to stretch to the ends of the earth. At the age of thirty, still grieving shattered dreams, my world no longer held endless possibilities. I wondered if my love for the nighttime would ever return.

Sometimes I feel certain I'm younger than forty-four. How different it is now to share the full moon with my daughter, Amanda, as we drive around our neighborhood and the surrounding vicinity, trying to find the orange globe, still too low in the sky to be seen clearly from our house. "Oh, Mommy, *there* it is!" Amanda exclaims, almost shrieking. Likewise, I delight in pointing out a half moon or even a special little sliver shining in the night. The sky is ours now. For me it is no longer associated with pain.

On the night before Amanda's second birthday, I stayed up decorating the house and blowing up balloons, knowing how it would tickle her to wake up on her birthday to colorful surprises. At 11:45 P.M., I went in to where she was sleeping and sentimentally seized the last chance to kiss my little Amanda in the second year of her life. At about 12:30 A.M., I went back in to plant a good-night kiss on the forehead of my big two-year-old, now entering her third year. I found it difficult to sleep in anticipation of Amanda's discovery of the room full of balloons. Having a little person to plan surprises for is so much fun, I thought as I fell asleep. I've since become aware that balloons can be aspirated and are dangerous for very young children, but I do hold fondly to that memory of the night she turned two.

There are many nights just before I drift into dreams, when I lie in bed thinking how much richer my house feels with a child asleep in the next room and the knowledge that another child is coming. Mind pictures roll by and I doze off watching Amanda run in the yard, contemplating how enjoyable it will be, however old she is, to watch her at play. I then think about her baby sister, and I enter dreamland watching the two of them sharing a pizza, digging in the sand, cuddling a little dog, wearing pretty dresses on a sunny day.

It would be nice if my daughters had a daddy. Occasionally Amanda, wearing a teasing smile, calls me "mommy-daddy" when asking for permission to do something. Recently she drew a picture of a daddy so cheerful-looking that we still have him taped to the wall! Nevertheless, I feel deeply thankful for my life, exactly as it is.

One thing is clear: I would never want to have missed the life I'm having with one daughter born in India and another on the way. How my life has been enriched and enlarged by them already!

The incredible struggles I have had over the years seem

distant now. Like everybody else, I'm sure I'll have to deal with pain again in my life, yet it is absolutely astonishing to me how much healing can take place when we are badly broken and how we can be restored.

CHERISHING THE SUNSHINE

My nursery-school-aged daughter and I are lying on the couch together. The winter afternoon sun is streaming into our living room, and we have just finished reading *Santa Mouse*, *Katie and the Smallest Bear*, *The Night Before Christmas*, and *Frosty the Snowman*. Our Saturday morning babysitter had to go Christmas shopping with her mother before Amanda was fully asleep, and I'm here trying to bring the "sandman" so I can get back to writing and finish this book. Our new baby, Ashley Anjali, was born in India nearly three months ago, and I'm working long hours, six and seven days a week, to finish the manuscript and give my tired body a rest before the baby arrives next month.

"Isn't this fun?" Amanda asks with a wide smile. She is referring to our napping on the couch together and the pleasure she gets from the sweet little conversations we have at such times.

"Yes, honey, go to sleep now," I reply, eager to return to the glassed-in sun porch where I write. The December sun is streaming into my writing room, too, I remember. It's a wonderful place to work, especially on a sunny day. I can look through the hemlock trees in the backyard that border on a spacious golf course and let God's warm, radiant sun nurture and inspire me.

Amanda is squirming. I am five foot nine, and even with my petite thirty-pound daughter it is hard to find sufficient room on the couch for both of us. "It's giggle time," she says, trying to tickle me.

"No, Amanda, it's time for your nap. When you wake up

Marylee is coming to help us hang the outdoor Christmas lights, and we may even go get our tree today. She's going to babysit with you tonight while Mommy plays cards with friends here at home. We're all going to have Indian food together first. You need to sleep now."

"Can I pat your back?" she goes on, her brown eyes looking overly awake and alert.

"Just for a little bit," I answer. "Then go to sleep, Amanda. If you want me to stay here on the couch awhile, you have to go to sleep *now*," I say, trying to be firm.

"You're the mommy I always wanted," Amanda says, choking me up.

"Thank you, Sugar Bear," I reply. "You're the daughter I always wanted. Please go to sleep."

"Mommy," Amanda chirps, "let's go to sleep with a big smile on our faces, okay?"

"Okay, honey," I reply. How could I not smile?

Finally, after about thirty minutes of my trying to figure out what to do with my long legs to make them more comfortable on this corduroy couch that was not made for a tall person, Amanda falls asleep. I look at her pretty little brown face and ponder the beauty of her. What a beautiful, lovable child she is—a "live wire" but so cherishable.

Carefully I sneak my body away from the couch and head for the sun room, my yellow legal pads, and my golden writing pen. "This is just what I always wanted," I think to myself, looking over my shoulder at my sleeping daughter. "My own child. My own family."

I say a prayer asking God to give my daughters long, healthy, and happy lives and I sit at my desk for a few minutes thinking about my baby. Ashley Anjali at this moment weighs about nine pounds and is one of 140 babies in a nursery in Calcutta, ten thousand miles away. She'll be coming home soon.

I am certain that when I was twenty-seven years old, devastated by the end of my marriage, it was completely outside of my ability to imagine that I could ever be so happy.

NOTES|

1. People Who Make Comebacks

1. Robinson Risner, *The Passing of the Night* (New York: Ballantine Books, paperback, 1975), p.3.
2. Ann Landers, *Daily Oklahoman*, May 2, 1986.
3. Gloria Gus Back, *Are You Still My Mother?* (New York: Warner Books, paperback, 1985), p. 6.
4. Ibid., p. 8.
5. Ibid., p. 9.
6. Ibid.
7. Anastasia Toufexis, "Dieting: The Losing Game," *Time*, January 20, 1986.

2. Dealing with the Pain Comes First

1. James Froehlich, O.F.M., Cap., in a paper written for the Pastoral Helping Relationship, a graduate course at Loyola College, Baltimore, fall 1984.
2. John Denver, from the album *Seasons of the Heart*, RCA, New York, 1971, 1982.
3. Daniel Goleman, "Mourning: New Studies Affirm Its Benefits," *New York Times*, February 5, 1985.
4. John Schneider, "Helping Grieving Families Help Themselves," a lecture, Kellogg Center, Michigan State University, East Lansing, Michigan, October 1, 1984.
5. Gerald Caplan, M.D., *Support Systems and Community Mental Health* (New York: Behavioral Publications, 1974), pp. 5, 6.
6. Gloria Gus Back, *Are You Still My Mother?* (New York: Warner Books, paperback, 1985), p. 15.

7. Ibid., p. 16.
8. Ibid., p. 15.
9. Ibid., p. 18.
10. Ibid., p. 21.
11. Robinson, Risner, *The Passing of the Night* (New York: Ballantine Books, paperback, 1975), p. 164.
12. Ibid., p. 166.
13. Ibid.
14. Rodney Barker, *Hiroshima Maidens* (New York: Viking Penguin, 1985), pp. 19, 29.
15. Risner, *op cit.*, p. 77.
16. Ibid.
17. Ibid., pp. 158–59.
18. Julius Segal, "Underestimating Hostages—What Psychologists Ignore Is Just How Tough They Are," *Washington Post*, June 30, 1985.
19. Ibid.

3. Getting Through Grief Takes Longer Than Most People Think

1. A. J. Stunkard, T.I.A. Sorenson, et al., "An Adoption Study of Human Obesity," *New England Journal of Medicine*, January 23, 1983, pp. 193–98.

4. Getting Unstuck by Recognizing What's Happening

1. Martin Seligman, *Helplessness: On Depression, Development, and Death* (San Francisco: W. H. Freeman & Co., 1975), pp. 169–70.
2. Mother Elise, CHS, "Summit of Forgiveness," *Community of the Holy Spirit*, St. Hilda's House newsletter, No. 44, February 1986, p. 4. The article first appeared in the newsletter of the Living Church, Milwaukee, Wisconsin, January 19, 1986.
3. Karen Brownstein, *Brainstorm* (New York: Macmillan, 1980), pp. 139–40.
4. Ibid.
5. Robert Weiss, "Recovery from Emotionally Traumatic Events," *Mental Health Letter*, Harvard Medical School, March 1985, pp. 4–6.

6. Ibid.
7. Ibid.

5. Turning Points

1. This information comes from interviews with members of Gloria Back's family and from her book, *Are You Still My Mother?*, p. 24.
2. Gloria Gus Back, *Are You Still My Mother?* (New York: Warner Books, paperback, 1985), p. 27.
3. Ibid.
4. Herman Wouk, *Inside Outside* (Boston: Little, Brown, 1985), p. 293.
5. Back, *op cit.*, p. 32.
6. M. Scott Peck, *The Road Less Traveled* (New York: Simon & Schuster, paperback, 1978), pp. 258–59.
7. Manny Lawton, *Some Survived: An Epic Account of Japanese Captivity During World War II* (Chapel Hill, N.C.: Algonquin Books, 1984), p. 50.
8. Ibid., p. 50.
9. Ellen Goodman, *Turning Points* (New York: Fawcett Crest Books, paperback, 1979), p. 167.
10. Frederick Kelly, "Daniel Brewster Savors His Turned-Around Life," *Baltimore Sun Magazine*, June 29, 1980, p. 6.
11. Blaine Taylor, "Phoenix—The Rise, Fall and Resurrection of Senator Daniel Brewster," *Maryland State Medical Journal*, Vol. 26, No. 7, July 1977, p. 38.
12. Ibid., p. 39.
13. Ibid.
14. Ibid.
15. Kelly, *op cit.*, p. 9.
16. Ibid., p. 6.
17. Robert H. Colvin and Susan C. Olson, *Keeping It Off* (New York: Simon & Schuster, 1985), p. 50.
18. Ibid., p. 59.
19. Ibid., p. 51.
20. Ibid., p. 61.
21. Ibid., p. 76.
22. Ibid.

23. Ibid.
24. Ibid., p. 178.
25. Ibid.

6. *Saying Complete Goodbyes*

1. Daniel Goleman, "Mourning: New Studies Affirm Its Benefits," *New York Times*, February 5, 1985.
2. Marilyn A. Carpenter, OSB, "The Importance of Ritualizing the Life/Death Event," unpublished master's thesis, Antioch University-West, Denver, Colorado, 1983, p. 42.
3. Naomi Sayer Shelton, *Mother Wit*, newsletter of the Consumer Task Force on the Childbearing Year, East Lansing, Michigan, April 24, 1982.
4. Shelton, unpublished poem written in 1983.
5. Shelton, unpublished poem written in 1984.
6. Karen Brownstein, *Brainstorm* (New York: Macmillan, 1980), pp. 67–68.
7. Ibid., p. 150.
8. Christopher Joyce, "A Time for Grieving," *Psychology Today*, Vol. 18, No. 11, November 1984, p. 46.
9. Alan Cunningham, "New York Stab Victim Eulogized in Denver Rite," *Rocky Mountain News*, Denver, Colorado, August 12, 1977.
10. The idea is taken from Dr. Robert Goulding and Mary Goulding, "Saying 'Goodbye,' " an outline (Watsonville, Calif.: Western Institute for Group and Family Therapy).
11. Ibid.
12. Ibid.
13. The idea is from the Reverend Gordon Spencer, Boston Avenue United Methodist Church, Tulsa, Oklahoma.
14. Ibid.

7. *The People Who Help*

1. George Vaillant, *Adaptation to Life* (Boston: Little, Brown and Company, 1977), pp. 29, 71.
2. Ibid., p. 269.
3. Gerald Caplan, "Stress Reactions: New Concepts and Opportuni-

ties" and "Practical Applications of Support Systems Theory: Interventions in Child and Adult Stress Reactions," lectures presented at the International Hotel, Baltimore-Washington International Airport, for the Health and Education Council, May 19, 1981.

4. Ibid.

5. C. E. Basch and T. B. Kersch, "Adolescent Perceptions of Stressful Life Events," *Health Education*, Vol. 17, No. 3, June/July 1986, p. 4.

6. "Support of Friends Can Do Much Good, but It Can Hurt, Too," *Baltimore Sun*, September 3, 1985.

7. Rodney Barker, *Hiroshima Maidens* (New York: Viking Penguin, 1985), p. 21.

8. Ibid., p. 55.

9. Ibid., pp. 58–59.

10. Ibid., p. 125.

11. Ibid., p. 130.

12. Ibid., p. 231.

13. Amy DePaul, "From Victim . . . to Victor," *Washington Post*, April 18, 1986.

14. Ibid.

15. Jennifer Barr, *Within a Dark Wood* (New York: Doubleday, 1979), p. 52.

16. Vaillant, *op cit.*, p. 344.

8. *Traits of the Survivor*

1. Gloria Gus Back, *Are You Still My Mother?* (New York: Warner Books, paperback, 1985), p. xi.

2. Ibid., p. xii.

3. Ibid., p. xiii.

4. Ibid., p. 30.

5. Kahlil Gibran, *The Prophet* (New York: Alfred A. Knopf, 1961), pp. 18–19.

6. A. J. Stunkard et al., "An Adoption Study of Human Obesity," *New England Journal of Medicine*, January 23, 1983, pp. 193–98.

7. Robinson Risner, *The Passing of the Night* (New York: Ballantine Books, paperback, 1975), p. 240.

8. Ibid.

9. George Vaillant, *Adaptation to Life* (Boston: Little, Brown and Company, 1977), p. 14.

10. Craig E. Taylor, "Where There's a Will," *Athletic Journal*, June 1945.

11. Bob Ibach, "What Handicap? Ask Ray Bevans," *Baltimore Evening Sun*, September 9, 1977.

12. Edward Kennedy, Jr., in a 1986 network television interview.

13. Back, *op cit.*, p. 15.

14. Ibid., p. 27.

15. Ibid.

16. Ibid.

17. Ibid., p. 26.

18. Karen Brownstein, *Brainstorm* (New York: Macmillan, 1980), p. 60.

19. Manny Lawton, *Some Survived: An Epic Account of Japanese Captivity During World War II* (Chapel Hill, N.C.: Algonquin Books, 1984), p. 76.

20. Stephen Wigler, "Elane Stein, Local Radio's Battlestar, Is a 'Living Institution,' " *Baltimore Sun*, August 17, 1986.

21. Al Siebert, "The Survivor Personality," *Association for Humanistic Psychology Newsletter*, August-September 1983, p. 19.

22. Ibid.

23. Ibid.

24. Ibid., pp. 20–21.

25. Ibid., p. 21.

26. Ibid.

27. Ibid.

9. Survivor Attitudes

1. Harold Bloomfield and Leonard Felder, *The Achilles Syndrome* (New York: Ballantine Books, 1986). This paperback is also published under the title *Making Peace with Yourself* (New York: Ballantine Books).

2. André Papantonio, class presentation in "Personal Psychology," Essex Community College, Baltimore County, Maryland, fall 1984.

3. Robinson Risner, *The Passing of the Night* (New York: Ballantine Books, paperback, 1975), p. 49.

4. American Health Magazine Service, "Ideas: Stress for Success," *Washington Post*, October 1, 1984.

5. Ibid.
6. Maya Pines, "Psychological Hardiness: The Role of Challenge in Health," *Psychology Today*, Vol. 14, No. 7, December 1980, p. 39.
7. Ibid.

10. How People Grow and Change

1. Paula D'Arcy, *Song for Sarah* (Wheaton, Ill.: Shaw Publishers, 1979), p. 99.
2. Viktor Frankl, *Man's Search for Meaning* (New York: Washington Square Press, 1963, 1985), p. 64.
3. Colette Dowling, *The Cinderella Complex* (New York: Summit Books, 1981), p. 31.
4. Dave Kindred, "Leonard Fights Because Life Without It Was a Knockout," *Baltimore Sun*, August 24, 1986.
5. Ralph Keyes, *Chancing It* (Boston: Little, Brown and Company, 1985), p. 7.
6. Ibid., p. 9.
7. Ibid., p. 10.
8. Ibid., pp. 10, 13, 15.
9. Ibid., pp. 286, 288.
10. Ibid., p. 51.
11. Ibid., pp. 154–55.
12. Ibid., p. 284.
13. David Viscott, *Risking* (New York: Pocket Books, 1979), p. 17.

11. The Best Life Within Reach

1. *Zoe Caldwell as Lillian*, a play by William Luce, directed by Robert Whitehead, performed at Johns Hopkins University, Baltimore, Maryland, December 4, 1986.

12. More Than Coming Back—Going Forward

1. Sandy Banisky, "Experts Think Most Hostages Will Adjust Easily to Freedom," *Baltimore Sun*, November 6, 1980.
2. Julius Segal, "Underestimating Hostages: What Psychologists Ignore

368 | NOTES

Is Just How Tough They Are," *Washington Post*, June 30, 1985.
3. Banisky, *op cit.*
4. Charlotte Sutton, "Couple Comes Through Tragedy with a Project to Help Others," *Washington Post*, September 13, 1984.
5. Norma Phillips, in a letter distributed nationwide from MADD in a fund-raising and education effort, December 6, 1985.
6. Theresa Saldana, *Beyond Survival* (New York: Bantam Books, 1986), pp. 81–82.
7. Ibid., p. 161.
8. Ellen Uzelac, "For Some, Comforting the Dying Leads to a New Life," *Baltimore Sun*, November 2, 1987, p. 1A.
9. Jonathan Fuerbringer, "To Dole, It Was an Education to Get Past Disability," *New York Times*, June 16, 1986.
10. Edward Kennedy, Jr., "Our Right to Independence," *Parade Magazine*, November 23, 1986.
11. Amy Goldstein, "Lonise Bias, 'On Mission,' Talks to UM Drug Abuse Class," *Baltimore Sun*, December 4, 1986.
12. Robinson Risner, *The Passing of the Night* (New York: Ballantine Books, paperback, 1975).
13. Gloria Gus Back, *Are You Still My Mother?* (New York: Warner Books, paperback, 1985), p. xiii.
14. Ibid., p. 30.
15. Nadine Brozan, "When a Son or Daughter Is a Homosexual," *New York Times*, March 12, 1984.
16. Ibid., pp. 230, 232.
17. Ibid., p. 26.
18. June Bailey, *Fat Is Where It's At*, was written and published privately.

ANN KAISER STEARNS holds a master of divinity from Duke University and a doctorate in clinical psychology from Union Graduate School with clinical training at the Pastoral Counseling Service, Washington, D.C., Eastpoint Medical Center, and the Johns Hopkins Hospital, Baltimore. She is a member of the National Academy of Certified Clinical Mental Health Counselors. She is professor of psychology at Essex Community College, Baltimore; an adjunct professor at Loyola College; and was for many years a member of the faculty of the Family Practice Training Program, Franklin Square Hospital. She has served as an associate chaplain at Michigan State University and lectures widely across America. Author of the popular *Living Through Personal Crisis*, she has also contributed a chapter to the book *Pastoral Counseling*. She lives in Baltimore with her daughters, Ashley Anjali and Amanda Asha.